10 0302218 6

# Busybodies, Meddlers, and Snoops

**Recent Titles in Contributions in Women's Studies**

"Nobody Wants to Hear Our Truth": Homeless Women and Theories of the Welfare State
*Meredith L. Ralston*

Spanish Women in the Golden Age: Images and Realities
*Magdalena S. Sánchez and Alain Saint-Saëns*

Russian Women in Politics and Society
*Wilma Rule and Norma Noonan, editors*

New Perspectives on Margaret Laurence: Poetic Narrative, Multiculturalism, and Feminism
*Greta M. K. McCormick Coger, editor*

Women Shapeshifters: Transforming the Contemporary Novel
*Thelma J. Shinn*

Petticoats and White Feathers: Gender Conformity, Race, the Progressive Peacc Movement, and the Debate Over War, 1895–1919
*Erika A. Kuhlman*

*With Her in Ourland:* Sequel to *Herland*
*Charlotte Perkins Gilman*
*Edited by Mary Jo Deegan and Michael R. Hill*

(Un)Doing the Missionary Position: Gender Asymmetry in Contemporary Asian American Women's Writing
*Phillipa Kafka*

Historical Nightmares and Imaginative Violence in American Women's Writings
*Amy S. Gottfried*

Dissenting Women in Dickens's Novels: The Subversion of Domestic Ideology
*Brenda Ayres*

Deprivation and Power: The Emergence of Anorexia Nervosa in Nineteenth-Century French Literature
*Patricia A. McEachern*

A History of Popular Women's Magazines in the United States, 1792–1995
*Mary Ellen Zuckerman*

# Busybodies, Meddlers, and Snoops

## *The Female Hero in Contemporary Women's Mysteries*

KIMBERLY J. DILLEY

Contributions in Women's Studies, Number 166
Kathleen Gregory Klein, *Series Adviser*

GREENWOOD PRESS
Westport, Connecticut • London

**Library of Congress Cataloging-in-Publication Data**

Dilley, Kimberly J., 1964–
Busybodies, meddlers, and snoops : the female hero in contemporary women's mysteries / Kimberly J. Dilley.
p. cm.—(Contributions in women's studies, ISSN 0147–104X ; no. 166)
Includes bibliographical references and index.
ISBN 0–313–30330–4 (alk. paper)
1. Detective and mystery stories, American—History and criticism. 2. Detective and mystery stories, English—History and criticism. 3. American fiction—Women authors—History and criticism. 4. English fiction—Women authors—History and criticism. 5. Women detectives in literature. 6. Feminism and literature. 7. Heroines in literature. I. Title. II. Series.
PS374.D4D55 1998
813′.0872099287—dc21 97–45670

British Library Cataloguing in Publication Data is available.



Library of Congress Catalog Card Number: 97–45670
ISBN: 0–313–30330–4
ISSN: 0147–104X

First published in 1998

Greenwood Press, 88 Post Road West, Westport, CT 06881
An imprint of Greenwood Publishing Group, Inc.

Printed in the United States of America

The paper used in this book complies with the Permanent Paper Standard issued by the National Information Standards Organization (Z39.48–1984).

10 9 8 7 6 5 4 3 2 1

For Jordan and Zoie
with love

# Contents

# Preface

In 1990, as a potential Ph.D. candidate, I had to find a research topic to make my own for the next four or five years. One evening I was watching an episode of "Mystery" on PBS television. The host, Diana Rigg, introduced the scheduled mystery with a few comments about its author, Margery Allingham. Allingham is a mystery author best known for her 1930s and 1940s detective novels featuring the aristocratic sleuth, Albert Campion. Rigg observed that the history of the modern detective novel is composed of, and has been greatly influenced by, many women authors. She hinted at the tension in such a seemingly incongruous mating. Society defines women as passive, morally superior to men, and emotional. Many women authors have, however, made great contributions to a genre characterized by violence, death, impropriety, and rationalism. I was attracted to the genre as an adolescent, but had failed to notice its connection with women. Rigg's comments sparked my interest, and I set myself the task of answering why women are so good at writing of mayhem. It was also a fine excuse for renewing my interest in good mysteries.

Since that evening many years ago, this project and I have spent quite a lot of time together. We were together when I married, had my children, and moved through four states, two houses, and four apartments. We've gone through at least three computers and several printers, as well as countless numbers of hardware, software, and operator crashes. Now we will soon be parted. (Does anyone know of an author version of "empty-nest syndrome"?) I do know that through these many years, a great number of people have assisted and supported me. I would like to thank Professor Helene Keyssar, the chair of my dissertation committee, for countless hours of help and nudging in the right direction. My thanks also extend to the members of my committee: Professors Robert Horwitz, Carol Padden, Don Wayne, and Page Du Bois. I thank, too, Kathleen

Gregory Klein for helping me see a book where before there was only a dissertation. I am especially grateful for the women of Sisters in Crime, who were more than willing to put up with my long-winded questions as I interviewed them by telephone. Their responses and words of encouragement helped to shape the direction of this work. It has been a privilege to share a few minutes with such interesting, intelligent, warm, and witty women. I would certainly be remiss if I did not make grateful mention of the public library system. Please support your local libraries. They keep the words of many wonderful writers alive.

Finally, it is my family who deserves the most thanks. Since 1990, I've added some in-laws, too. Along with my parents and brothers, they have all been very supportive. I'm not sure what would have happened if my parents had not used the well-worn, but still effective, words of encouragement, "You've come this far, you might as well just finish it." I would also suggest to them that next time they find themselves unsure how to explain what subject I got my degree in and what I do, they should just say, "She's a writer."

To Steve, Jordan, and Zoie: I thank you very much for your love and support. I promise to clean up my mess now and put away all those books. I love you.

# Introduction

> It is not always necessary to demonstrate the importance of a body of literature. If literature, any literature, helps us decode our environment as we wish to relate to it, it is valuable. If it carries us outside ourselves, to return us to ourselves enlarged, surely that is enjoyable—Robin Winks[1]

Many popular fiction critics designate the 1980s and 1990s as the "Second Golden Age" of the mystery novel. The 1930s and 1940s were the original Golden Age. The form experienced significant growth and expansion during these earlier years. Women authors were among the genre's most prolific and economically rewarded, as well as critically acclaimed. Many of the conventions of the modern mystery novel developed during this period. The books of Agatha Christie, one of the period's most acclaimed authors, may appear cliché to today's audiences, but only because admirers have copied her literary inventions, plots, and character types for decades. The women writing during this period—Agatha Christie, Josephine Tey, Dorothy Sayers, Margery Allingham, Ngaio Marsh—had no sense of themselves as belonging to a group. They did not write as "Golden Age" authors. Each found that the genre offered a means of income for her family's survival. It had a structure that could be learned and mastered relatively easily. Finally, the conventions were still flexible enough to allow for creativity and commentary.

The women of this time period made unique contributions to the direction of the genre that have persisted to the present. The narratives created for their characters and the authors' commentary on the roles of community, family, society, and authority continue to resonate with contemporary audiences. Women mystery authors of the 1980s and 1990s are building on the lessons of their

Golden Age sisters. They are expanding on the classic characters and story lines, revealing the continued potency and flexibility of genre fiction, and making a living from their words. The detective fiction of the 1980s and 1990s critiques stereotypic assumptions of gender and expands the vitality of the everyday. The characters use wit and humor as they deal with social issues. The women heroes are resourceful, strong, and independent. "Now the women don't pass their problems onto men; they solve them all by themselves. Often they protect other characters along the way and they certainly don't defer to men."[2] Susan Sandler, of the Mystery Guild, reports: "Having a woman detective puts special demands on the writer to be more imaginative. For example, females don't generally shoot from the hip and writers are forced to come up with more creative plot and action ideas."[3] Heroism for the woman mystery detective is not in the extraordinary. It is lived in the ordinary.

The analysis that follows focuses on the mysteries of contemporary American women authors whose novels include a serial detective. The novels were published between 1978 and 1997.[4] The type of sleuth central to the texts—private eye, police-trained investigator, and amateur sleuth—is used to delineate the texts. To arrive at a final selection of five authors for each category out of the hundreds published, I used a general definition of "popular." Commenting on mass-market fiction, I would argue, requires the critic to find the texts that are popular with readers, and in turn, with authors, booksellers, and popular fiction literary critics. These are the narratives that resonate with readers' lives. My selections were based on numerous conversations with readers at book signings and mystery conventions; award nominations from critics, peers, and readers; and the suggestions of a mystery bookseller in Dallas, Texas. The final selection, of course, is my own. The novels of the authors chosen best illustrate trends and patterns common to many of the works published by other women mystery writers.

The serial detective provides the scholar with the unique opportunity to examine an author's narrative as it changes over time. As will be discussed in more detail, serial mystery novels developed as a marketing tool. Once an author has attracted an audience for her characters, subsequent books are easier for the publisher to market and sell. It is also easier for the author to sell subsequent manuscripts since she already has a publisher eager for the next work in the series. This marketing tool allows authors and readers the possibility of exploring complex issues such as maturity, relationships, growth, and the consequences of actions on the future. Characters and their situations are dynamic rather than static, as in the single occasion detective novel. The characters live lives that continue on after the book ends. Readers and authors connect with characters and situations that are never totally complete or known. New novels bring them the opportunity not only to become reacquainted with old "friends," but to explore the women's lives further. The literary critic, too, becomes part anthropologist, studying a community and its codes over time.

Discussing women's language and perceptions is complicated by trying to find the exact line between biology and culture. Stereotypic "femininity" and "masculinity," as they have been perpetuated by cultural mythology, represent the "ideals," or extremes, of human qualities. Women and men adopt varying degrees of the qualities they are told should be important to them, often striving to be more "perfect" or at least understand why they are not as they are "supposed" to be. Different women have different degrees of passivity, nurturing, and subservience. They also have differing degrees of independence, physical aggression, and drive for success. In the discussion that follows I do not try to locate where "femininity" and "masculinity" come from, except to say that they exist as a product of socialization. Second, just because the qualities associated with women and men are encouraged by society, this does not mean that they are inappropriate or unwanted by the bearer. As will become clearer over the course of this discussion, the woman detective puts a very high priority on her feelings of responsibility and empathy. She wants to expand her reach from the home to the larger society. Qualities such as passivity, for example, she finds inappropriate and, in many ways, dangerous. Rather, the woman detective endeavors to reach out into the world and demand that it take her seriously. She learns to defend herself. She also learns how to understand that needing help is not the same as being helpless. In either case, gender mythologies must change from being taken for granted, and therefore "invisible" to human intervention. It is necessary for both men and women to recognize and question their feelings and priorities and make them their own. Even where the woman sleuth grasps hold of attributes traditionally associated with "femininity," she works to revitalize the definition. She takes the image and definition back and endows them with renewed strength and meaning. This act of reconfiguring the nature, history, and role of women in Western society is defined, for the purposes of this analysis, as "feminism." Following the lead of Maureen Reddy, feminism is defined as a way of looking at the world that puts women's experiences at the center. Women are capable of intelligence, moral reasoning, and independent action, while they also attend to the limitations placed on them by patriarchal society. Moreover, feminism is aware of the complexity, diversity, and dissimilarity of women's lives. Women may be different from men, but few of these differences are biologically determined. "Different" does not, in any way, mean "lesser."[5]

The analysis that follows is in three parts. The first chapter locates the mystery novel as a commodity in a free market economy. As an artifact of popular culture, the mystery novel is part of a much larger enterprise—private enterprise. Format, marketing strategies, and, to a certain extent, content are shaped by forces invisible to readers. The modern detective story was originally created to attract a wide market for emerging popular magazines and publications. Authors and publishers developed conventions for the genre in order to make it accessible to a wide audience and to attract more authors. Today, corporate publishers with a priority on the economic bottom line continue to shape the genre. Readers and authors do not just interpret texts in isolation as they read; choices and influences in the industry shape their experiences before the cover of the book is opened.

The subsequent three chapters build on this background and become the second part of my discussion. Part 2 is a textual analysis of the three types of detective novels delineated—featuring either the private eye, the police-qualified investigator, or the amateur sleuth. Issues in these chapters include how authors find flexibility in the conventions of the genre to expand and debate issues of violence, women in society, social expectations, heroism, feminism, and responsibility. Mystery fiction allows women space and opportunity to imagine themselves as the hero. Rather than the traditional definition of "femininity" and its restrictive set of codes for behavior, expectations, and responsibilities, many women's mysteries illustrate the potentially dangerous realities in this definition and the lives that are possible outside of the stereotype.

Since the eighteenth century, literature has been a largely feminine pursuit. Upper- and middle-class women, excluded from many activities outside the home, filled their leisure hours with reading. Women in the lower classes found more leisure time to read as manufacturing and industry took over the duties they had previously performed. Apprentices and household servants were exposed to books in the homes of their employers and had the time and a comfortable space in which to read. Women were the primary audience for fiction, but society had clear rules about what was appropriate for them to read and write.[6]

Many of the early works by women authors have been lost, dismissed, or overlooked by historians and critics. The fact that a majority of eighteenth-century novels were written by women, for example, is dismissed by critics as merely an issue of quantity and not quality:[7]

> American literature is male. To read the canon of what is currently considered classic American literature is perforce to identify as male. Our literature neither leaves women alone nor allows them to participate. It insists on its universality at the same time that it defines that universality in specifically male terms.[8]

The result is a paradox. To be a writer of great works, a woman author has to "write like a man," but in order for a woman to be considered a legitimate author by critics, she has to "write like a woman."

Women's novels were expected to reflect "feminine" sensibilities—gentle language, a focus on the home, and romance without passion.[9] Consequently, women's works were criticized and passed over by critics for lacking real (i.e., "masculine") feelings and expressions. In "The False Morality of Lady Novelists," critic W. R. Greg argues that woman's sexual innocence prevents her from writing great novels:

> She is describing a country of which she knows only the more frequented and the safer roads, and a few of the sweeter scenes and the prettier by-paths and more picturesque detours which be not far from the broad and beaten thoroughfares; while the rockier and loftier mountains, and more rugged tracts . . . are never trodden by her feet, and scarcely ever dreamed of by her fancy.[10]

John Stuart Mill suggested that literary utopia for women would involve them living in a different country than men, and therefore, never having read any men's writings. In such a place, women would be able to have a literature of their own, and thus could be innovators rather than the imitators Mill was sure they would otherwise always be.[11]

Feminist literary critics have, in more recent years, taken on the project of recovering women's writings that were lost to history and the masculine tradition of literary criticism. Recovery also includes redefining the language of literary criticism in order to recognize how it has traditionally privileged the masculine and demeaned the feminine. "Language has been a powerful social force, male, that undermines the autonomy of the individual, female."[12] Language and narratives are redefined as systems that construct arbitrary differences. The task of the literary critic is no longer to arrive at the absolute meaning of a text, but to discuss it in terms of power relations. The struggle over language is a struggle for dominance over meaning. The "great works" are not the only locations for analyzing power relations. Feminist literary critics have been among the scholars expanding the field of literary research to include popular culture. They have reviewed the history of their own discipline and adapted theories and models to their contemporary objectives. New perspectives have led to new applications for traditional models.

Women have begun to take on the mystery genre as literary critics. Traditionally, the field was dominated by men and reviews of the genre were more concerned with constructing lists of "the best" and charting the history of the genre as a product of these lists. Most debate was usually limited to defining the boundaries of detective fiction—as opposed to the "mystery novel," "crime novel," or "thriller." The critic's job was to determine who was good enough to belong and just what "being good enough" meant. The American male private eye novels of the 1940s and 1950s tend to be regarded as the genre's apex and served as the conclusion of most traditional reviews of the literature. Because they are mass-produced for a general and widespread audience, critics tend to focus on the formulaic quality of the novels. The popularity of the form is most often explained as the audience's positive feelings for conservatism, law and order, and maintaining the status quo.[13]

Feminist literary critics question the theorist's place of privilege in traditional analyses. The critic's role is not to determine meaning but rather, according to Patrocinio P. Schweickart, to change society. Feminist criticism is a way of reading. Literature acts on the world by acting on its readers.[14] Human language reflects the struggles for power in society. The novel captures the struggles over the primacy of meaning in language, which is not represented in the novel as unitary or finished. History and society are part of the text; the text is a part of society. The language of the novel is at once unique and familiar as the author exploits these components to create new meanings and allows room for the audience to be part of the text.[15]

Elizabeth Long, in *The American Dream and the Popular Novel*, highlights the relationship that readers experience with the novel. The novel is the story of individual lives: how individuals take in the world, how it shapes them, how they perceive it (with relative degrees of accuracy), and how it presents them with choices and constraints. Readers see how individual choices, desires, and fears impact the lives of others and stretch or tear the moral fabric of society. Contrary to views of traditional literary criticism, within the novel, ordinary people continually remake their culture—redefining the past, reconstituting the present, and reconceptualizing what they desire from the future.[16] Writers and readers are part of a community of shared meanings. A novel is not just an author's view of the world; it implicates the perceptions of the audience to whom the author writes. The social world is not simply "reality," but a "web of significance," built, in part, on our perceptions of the world. Literary conventions, such as those that have historically defined the mystery novel, are the areas of commonality between the imagined world of the novel and the perceptions of the world held by the audience.[17]

The conventions of the mystery novel comprise the system of codes that make meaning possible. The writer reaches out to the reader and society through the genre's codes. Readers and writers expand the conventions of genre by drawing attention to them and employing them in new situations. Genre fiction comments on society and its own conventions. Thus, it is both a reflection and a critique. Interpretation by the critic, reader, and writer is political. Language constructs meanings that implicate distributions of power rather than absolute truths. “If the world is the product of interpretation, then who or what determines which interpretive systems will prevail?”[18]

Feminist literary critics analyzing women's texts are a part of recovering, articulating, and elaborating expressions of women's points of view. They celebrate the survival of these points of view in spite of the formidable forces that have ranged against them. In analyzing the mystery writing of women, critical emphasis is placed on the recovery and cultivation of their culture and the struggle against patriarchy. It involves women reading women's texts and encountering, not just another text, but the "heart and mind" of another woman. Traditional models of interpreting texts are preoccupied with partition and control—where meaning is and who has it. The feminist reader and text are defined by the drive to connect and develop a relationship across the text.[19]

Literary analyses by women in the field of popular culture have illustrated the models of feminist literary criticism. Their works have expanded the critical understanding of women and their relationship with "women's texts"—namely, romance novels, gothic romances, and mystery novels. None are complete in and of themselves, but each adds to and expands the debate, pointing out new questions and highlighting new areas of inquiry. Literary critics such as Tania Modleski and Janice Radway began their investigations in response to earlier analyses of women's fictions, which concluded that women enjoyed their subjugation and were not "smart enough" to handle serious drama or fiction.

> Their [romance, gothic, and soap opera narratives'] enormous and continuing popularity, I assume, suggests that they speak to very real problems and tensions in women's lives.

> The narrative strategies which have evolved for smoothing over these tensions can tell us much about how women have managed not only to live in oppressive circumstances but to invest their situations with some degree of dignity.[20]

Women use mass-produced texts to make potentially radical statements about themselves and their society.

Modleski is not completely comfortable with the subject of women and romance novels. Ultimately, she concludes that the women reading romance novels, such as those marketed under the name "Harlequin Romance," would be better served by channeling the energies they exert to belittle themselves by reading romances into something more constructive. Revolutions are "real" when manifest in outward social movements. "Real" reading occurs with "great literature."[21] There is an important connection that takes place between women and certain types of genre fiction and popular culture, but Modleski only touches the surface of the relationship. External forces, for example, that mediate women's experiences with the romance are left out of her examination.

"Popular" fiction is not simply a product of the reader enjoying the novel, but also of its attraction to agents, editors, and publishers as a product that will generate revenue by attracting an audience with disposable income. Janice Radway integrates the history and background of the romance novel into her psychological and literary analysis of texts and readers. Readers, too, are specified. Unlike Modleski, Radway interviews them for their own explanations and evidence. Thus, the novel is analyzed as a part of the life of its readers. Radway finds that "although ideology is extraordinarily pervasive and continually determines social life, it does not preclude the possibility of firm, though limited, resistance."[22] In Radway's population of romance readers, there is resistance to the patriarchal order that traditionally defines the lives of the women.

Most traditional literary critics discuss the novel in terms of "the" reader, thus assuming reading to take place as a solitary activity isolated from other influences or readers. Radway "rediscovers" the community of the reader by constructing focus groups in order to talk to the women about their reading. What becomes clear through their conversations is that while the group was artificially created, the discussion comes out of the women's everyday experiences with the novel. The women have special friends with whom they talk about and share books. For example, the neighborhood bookseller talks with the women about new titles and makes recommendations based on conversations she has with them about previous titles. Reading is an activity the women do just for themselves, often stealing moments away from household duties for it. To those moments they bring a host of conversations with their friends about romance novels. Community and connection enrich the women's reading experience.

The task of the feminist scholar with regard to the mystery novel is twofold. A great deal of women's history in the genre has been forgotten by critics and readers. Scholars such as Patricia Craig and Mary Cadogan, Victoria Nichols and Susan Thompson, and Jean Swanson and Dean James have set out to retrieve women's contributions. Their reinterpretations of history record the work of many more women authors and show how they, too, helped shape the genre. In addition, their bibliographies point new readers toward the stories of women, increasing awareness and potential market size.[23]

The second task of feminist scholars is to analyze popular texts with regard to women and their relationship to the narratives. Jessica Mann, Kathleen Gregory Klein, and Maureen T. Reddy are several of the women who have taken on this task. Jessica Mann, for example, was inspired by the question, "Why are respectable English women so good at murder?" This question has been asked by many who are interested in the mystery genre, particularly in the Golden Age; however, Mann's conclusions are unfulfilling. According to Mann, the answer is "fantasy." Since most English women authors have probably never met a criminal, they probably fantasize about such a character.[24] Mann brings the question into the arena of scholarly debate, but fails to develop a rigorous answer.

Kathleen Gregory Klein's focus is the woman private eye in detective novels written by men and women authors between 1864 and 1987. She establishes archetypes based on historic male detectives: Sherlock Holmes, Sam Spade, and Spenser.[25] Women fictional detectives are compared and contrasted with these models. Klein concludes with criticism toward the women detectives for being incomplete with regard to the models she designates. The woman private eye is not allowed to act like a private eye in the detective novel, according to Klein, because the genre is inherently conservative. The mystery novel upholds dominant ideas of power, privilege, and law and order: indeed, "the underlying plot in almost three hundred novels denies these characters either as detectives or as women."[26] Women in detective novels are forced by the genre to be either inadequate women or inadequate detectives. Because mystery novels are produced by the market for mass consumption, they are necessarily incapable of critical reflection or serious consideration, according to Klein. The message for the reader regarding women is traditional, stereotypic, and restrictive. Klein dismisses the current state of the genre and calls for scrapping it in favor of a "women-centered, gender-aware" detective fiction.[27] Feminism and the mystery genre are thus declared incompatible.

Klein's analysis is inconclusive about what the "new" mystery genre would be. She assumes masculine models to be universal. Women are criticized for not being like men and then called on to provide new, "woman-centered" narratives. The task of the feminist critic is not to find the single answer or meaning in a text or body of work. There is no one explanation for women's relationship to the mystery novel —multiple truths exist. Klein offers one set of explanations for the "facts." Using a feminist perspective, Klein constructed one story to fit the evidence. Successive feminist critics have searched to find a story that is more satisfactory in its fit.

Maureen Reddy's *Sisters in Crime* repositions the detective genre in the history of women and feminism. Reddy reviews women mystery writers who have created series female protagonists. More clearly than Klein, Reddy emphasizes the role women have played in developing and expanding the genre. She reviews the history of the mystery genre and draws attention to women authors who have traditionally been overlooked by critics and historians. Authorship is an important criterion in this analysis. The detective novel did not simply emerge, fully formed, from the pens of Edgar Allen Poe and Sir Arthur Conan Doyle. Reddy's feminist analysis highlights the contributions of women's gothic and sensationalistic novels of the eighteenth century to the development of the modern mystery. The themes of women's imprisonment, escape, and the constraining social roles common to women's gothic fiction of the eighteenth century set the stage for contemporary women's mysteries.[28]

Bringing feminist literary criticism to the mystery novel, Reddy expands the definition of "reader" to include the detective in the mystery novel. The text presented to the detective is a fragmented one; her job is to read and write the text in order to bring the narrative to a conclusion that makes sense. She locates meaningful signs (clues) and turns them into a coherent narrative for herself as well as the other characters in the novel. The text of the crime is made whole again (the first time being when it was executed); the text of the novel is made whole and legible to the reader for the first time. The detective appears to have the privileged voice because she tells the characters and readers what the text means, but she acknowledges that the narratives and signs are capable of supporting multiple, and conflicting, interpretations.[29]

Reddy's feminist analysis of women's mystery novels is instructive to the scholars who follow her for its emphasis on multiple truths within the novel and how this is significant for women readers. The detective's presence is an indicator that no event will be without significance, no problem too slight, and no mystery too simple.[30] Everything is a potential sign (clue)—a potential location for interpretation, domination, misdirection, and debate—by virtue of the detective's presence in the story. Mystery novels—in particular, the novels of women—highlight the process of reading, multiple truths inherent in language, and the subjective nature of truth. The detective novel is well suited to women's struggles over social definitions and the power of language to control and define, according to Reddy. In her analysis, Reddy focuses on women—women writers, women characters. Unlike Klein, she is able to isolate women's voices in the creation of their narratives. Reddy develops a model of interpretation that emphasizes focusing on women's creation of narratives and the subjective nature of truth and language.

The analysis that follows continues in the footsteps of Reddy. I illustrate how the mystery novels of women have provided a fertile venue for women's discussions about their own lives and their place in a society where gender prescribes behavior, expectations, and limitations. Contemporary women readers and writers have made significant contributions to the conventions of the mystery novel. The current wave of economic tightening by publishing houses will not be able to erase the significant changes women have made to the genre. The definitions of what constitutes the mystery market, mystery plotting and char-

acterization, and valid mystery themes will continue to expand as women venture further into the field and those areas held tightest by masculine domination.

## NOTES

1. Robin W. Winks, ed., *Detective Fiction: A Collection of Critical Essays* (Woodstock, VT: Foul Play Press, 1988), 4.

2. Edie Gibson, quoting Janet Hutchings, a mystery editor at Walker & Co., "The Sisterhood of Sleuths," *Publishers Weekly* 235.18 (5 May 1989): 37–38.

3. Quoted in Carolyn Anthony, "Crime Marches On," *Publishers Weekly* 237.15 (13 April 1990): 28.

4. British women authors have also made valuable contributions to the current Golden Age. P. D. James, Antonia Fraser, Ruth Rendell (Barbara Vine), and Deborah Crombie are a few examples of British authors who are critical and popular successes in the United States and Britain. In order to focus on the connections between cultural assumptions and definitions, I limited my analysis to contemporary U.S. authors and their U.S. readers. This leaves a great deal of critical space available for scholars to expand this analysis and include a global perspective with regard to mystery authors and readers.

5. Maureen T. Reddy, *Sisters in Crime: Feminism and the Crime Novel* (New York: Continuum, 1988), 9.

6. Ian Watt, *The Rise of the Novel: Studies in Defoe, Richardson, and Fielding* (Berkeley: University of California Press, 1965), 43–47.

7. Watt, 298.

8. Judith Fetterly, *The Resisting Reader: A Feminist Approach to American Fiction* (Bloomington: Indiana University Press, 1978), xii.

9. Carolyn G. Heilbrun, *Toward a Recognition of Androgyny* (1973; New York: W.W. Norton & Co., 1982), 54.

10. W. R. Greg quoted in Elaine Showalter, *A Literature of Their Own: British Women Novelists from Brontë to Lessing* (Princeton, NJ: Princeton University Press, 1977), 26–27.

11. Showalter, 7.

12. Carolyn G. Heilbrun, "Women, Men, Theories, and Literature," in *The Impact of Feminist Research in the Academy*, ed. Christie Farnham (Bloomington: Indiana University Press, 1987), 221.

13. Examples of traditional literary critiques of the mystery novel include: Thomas Gilbert, *How to Enjoy Detective Fiction* (London: Rockliff, 1947); Ralph Harper, *The World of the Thriller* (Cleveland, OH: Press of Case Western Reserve University, 1969); Howard Haycraft, *Murder for Pleasure: The Life and Times of the Detective Story* (New York: D. Appleton-Century Company, 1941); Ernest Mandel, *Delightful Murder: A Social History of the Crime Story* (London: Pluto Press, 1984); Glenn W. Most and William W. Stowe, eds., *The Poetics of Murder: Detective Fiction and Literary Theory* (San Diego, CA: Harcourt Brace Jovanovich, Publishers, 1983); Dennis Porter, *The Pursuit of Crime: Art and Ideology in Detective Fiction* (New Haven, CT: Yale University Press, 1981); Ellery Queen, *Queen's Quorum: A History of the Detective-Crime Short Story as Revealed in the 106 Most Important Books Published in the Field since 1845* (New York: Biblio and Tannen, 1969); Vince Starrett, ed., *Fourteen Great Detective Stories* (New York: Modern Library, 1928); R. F. Stewart, . . . *And Always a Detective: Chapters of History of Detective Fiction* (Newton Abbot. U.K.: David & Charles, 1980); Jul-

ian Symons, *Bloody Murder, From the Detective Story to the Crime Novel: A History* (London, U.K.: Viking, 1985); H. Douglas Thomson, *Masters of Mystery: A Study of the Detective Story* (New York: Dover Publications, 1978); and Colin Watson, *Snobbery with Violence* (New York: St. Martin's Press, 1971).

14. Patrocinio P. Schweickart, "Reading Ourselves: Toward a Feminist Theory of Reading," in *Gender and Reading: Essays on Readers, Texts, and Contexts*, ed. Elizabeth A. Flynn and Patrocinio P. Schweickart (1986; Baltimore, MD: Johns Hopkins University Press, 1992), 39.

15. M. M. Bakhtin, *The Dialogic Imagination*, ed. Michael Holquist (1981; Austin: University of Texas Press, 1987).

16. Elizabeth Long, *The American Dream and the Popular Novel* (Boston: Routledge & Kegan Paul, 1985), 200–202.

17. Long, 3–5.

18. Jane P. Tompkins, "The Reader in History: The Changing Shape of Literary Response," in *Reader-Response Criticism: From Formalism to Post-Structuralism*, ed. Jane P. Tompkins (Baltimore, MD: Johns Hopkins University Press, 1988), 226.

19. Schweickart, 52, 55.

20. Tania Modleski, *Loving with a Vengeance: Mass-Produced Fantasies for Women* (New York: Routledge, 1985), 14–15.

21. Modleski, 57–58.

22. Janice Radway, *Reading the Romance: Women, Patriarchy, and Popular Literature* (Chapel Hill: University of North Carolina Press, 1987).

23. Patricia Craig and Mary Cadogan, *The Lady Investigates: Women Detectives and Spies in Fiction* (London: Victor Gollancz, 1981); Victoria Nichols and Susan Thompson, *Silk Stalkings: When Women Write of Murder* (Berkeley, CA: Black Lizard Books, 1988); Jean Swanson and Dean James, *By a Woman's Hand* (New York: Berkley Books, 1994). Other women who have published histories and critiques of the genre include: Elaine Budd, *13 Mistresses of Murder* (New York: Ungar Publishing Company, 1986); Hanna Charney, *The Detective Novel of Manners: Hedonism, Morality, and the Life of Reason* (London, U.K.: Fairleigh Dickinson University Press/Associated University Press, 1981); Linda Herman and Beth Stiel, *Corpus Delicti of Mystery Fiction: A Guide to the Body of the Case* (Metuchen, NY: Scarecrow Press, 1974); Bobby Ann Mason, *The Girl Sleuth: A Feminist Guide* (New York: Feminist Press, 1975); Michele B. Slung, *Crime on Her Mind: Fifteen Stories of Female Sleuths from the Victorian Era to the Forties* (New York: Pantheon Books, 1975); and Dilys Winn, ed., *Murderess Ink: The Better Half of the Mystery* (New York: Workman Publishing, 1979).

24. Jessica Mann, *Deadlier than the Male: An Investigation into Feminine Crime Writing* (London: David & Charles, 1981).

25. Kathleen Gregory Klein, *The Woman Detective: Gender and Genre* (Urbana: University of Illinois Press, 1988), 2.

26. Klein, 1.

27. Klein, 201, 225, 229.

28. Reddy, 2–9.

29. Reddy, 10.

30. Richard Martin, *Ink in Her Blood: The Life and Times of Margery Allingham* (Ann Arbor, MI: UMI Research Press, 1988), 28.

## *Chapter 1*

# The Mystery Novel as Mass-Market Construction

The relationship between the publishing industry and the contemporary detective novel is contradictory and complicated. Publishers today actively seek out new mystery manuscripts, yet most mystery authors earn little from advances and royalties and their books have limited print runs. Mystery editors (and trade division editors pressed into service as "mystery editors") work for corporate-owned publishing houses. Their first priority is the company's fiscal bottom line, but each works personally with the authors and is often a fan of the genre. Corporate conglomerates have taken over much of the publishing industry, which is increasingly being concentrated into a handful of powerful companies. Small publishing houses with limited resources have, however, successfully published mysteries and been able to maintain a share of the audience. Corporate attention to financial rationality has taken place during the same time period as the recent boom in the detective novel. The boom is marked by an increase in the number of titles sold and in literary worth; attracting a wider audience has not diluted quality, it has improved it.

Most historians of the mystery novel credit Edgar Allen Poe with writing and publishing the first modern detective story in 1841. Stories have always been told about crime, violence, and murder, but Poe structured his story around one man's, the "detective's," investigation of a murder. The detective employed logic and "ratiocination" to the clues found at the scene. "The Murder at the Rue Morgue" was published in the first mass-circulating magazine, *Graham's*. Poe, Wilkie Collins, and Sir Arthur Conan Doyle first found success with their detective stories in the mass-circulating magazines of the United States and Great Britain. Their wildly popular stories were often subsequently published in small booklets or volumes to capitalize on their popularity and expand sales figures. The large daily newspapers, too, ran serializations of popular mystery stories in the late 1800s. From its inception, the detective stories had an economic function: to attract a mass audience in order to sell a product—magazines and, later, books. Popular fiction is market driven. Its stories need to be easily accessible to the public. Few may reach best-seller status, but many afford publishers stable and predictable markets on which to depend for revenue. Since 1945, at least 10 billion copies of crime stories have been sold worldwide. Agatha Christie's novels, for example, have been translated into almost all known written languages. Libraries report readerships of between fifty and one hundred readers for every new mystery published. Today, the detective story is one of the most widely read and steadily consumed forms of modern literature—while individual sales of titles are negligible.[1]

Anna Katharine Green created the first book-length mystery story. Other authors of the time had their stories put together into books at the end of their serialization. Green's *The Leavenworth Case* was written as a mystery novel. Most mystery readers are vaguely, if at all, familiar with the name Anna Katharine Green, yet she published her novel a decade before Conan Doyle penned Sherlock Holmes. Green had no traceable literary antecedents. Her story contained a substantial police detective in a convincing plot and was not just a story that contained an element of detection. According to mystery historian Howard Haycraft, Green is one of the all-time best-sellers in literature. While most women were writing primarily romantic prose, Green brought the detective story into the novel.[2]

For the first seventy-five or eighty years of the modern mystery, there were only a handful of women writers in England and the United States. World War I was a watershed for women writers. This Golden Age is the foundation for many contemporary American women writers. The struggles and successes of these earlier women encouraged and instructed those who came later to the genre. Whether the 1930s or the 1980s, convincing publishers that women could write interesting stories and that other women existed as a market for the mystery was the first step. Agatha Christie had a difficult time finding a publisher for her first Hercule Poirot book. Its success was moderate, but it was enough to encourage Christie to continue writing. Christie's mass appeal came with the serialization of her novels. The publication of *The Murder of Roger Ackroyd* (1926) marked the start of her popular success. The publication coincided with Christie's own mysterious disappearance and the nationwide search for her. The press picked up the story and its sequence of events, which seemed to come straight from one of her novels. During her sensational nine day disappearance, two newspapers began to serialize previous publications and reprints of her earlier works sold out. In little more than two decades from her entrance into the field, Agatha Christie reached the pinnacle of financial success achieved from book and magazine rights by any writer of exclusively detective fiction of the time.

Dorothy L. Sayers is another Golden Age author who dramatically affected the form of the genre and influenced young women readers who would later become practitioners of the craft. Sayers owed much of her popularity in the

United States to magazine serialization. The American women's magazines that picked up her latter books significantly increased her readership. *Murder Must Advertise* sold approximately 9,000 copies in its original U.S. edition. The later *Busman's Honeymoon* reached a total of 20,000 copies due to Sayers's new "women's magazine" audience. Eventually, the profits from her book, magazine, and motion picture rights made Sayers such a wealthy woman that she and her family were able to live off of her work as an author.[3]

For several decades, "women's mysteries" were the almost exclusive domain of the British women of the Golden Age. Agatha Christie, Dorothy L. Sayers, Josephine Tey, Margery Allingham, and Ngaio Marsh set the standard for the traditional mystery. Their stories told of murder, intrigue, and the skills of investigation, but they also gave women a look at other possible narratives. There was marriage and proper English gentility, but there were also women with intelligence, wit, and independence. The authors explored relations between men and women, as well as how women understood themselves and their place in society. The reader, as well as the women characters, was granted the permission to freely travel throughout a wide range of social classes and situations. The criminal investigation was the vehicle for women's adventures.

Publishing changed in the 1950s, and with it, the mystery novel underwent substantial changes, as well. Most mystery publishing prior to the 1950s focused on mass-circulating pulp magazines and hardcovers of British authors. The mass-marketing techniques of the pulp magazine encouraged paperback publishers to offer series of low-cost mystery titles. Simon & Schuster and Penguin Books in the United Kingdom were the first to adopt the magazines' techniques for mass marketing and distribution.[4] From the 1950s there was a marked decline in the pulp magazines, and softcover mystery novels took their place as the format preferred by publishers.

In May 1950, Fawcett's Gold Medal Books was established and began to publish mystery paperback originals. Paperback houses traditionally buy the rights to hardcover editions. A full 50% of the royalties from reprints go back to the hardcover publisher, and the rest are the author's. Since most profits come from paperback sales, authors share a large percentage of a book's profits with hardcover publishers. Gold Medal's publication of paperback mystery originals meant that authors were able to receive 100% of their royalties. The hardcover publishers' control over mystery publishing was thus challenged. Many of Gold Medal's mysteries sold over 1 million copies, at a time when sales of such magnitude were rare.[5]

Hardcover publishing remained the vehicle for attaining any critical success. Women mystery authors primarily remained with hardcover publishers and were among the most critically successful authors. Most of the paperback mysteries published by Gold Medal were masculine stories about tough men and manipulative and sexy women, which were most often written by men. They were the descendants of the nineteenth century action-adventure dime novels and pulp magazine private eyes. The men who dominated the early popular paperback market were able to shape the perceptions of publishing houses about the make up of the mass of the mystery audience.[6] Lee Wright was an editor at Random House in 1960. She notes that she was both the mystery and cookbook editor since "mystery stories and cookbooks were considered the same, in that they had predictable sales." Author Donald Westlake remembers that at the time hardbound mysteries were aimed at libraries and the educated masses. Publishers assumed that paperback mysteries were only bought by "virtually illiterate men."[7]

The publishing industry, and subsequently, mystery publishing as part of what publishers call the trade division, went through a fundamental shift in how it conducted business in the 1960s. Traditionally, most publishing was family owned and operated. Trade book publishing was considered a "gentlemanly" way to make a living. While not consistently profitable, trade publishing did allow publishers to sustain a love of books and professional independence. Publishing houses were mostly independent organizations. They maintained stable and close relations with authors, agents, and booksellers. The titles published by a house were a reflection of the publisher and his tastes and ideas of scholarship.

In the early 1960s, Alfred A. Knopf was absorbed by Random House. With this merger began the trend toward the concentration of ownership, corporate ownership, and mergers between paperback and hardcover publishers.[8] In 1958, 65% of trade books sold in the United States were from the fifty largest trade book publishers, yet by 1977, 60% of trade books were issued by the ten largest trade publishers.[9] Eight of the largest mass-market paperback houses—all conglomerate owned—accounted for 84% of all mass-market paperback sales.[10] The Authors Guild, in recent years, complained to the U.S. Federal Trade Commission, the U.S. Department of Justice, and the judiciary committees of both houses of Congress that the trend toward concentration and conglomeration in book publishing has gone beyond the limits of fair competition. It threatens the survival of the remaining independently owned publishers and is contrary to the "'uninhibited marketplace of ideas' guaranteed by the First Amendment." In addition, it jeopardizes or diminishes an author's marketing power with publishers and the opportunity for many authors of artistically meritorious work that lacks immediate commercial appeal to be published. In response, the American Association of Publishers (AAP) claimed that the industry is "amazingly diverse, flexible, and open." They reported a more plentiful supply of good books, reflecting a greater diversity of subject matter and treatment. According to the AAP, the number of American publishing companies increased by more than 30% in the last twenty years.[11]

Rather than looking at the numbers of publishing houses in the United States, a more accurate understanding of the concentration of power in the publishing industry looks at publishing revenues. Revenues and, subsequently, power have become concentrated in the hands of fewer and fewer publishing houses. Recent mergers and acquisitions have created seven giant trade publishing houses with revenues of over $250 million. The category of "moderate to large" publishers (those with sales between $100 and $250 million) now includes only two.[12] Critics watching the developments in the publishing industry note, "[T]here are still more than a handful, but more power has indeed accrued to the half-dozen largest publishers in New York, which publish the lion's share of books and receive a commensurate amount of attention."[13]

Multi-million dollar corporations have moved into publishing from other entertainment fields—such as television, cable, cinema, amusement parks, toys, and music—as well as unrelated business interests—including finance, electronics, fine china, submersible pumps, oil recovery, and real estate. These conglomerates were originally attracted to the publishing industry's growth. Millions of dollars were pumped into publishing as a result of their interest. The returns on this investment have not always been as high as expected: "From a business standpoint, making and selling books is an annoyingly quaint and fiddly industry."[14] The amount of money consumers spend on books has not risen in relation to costs. A 1992 study released by the American Book Industry reported that 60% of American households bought no books over the course of an entire year.[15] Publishing looks like any other entertainment industry: high fixed costs, heavy reliance on a few "hits" to pay for the many "misses," and no way of predicting what will hit and what will miss. In the entertainment industry, the solution for conglomerates is to be big. The result for book publishing has been overspending and overproduction. Corporations looking to unload some of their debt have restructured their publishing divisions, decreased the number of employees, reduced the number of imprints within the publisher's label (and subsequently, the number of editors leaving their personal marks on the lists put out by the publisher), and found buyers for portions of their book divisions.

Profit margins in trade publishing are thin, as they are a function of volume. A trade publisher pays all fixed, front-end costs of a book. A small initial print run results in a high total cost per unit. The cost of acquiring the paperback rights to a successful hardcover title can be expensive and varies widely from title to title. All unsold books are returned by retailers to the publisher. About 30% of trade books and 42% of mass-market paperbacks are returned. Millions of dollars are spent shipping unsold books to publishers and discount vendors. U.S. bookstores and wholesalers receive an average discount of approximately 50% from the suggested retail price of a book. Marketing, a previously negligible expense, now accounts for 5% to 10% of publishing costs. Royalties have increased from 10% to 15% or more. In the early 1960s, 200,000 copies of a novel were enough for best-seller status. Today, it takes ten times as many. Only one out of five new books is successful. The publisher's share of a book's cover price has shrunk from 30% five years ago to closer to 20%. As the amount of money being spent by the public on books shrinks, publishers struggle to get 5% profit on books that used to net 5% to 10%. Backlist titles (titles already published to which the publisher still retains rights) are one of the few areas where publishers can find profit margins as high as 15% to 17%. As much as 25% to 30% of an average publisher's sales come from backlist titles, but with rising costs in shipping and warehouse storage, backlist titles are having a more difficult time reaching bookstore shelves.[16]

The fierce competition among publishers for profit and the attention by corporate owners to the bottom line have meant an increased effort to find and market best-sellers. The number of copies that can be potentially sold becomes as important, if not more so, than literary merit. Conglomerate owners of publishing houses have little direct connection with "the product." Corporate interests are primarily efficiency and profit. This sense of remoteness is communicated to the people directly in charge of the publishing houses. Books are regarded as interchangeable products; all are promoted as best-sellers. Each new book is advertised like the one that came before it, and there is a uniformity under the brand name, "best-seller." Good books written by talented artists sell well, but the nature of the hype obscures such distinctions.[17] Literary agent Debra Schneider warns that the conglomerate-owned publishing house accountants focus on the bottom line and force the selection of commercial works with "blockbuster" potential over those that will build an author's career. For authors who are starting out, the situation is "brutal"; those with an established career do a little better. Editors still buy manuscripts, but agents are finding it more difficult to sell their clients' books.[18] Agent Nancy Yost optimistically calls the current state of publishing a "thinning out" period where only the best, and not merely the average, get to market.[19]

Despite corporate ownership, mystery editors report that at the editorial level, publishing in the 1990s still has much in common with traditional publishing. The decision to buy a manuscript tends to be made by a single editor or small editorial board, depending on the house. Today's editors do have to pay closer attention to costs and expenses than their predecessors. Where it still exists, an imprint at a large publishing house assures both agents and authors that a book will receive individual attention and not become lost as it goes through the publishing process.[20] Mysteries are seldom in the best-seller category—titles that do make it to best-seller status are more likely shelved and marketed as best-sellers rather than category mysteries. Mystery novels tend to have limited print runs and realize moderate, yet stable, sales. Most mystery authors do not receive large advances. As long as an editor's mystery list is profitable for the house, most mystery editors do their job without corporate intervention.

Traditionally, publishing houses put out lists of titles that reflected editors' personal tastes, and even today, mystery editors can often shape a house's list to reflect their own personal ideas about writing, mysteries, and the mystery audience. Once an editor becomes known for a certain type of mystery, agents and authors follow with more of that type. For example, Joe Blades, an editor at Ballantine Books, has been a longtime mystery reader. While at Avon, he became known as the "inveterate mystery reader on the premises," and mystery manuscripts were generally sent to him for review. He was able to shape Avon's list for several years.[21] Kate Miciak, an editor at Bantam Doubleday Dell Publishing Group, is another example. When she joined Bantam, the mystery list consisted primarily of titles by male authors who had written in the 1940s and 1950s and were no longer living. She took as her first task signing up more contemporary authors. Second, and more in line with her own interests, Miciak included more strong women authors. She met with skepticism from her superiors, but today Bantam is recognized as one of the first publishers to pay serious attention to women's detective fiction.[22] Under the urging of Sara Ann Freed, Mysterious Press developed a list with stories that include strong female protagonists.[23] As women become more commercial both as authors and protagonists in mystery novels, editors find more support for their editorial choices.

Mystery editors receive hundreds of manuscript submissions. The numbers of openings on publishers' lists, however, are decreasing. It is no longer enough for the stories to be good or resemble something that already exists. "There are too many books to just publish the competent."[24] One result of the glut of manuscripts and publishers' tight focus on fiscal responsibility has been the mass marketing of the unique in mysteries. Each publishing house is looking for something new to give it an edge in market share. Fresh voices are more marketable than many published authors who attract midsize audiences: "It's bad to have a track record unless it's excellent."[25] Thus, editors report more chances than ever for an author to find a publisher for a first novel. Publishers market books with the hook that they are "new" and "hot." In an industry where money constitutes worth, the publisher's cost of acquiring the rights can also be a convincing marketing tool.[26]

While the publishing industry has been undergoing dramatic changes in how it conducts business, women authors have been undergoing changes of their own: they are taking more responsibility for their own work and how it reaches the public. Traditionally, women had little sense of authorship as a business and would wait for their publisher to tell them what to do. Most of the time, the answer was, "Nothing," as prior to the 1980s, publishers did very little to promote their mystery lists. Consequently, women authors had little control over the direction of their careers. For example, Marcia Muller is one of the first contemporary U.S. women to write a detective novel with a female private investigator. She published her first Sharon McCone mystery in 1978. Looking back, Muller notes that the problems she had in getting her work published were largely due to her failure to take control of the process.[27]

The new breed of woman author is very savvy about business and the mystery genre, according to literary agent Debra Schneider.[28] Authors' groups, such as Sisters in Crime (an authors' organization that is devoted to ending the discrimination toward women in the mystery field), have made resources available to women writers. Sisters in Crime, for example, publishes booklets on marketing and promotions. Their newsletter relays information from published authors about their own experiences. Moreover, the organization creates a sense of community among authors and their fans, which was historically not available. In the 1970s and early 1980s, authors Marcia Muller, Sue Grafton, Sara Paretsky, and Maxine O'Callaghan were all writing detective stories with strong female protagonists, yet none of the women knew about each other. As mystery fans, they were unable to find mysteries with interesting women characters, which was one reason why they decided to write their own detective stories.[29]

For women writers, contemporary models were not well publicized or made available.

Part of women's education in the publishing industry has included an increased awareness of the role of marketing. If the marketing department cannot locate a book as a recognizable type, chances are good that the manuscript will be overlooked. Author P. M. Carlson originally planned to do a series about a woman's life that spanned the character's lifetime. Carlson wanted to explore how a woman, under specific kinds of situations, could develop and grow over time. In the first Maggie Ryan manuscript, Ryan was fifteen years old. Publishers had a difficult time determining a marketing strategy. The main character was a juvenile ("young adult fiction"), but the themes were adult ("adult mystery"). In the second manuscript, Ryan is in college, making her "adult" enough for the work to be marketed as an adult mystery. Carlson was able to sell the second book, but not the first. She was upset that she could not write a particular story because publishers did not know how to market it, but, she notes, there is still a great deal to write about within the genre. Carlson's second book became the first in the successful Maggie Ryan series.[30]

Marketing is also largely responsible for the serial nature of mystery publishing. Many mystery writers continue their characters and locations across several books.[31] Authors who intended their stories to be complete as one book often find themselves asked by publishers to continue the characters in subsequent books. Editors project forward with many of the manuscripts they receive for review: "Are these characters going to last over several books?" Most first mysteries do not turn a profit. If they are not to simply go after the best-seller, publishers have to develop a steady and reliable audience. By the time an author has published two, three, or four books, reviews and word of mouth can influence the quantity of books purchased by retail outlets.[32]

The series is not without complications for authors and publishers. In particular, authors have no control over their backlist titles; a series can become scattered over several publishing houses. To recoup expenses, hardcover publishers tend to sell the paperback rights.[33] Even when an author has regained the rights to earlier titles, finding a publisher to reprint them can be difficult. Linda Grant's Catherine Sayler series began almost ten years ago. The first volume, *Random Access Murder,* is no longer in print. Grant has the publishing rights, but her current publisher is not interested in reprinting it until there are several more titles in the series. New titles must build an audience to guarantee sales for the first.[34] Authors who try to get a new publisher for their series have a difficult time, as well. Publishers are often reluctant to pick up a series in the middle unless they are sure it will be successful and can get the rights to the entire series.[35]

Authors can use publishers' marketing strategies to their own advantage. While some new authors have found receptive publishers, it can still be difficult to persuade publishers to take on new titles not already known to be of commercial value. Publishers have reduced their mystery lists, which generally means that new authors must convince publishers to replace an existing author. Author Barbara Neely is illustrative of how contemporary U.S. women mystery writers are taking more control over the business of their authorship. Neely had to show publishers there was a market in the African-American community for her stories. Traditionally, little shelf space is allocated to African-American literature. Neely used what she terms publishing's "flavor of the month" tendency to her advantage. Once her manuscript sold she had to remain vigilant to ensure the continued authenticity of her story. The publishing industry is 99% nonblack, and cultural differences can lead to misunderstandings. For example, the skin color of Blanche, the protagonist in Neely's mystery (shown on the book's cover), is significant. Neely has to make the publishing process work for her so that more publishers will follow with mysteries by African-American women.[36]

Ultimately, marketing involves getting mysteries to readers, who gain access to the books through bookstores, retail outlets, and libraries. The degree to which these venues bring in revenue influences their ability to make demands on publishers. According to Richard Snyder, formerly of Simon & Schuster, it is the giant bookstore chains that has really changed the face of publishing, not conglomerate ownership.[37] Agent Raphael Sagalyn, too, credits the rise of the chain bookstores with the most profound changes taking place in the publishing industry: "It was feared, and proven true, that their proliferation would make publishers streamline their lists." The demand for fast-moving titles has intensified and mid-list books are losing out, even though they were often strong sellers in the library market.[38]

Retail book chains, such as Barnes & Noble, B. Dalton, and Borders-Walden, grew rapidly in the 1980s. Concurrently, there was a sharp rise in the number of book outlets located in shopping malls, which linked book sales with mall traffic. Bookstores became a familiar part of the consumer environment and were able to deliver books to the public in the same manner as goods in a drugstore or supermarket. Malls also tied bookstores to consumer economic conditions. Book sales were sluggish in the weak economy of 1990—hardcover and paperback sales each rose slightly more than 4%. By 1992, the industry was able to get back to the 13% annual growth experienced from 1984 to 1989. Part of this jump in growth came from discounting programs instituted by the major chain bookstores, which often reduce the prices of new hardcover best-sellers by, for example, 25% to 40%.[39]

The big chain bookstores take an active role with publishers by signaling them on what is and is not likely to sell in their stores. The *B. Dalton Merchandise Bulletin* is a weekly publication containing brief reviews of recommended current books, up-to-date lists of "what's hot" compiled from data taken from computers directly linked to the B. Dalton cash registers, and author tour information for store displays. The bulletin is sent to all B. Dalton stores and is closely studied at trade publishing houses. It has developed into one of the most influential publications in the book-publishing business.[40]

The majority of books sold to the public are sold by bookstore chains, independent bookstores, and general retailers. These outlets account for 35% of publishers' domestic sales in 1991. National bookselling chains have increased their share of the market in recent years at the expense of the independent bookstores.[41] According to publishing historian Thomas Whiteside, in 1972 the four largest bookstore chains accounted for about 11½% of all trade book sales in the U.S., and by the end of 1979, just the two largest chains accounted for approximately 33% of all trade and mass market paperback sales.[42] Revenues from the largest U.S. bookstore chains increased by 18.2% in the year ending January 31, 1994—increasing from $2.7 billion to nearly $3.2 billion. This growth by the top chains surpasses the expansion reported by the entire retail bookstore segment—retail bookstore sales increased 5.5% during this same time, to total $9.29 billion. The market share of the five largest chains (Borders-Walden, Barnes & Noble, Crown Books, Books-A-Million and Encore Books) is becoming an increasingly large segment of the retail bookstore industry. Since 1992, the chains' share of sales has grown from 30.4% to 34.0%.[43]

Independent booksellers were the traditional venue for book sales, but their ability to compete in today's market has been drastically reduced by the increase in bookstore superstores, with their deep discounts and extensive inventories. In 1958, one-store independent booksellers were responsible for 72% of the trade books bought in the United States. By 1980, however, they accounted for less than 40% of the market.[44] There are more than 4,300 independent general bookstores in the United States. They see themselves as upholding a 300 year old tradition as guardians of diversity and free expression in the marketplace of books. They set themselves the tasks of nurturing new authors, continuing support for authors who do not make the best-sellers' list, establishing long-term relationships with hundreds of publishers—especially the small or regional presses—and providing reading recommendations to their customers. The independent bookstore builds a community for authors and readers. In contrast to the bookstore chains, the independents have very low return rates, give books longer shelf lives, and lobby publishers to keep books in print and increase promotional support.[45]

The first dedicated mystery bookstore opened June 14, 1972—Dilys Win's Murder Ink in New York City. In 1993, the number of mystery bookstores had grown to approximately eighty stores and close to thirty mail order or by-appointment dealers.[46] Mystery publishing is one area of trade publishing closely associated with the independent bookstore market. Lyssa Keusch, an assistant editor at Avon Books, notes that while the chain bookstores are a very important outlet for romance novels, Avon Books needs to sell its mysteries to the specialty stores, too.[47] According to editor Sara Ann Freed, Mysterious Press has a stronger relationship with the independent bookstores than with the chain booksellers.[48] This type of attention to independent booksellers by mystery publishers is reported by other editors as well.

Mystery author Carolyn Wheat, who started her career as an author in 1981, credits the boom in women's mysteries to the quantity of independent mystery bookstores across the country. In was unusual for anyone to go on the road and tour in the early 1980s.[49] Publishers today utilize the resources of these stores and push authors to tour with their books. St. Martin's Press editor Ruth Cavin, too, links the boom in women's mysteries with the spread of mystery bookstores across the country. Cavin observes that many specialty bookstore owners and clerks are women. They promote the books that interest them, including mysteries with strong female characters.[50] The staff at mystery bookstores read most of the books they stock, paying close attention to lesser-known authors who have not received media attention. The staff hand-sells books by suggesting new authors and being aware of what their individual clients look for in mystery novels. Mystery bookstores have very low return rates and keep as many of an authors' books as possible on the shelf. Author signings and reading are popular events that expose new readers to the author and the store. Specialty bookstores work to persuade publishers to keep books in print longer and increase promotional support.[51] The career building provided by the mystery bookstores is beginning to be noticed by the chain bookstores, which are most often concerned with the most current titles and with authors who produce high-volume, rapid sales. Authors must be popular within the mystery reader community and have crossed over into the mainstream public to have the sales figures necessary to attract the chains' attention. The staff of chain bookstores cannot devote a great deal of time and attention to what is just a percentage of their book stock, but several have begun to take advantage of the increased publicity. Waldenbooks designated October 1994 as Sisters in Crime month at their stores. The month included special displays, increased new and backlist titles, and a telemarketing telephone number for authors who were available for in-store promotions.[52] Chain bookstores follow the trends; their sales are made after an author becomes popular and customers start to request particular kinds of books.

Retail outlets are only part of the mystery-publishing picture. The library market also plays a major role in career building for mystery authors. Before mystery bookstores spread across the country, libraries supported mid-list authors and introduced new authors to the public. Libraries are the principle market for hardcover mystery titles, and mysteries are the most circulated collection in most public libraries. Author Nancy Pickard put the influence of the libraries on the mystery genre into perspective with the following "tongue-in-cheek" observation made at the 1994 American Library Association (ALA) Conference in Miami, Florida: she asserted that for a mystery hardback with a first print run of six thousand copies, four thousand go to libraries, one thousand go to friends and family, and the remaining thousand are returned to the warehouse.[53] Hardback mysteries are sold by bookstores, too, but the numbers do not compare to their library sales.

Libraries help to maintain an author's career during a time when books are going out of print quickly and only the most popular and latest titles can be found on most bookstore shelves. At a Sisters in Crime panel discussion, "Mystery Writing as a Second Career" (held at the 1994 ALA Conference), author Marlys Millhiser credited libraries with keeping her career alive. Millhiser began her writing career in 1972 but took a prolonged break and has only recently returned to mystery writing. Because of the attention library patrons paid to her first book, Millhiser was able to come back to her career with some degree of success. Her first book, *The Mirror*, has been out of print for several years, but library copies continue to circulate.[54]

Many mystery titles would not be published if there were no library market to guarantee a minimum of sales. Hardcover publishers, such as St. Martin's Press, have traditionally looked to libraries for the bulk of their sales. A full 95% of the general titles published in a given year sell fewer than 20,000 copies, and 55% of the copies sold of these nonbest-sellers are sent to libraries. More than half of all libraries spend 10% to 20% of their book budgets on backlisted books to replace worn or stolen copies and to fill special requests by patrons. More than 29,000 private, public, academic, and specialized libraries exist in the United States. They account for approximately 12% of the total dollar value of publishers' book sales and about 5% of units sold in any given year. For publishers, libraries make good business sense. Libraries operate with very low overhead. Publishers spend a significantly lower percentage of sales dollars to advertise and promote books to libraries than to bookstores. Libraries are also less likely to overstock titles, reducing the number and expense of returns. In 1991, libraries purchased over 125 million books, for more than $2.1 billion.[55] For mystery publishers, libraries are the place to sell the first mystery by an author—and even the second or third.[56] While superstore bookstores continue to grow, focusing publishers' attentions on the most current and fast-selling titles, libraries and mystery bookstores work to balance the equation for mid-list and new authors.

In the 1980s, publishers looking to make a profit rushed to publish a "hot" new trend—mysteries by women with stories that focused on strong, independent women. The economics of publishing in the 1990s faces a slowdown. Corporate owners are not realizing the expected profits and publishing houses continue to merge. Publishing houses also perceive their lists to be oversaturated with women's mysteries and are limiting the number of manuscripts purchased. In the 1990s, however, women's mysteries and the strong market of women readers they galvanized have become a staple of the genre. The "Second Golden Age" has indeed reshaped the mystery for generations of writers and readers to come. The types of characters, locations, and plots developed will be imitated until they, too, will risk becoming cliché.

Mystery readers and writers do not arrive at the novel free from influence or expectation. Popular fiction is a product of the market. The history of the mystery novel is of a form constructed for mass appeal. Its format, conventions, style, and look were developed with an eye to reaching the widest possible audience. Editors are employees of publishing companies. They must select books that meet with perceived audience expectations of the genre as well as meet corporate criteria for profitability. Conglomerates have taken over publishing houses and merged them with their other market ventures. Publishing has become one of many corporate interests; each responsible for producing a product and showing a profit. Publishers struggle to turn a potential audience into mystery readers by making their books in some way stand out from the others on the shelf. What readers react to are not just the words between the covers. Decisions are made that affect the text before the reader lays a hand on the book. The mystery novel is a mass-produced narrative written according to accepted genre conventions. How well a text follows conventional standards influences a publisher's expectation of its profitability. The analysis of the mystery novel that follows continues to look at the issue of popularity. The industry both shapes, and is shaped, by the relationship that develops between the novels, the authors, and their readers. Decisions by publishers determine which books reach the public, but at each step in the process, publishers look to the public for what will sell. The authors and texts that are a part of my analysis illustrate the flexibility of genre conventions and how popularity can include the element of revolution.

## NOTES

1. Ernest Mandel, *Delightful Murder: A Social History of the Crime Story* (London: Pluto Press, 1984), 66; James D. Hart, *The Popular Book: A History of America's Literary Taste* (New York: Oxford University Press, 1950), 259; Howard Haycraft, *Murder for Pleasure: The Life and Times of the Detective Story* (New York: D. Appleton-Century Co., 1941), 262.
2. Haycraft, 83–84.
3. Haycraft, 139.
4. World War I was part of the paperback revolution since it created a need for large numbers of cheap books for the U.S. armed forces. Mandel, 66.
5. George Tuttle, in "The Golden Era of Gold Medal Books," *The Fine Art of Murder: The Mystery Reader's Indispensable Companion*, ed. Ed Gorman, Martin H. Greenberg, Larry Segriff, and Jon L. Breen (New York: Carroll & Graff Publishers, 1993), 343.
6. Jon L. Breen, introduction to *The Fine Art of Murder: The Mystery Reader's Indispensable Companion*, ed. Ed Gorman, Martin H. Greenberg, Larry Segriff, and Jon L. Breen (New York: Carroll & Graf Publishers, 1993), 3–4.
7. Rosemary Herbert, "Mystery Books Today: The Evidence Points to a Rise in Crime," *Publishers Weekly* 234.2 (8 July 1988): 17.
8. Thomas Whiteside, *The Blockbuster Complex: Conglomerates, Show Business, and Book Publishing* (Middletown, CT: Wesleyan University Press, 1981), 1–2.
9. Whiteside, 40–41.
10. Whiteside, 49.
11. Whiteside, 10–11.
12. Jim Milliot, "New Alliances for New Media," *Publishers Weekly* (3 January 1994): 51.
13. Sarah Lyall, "After the Sale of Macmillan, Fears of Concentrated Power," *New York Times*, 15 November 1993, D10.
14. "The Diseconomies of Scale," *Economist*, 7 April 1990, 25.
15. "Reading between the Videos," *Economist*, 29 February 1992, 29.
16. "How Publishers Turn a Profit," *Standard & Poor's Industry Surveys* 161.6 (1993): M36-M37; "The Diseconomies of Scale," 26; John F. Baker, "Reinventing the Book Business," *Publishers Weekly* (14 March 1994): 40.
17. Whiteside, 191–92.
18. Debra Schneider, telephone interview, 28 January 1994.
19. Nancy Yost, telephone interview, 2 March 1994.

20. Ruth Cavin, telephone interview, 31 January 1994.

21. Lauri Miller, "Joe Blades of Ballantine Books," in *Mystery Writer's Marketplace and Sourcebook*, ed. Donna Collingwood (Cincinnati, OH: Writer's Digest Books, 1993), 114.

22. Robin Gee, "Kate Miciak of Bantam Doubleday Dell," in *Mystery Writer's Marketplace and Sourcebook*, ed. Donna Collingwood (Cincinnati, OH: Writer's Digest Books, 1993), 118.

23. Jack Heffron, "Sara Ann Freed of Mysterious Press," in *Mystery Writer's Marketplace and Sourcebook*, ed. Donna Collingwood (Cincinnati, OH: Writer's Digest Books, 1993), 146; Sara Ann Freed, telephone interview, 25 February 1994.

24. Hope Dellon, telephone interview, 24 February 1994.

25. Quote from Ginger Barber, Virginia Barber Literary Agency, in Barbara Hoffert, "Getting Published: A Report from the Front," *Library Journal*, 15 February 1990, 155.

26. Freed interview.

27. Marcia Muller, telephone interview, 27 January 1994.

28. Schneider interview.

29. Muller interview.

30. P. M. Carlson, telephone interview, 5 November 1993.

31. Most writers of serial mysteries have a primary protagonist that carries across the series, but there are other possibilities. Author M. D. Lake, for example, uses a primary location. The characters vary across the series, but the town is always the same.

32. Donna Collingwood, Hal Blythe, and Charlie Sweet, "Susanne Kirk of Charles Scribner's Sons," in *Mystery Writer's Marketplace and Sourcebook*, ed. Donna Collingwood (Cincinnati, OH: Writer's Digest Books, 1993), 166–67.

33. Maxine O'Callaghan, telephone interview, 24 January 1994.

34. Linda Grant, telephone interview, 2 February 1994.

35. O'Callaghan interview.

36. Barbara Neely, telephone interview, 24 January 1994.

37. John Berry, "On Commerce and Conscience: A Conversation with Richard Snyder," *Library Journal*, 15 February 1990, 151.

38. Hoffert, 155.

39. "Near-term Sales Outlook Bright," *Standard & Poor's Industry Surveys* 162.19 (1994): M24–M25; "Sales Aren't Impervious to Economic Slump," *Standard & Poor's Industry Surveys* 159.5 (1991): M31; "Adult Trade Books Set the Pace in '92," *Standard & Poor's Industry Surveys* 161.6 (1993): M35.

40. Whiteside, 45.

41. "How Publishers Turn a Profit," M37.

42. Whiteside, 40.

43. "Chain Sales Rise 18% in Year; Market Share Increases," *Publishers Weekly* (11 April 1994): 10.

44. Whiteside, 40–41.

45. Lorraine Petty, "Plugging into the Independent General Bookstore Network," *Sisters in Crime Newsletter* 5.3 (1993): 6.

46. Elaine Raco Chase, "Waldenbooks to Promote SinC Authors," *Sisters in Crime Newsletter* 5.3 (1993): 6; Jan Grape, "The Care and Feeding of a Mystery Bookstore," in *The Fine Art of Murder: The Mystery Writer's Indispensable Companion*, ed. Ed Gorman, Martin H. Greenberg, Larry Segriff, and Jon L. Breen (New York: Carroll & Graf Publishers, 1993), 377–79.

47. Lyssa Keusch, telephone interview, 1 March 1994.

48. Freed interview.

49. Carolyn Wheat, telephone interview, 20 December 1993.

50. Cavin interview. Women working in mystery bookstores enjoy and sell books by men, but the novels tend to be stories without excessive or gratuitous violence or sex. The boom in women's mysteries has resulted in a "softening" of many mysteries by men.

51. Petty, 6.

52. Chase, 6.

53. Nancy Pickard, "Mystery Writing as a Second Career," panel discussion, American Library Association (ALA) Conference, Sisters in Crime ALA Breakfast, Doral Hotel, Miami, Florida, 26 June 1994.

54. Marlys Millhiser, "Mystery Writing as a Second Career," panel discussion, American Library Association (ALA) Conference, Sisters in Crime ALA Breakfast, Doral Hotel, Miami, Florida, 26 June 1994.

55. "Library Market Is Crucial to Book Industry," *Standard & Poor's Industry Surveys* 160.7 (1992): M35.

56. Barbara Hoffert, "St. Martin's: A Genius for Genre," *Library Journal*, 1 September 1993, 140.

## *Chapter 2*

# The Private Eye

In 1978, Marcia Muller broke into the traditionally male-dominated domain of the hard-boiled private eye novel with her detective Sharon McCone in *Edwin of the Iron Shoes*.[1] McCone is a private investigator (PI) with a license and a gun, but little else in common with the archetypal PI, Sam Spade. Muller has subsequently been dubbed by the media as the "mother" of the "soft-boiled" woman-centered private eye detective novel.[2] Authors Sue Grafton and Sara Paretsky followed shortly behind Muller with their own fictional women private eyes. Each of these women came to a point in their lives and their reading where they were no longer fulfilled by the traditional narratives for women. Each imagined other possible stories. What the market was not providing, these women set out to write. Since their entry into the field, other women authors have followed to further expand, develop, complicate, and enrich the PI genre for women and men. I have selected five women authors of PI series to illustrate how women have contributed to the possible narratives of women through the private eye novel. The authors (and their characters) chosen for this discussion are: Marcia Muller (Sharon McCone), Sue Grafton (Kinsey Millhone), Sara Paretsky (V. I. Warshawski), Linda Grant (Catherine Sayler), and Sandra Scoppettone (Lauren Laurano). The traditional male private eye is a loner living on the mean streets. He is forced to confront corrupt individuals and must be quick to action—usually with fists or guns. Relationships are hostile; rampant individualism is the rule. The women authors, in contrast, raise questions about these fictional portrayals of reality, including conventional definitions of "appropriate" roles for women. The authors reveal new possibilities for the heroic. Feminist literary critic (and a mystery writer, under the pseudonym Amanda Cross) Carolyn

Heilbrun suggests that the private eye novel is a story about how everyone can be anyone.[3]

The male private eye was introduced in the pulp magazine *Black Mask*, in the 1930s and 1940s.[4] Its U. S. authors made a significant break with traditional English mysteries. The male PI was not a direct descendant of the cerebral detective (i.e., Edgar Allen Poe's Dupin or Sir Arthur Conan Doyle's Sherlock Holmes). Instead, he came from the action-oriented adventurer common in the dime novel.[5] The new style was dubbed "hard-boiled." It was an abrupt break with the gentility of the classic detective story of the Golden Age—now marketed by publishers and booksellers as "traditional" or an "English Cozy." The new plots centered around brutality and social corruption, especially among the rich, rather than the psychological motives of greed or revenge in traditional mysteries.[6] Plotting and locations were culled from the streets of urban America.

Spy novels boomed in the 1960s and almost killed off the private investigator in the 1960s and 1970s. The 1960s and early 1970s were also a time of great change for women, and indeed, most of the women mystery authors who emerged in the 1980s and 1990s credit the contemporary women's movement for their success. Marcia Muller, for example, considers herself to have been "part of the whole thing." She was active in the movement and in consciousness-raising.[7] Sue Grafton started her own business, Homemakers Unlimited, in the late 1960s to run consciousness-raising sessions about attitudes toward housework. The business closed a few years later, but for Grafton it was an important breakthrough: for the first time, she had made money from her own ideas.[8]

The contemporary fictional woman private eye appeared in the 1970s. The decline in the popularity and importance—to publishers—of the private eye novel, coupled with women's discovery of the strength of their own voices, proved a fertile combination. Maxine O'Callaghan was the first woman to write about a contemporary woman private investigator. Her short story about Delilah West, PI, appeared in *Alfred Hitchcock* magazine in November 1974. Subsequently, Marcia Muller created the first novel-length story of a woman PI in 1978. Over time, the form found new vitality and popularity. In the 1980s, the Private Eye Writers of America was formed and its annual award, the Shamus, was created.[9] American women were at the forefront on the PI novel's renewed vitality.

The continuing challenge to women writers is to break through the traditionally narrow scope of the PI novel, which is a result of its perceived predominantly male market.[10] Women writers of the 1930s to 1960s were most often confined by the industry to writing about two basic types of female characters: "genteel old ladies who solved crimes between cups of tea and sultry dames who happened to be victims, girlfriends, murderers, or all three."[11] Muller credits the expanding opportunities for women that came in the wake of the women's movement of the 1960s and 1970s as the spark for women mystery writers. More women became police officers, private detectives, attorneys, business executives, and technical workers. Women began to try and shed old conventions and restrictions. They spoke their minds and experimented with alternative ways of living. Fiction slowly began to reflect women's new roles and struggles, as well as the consequences felt by society.[12] Ironically, it was an earlier women's movement that mystery critic Anne Cranny-Francis credits with giving the traditional hard-boiled male private eye his misogynist edge. Sam Spade and his PI counterparts were a fictional response to the challenge of the early twentieth century women's movement to the patriarchal system. They encapsulated male fantasies of denial and dominance and their sexual activity was a strategy to achieve power and dominance over women.[13]

Contemporary women mystery writers' stories of how they were inspired to write mysteries about a woman private eye are all very similar. As a group, the women came to many of the same conclusions about their lives and opportunities. Growing up, they were excited by the stories of male adventurers in private eye novels. The language of the stories was tough, cynical, and daring. As authors, the women found the books to be interesting models to learn from, but unsatisfying for female identification. Thus, they took it upon themselves to write the kinds of stories they wanted to read but could not find. All five of the authors selected chose the PI form in order to find a fictional voice closest to their own.

Marcia Muller was an avid read of the private eye novels of Ross Macdonald and Raymond Chandler, but she learned her craft by reading the girls' series books of Margaret Sutton (the Judy Bolton series). As a literature major in college, Muller moved away from the authors she had considered to be her heroes in popular fiction. As a college student, that was what she was "supposed to do." However, she came back to these authors as an adult. Muller got the idea of writing a mystery from reading Ross Macdonald. She was attracted to developing a female character who was a dry-witted, quick-thinking, legal investigator since she had not been able to find any such characters in fiction. Sharon McCone was created in 1972, but it took five years to find a publisher.[14]

As a child, Sue Grafton read all the time. She read Mickey Spillane instead of the more "girl-appropriate" Nancy Drew-type books. She wanted to write mysteries in the tradition of Raymond Chandler, Dashiell Hammett, and Ross Macdonald. Grafton liked the "down-and-dirty, dark, cynical world" they portrayed. However, she did not know how to plot a mystery or what a private eye really did, so she did not want to take on the extra burden of trying to write from a male point of view. Instead, Grafton decided to rely on her own experiences and perceptions: "[W]hat I did in essence was to make myself my prime character."[15] In the first draft of her first novel, Grafton thought Kinsey Millhone "sounded too much like Mae West." Subsequently, after Grafton stopped trying to spoof the genre, she was able to find the right voice. "I don't have to insist so much on her [Kinsey Millhone's] toughness because I know readers believe in her and enjoy her company."[16]

Sara Paretsky was inspired to write a mystery of her own after reading the works of Raymond Chandler. She read his books in 1970 and began to imagine a woman private eye who could overturn some of the stereotypes about women that pervade the work of Chandler and other noir novelists.[17] Paretsky published *Indemnity Only* in 1982. Years earlier she had received her Ph.D. in history and realized that what she really wanted to do was write a novel. Seventy pages into her first V. I. Warshawski novel, Paretsky signed up for a detective fiction-writing course taught by mystery author Stuart Kaminsky. His advice was to write like a woman. The women in Paretsky's novels behave like women, not women trying to behave like men.[18]

> As a reader of mysteries, I always had trouble with the way women are treated as either tramps or helpless victims who stand around weeping. I wanted to read about a woman who could solve her own problems. I was determined to write about a hard-boiled sleuth who was both a woman and a complete professional. Someone who could operate successfully in a tough milieu and not lose her femininity.[19]

Linda Grant began writing mysteries in 1984. She grew up with the fiction of Chandler and Hammett and liked the PI novel. She wanted to create a female protagonist and explore what would happen to the male PI archetype if it was turned on its head. In the early 1980s, women's mysteries were still poorly distributed. Grant did not find books by women authors such as Marcia Muller, who were interested in the same issues as she, until she was halfway done with her own manuscript. Grant knew that as an author, she wanted to write a new kind of story for the woman hero.[20]

Sandra Scoppettone has, professionally, always been a writer. However, crime writing came relatively late in her career. Her early crime novels dealt with male detectives. Scoppettone used the pseudonym Jack Early for these early mystery novels. Scoppettone recognizes with hindsight that her masculine alter ego brought with it a great deal of power. Her books received great critical reviews and attention. After the Jack Early book, *Donato & Daughter*, Scoppettone struggled to find a new voice for expressing herself through her writing, and thus the character of Lauren Laurano emerged. Scoppettone put her own name on the Laurano series and this new character's voice comes closest to Scoppetone's own, according to the author.[21]

The women authors discussed here were not satisfied with the traditional narratives for female readers. Traditional male PI novel authors were using language and action to give readers a sense of adventure that these women found lacking in other "female" stories. Not all the women set out to create a feminist critique of the PI novel and character. The authors differ in the degree to which they recognize their writing as a direct confrontation of the male model. What they have in common is an attraction to the fictionalized adventure and a realization that it was not meant for them as females. Without role models or a sense of the outcome of their efforts, the women worked to create their own definitions of heroism, adventure, and what is "appropriate." The books are not a treatise on feminism, but rather a window on the feminisms of many women living their lives in a masculine-dominated Western society.

Genre writing requires authors to make their work recognizable to readers by using or implicating conventions. If the conventions remain static, the form will lose its viability with readers. Tensions are created between traditional and expected models and the language of the author. The conventions of the hard-boiled private eye novel do not reflect the concerns and experiences of the contemporary Western woman. Women writing about female characters who are tough, intelligent, and independent have a difficult time with traditional PI novel conventions. A new genre has been created out of the tensions between the traditional PI novel and the narratives of contemporary women—the "soft-boiled" PI novel. These new mysteries tend to include less gratuitous violence and sex, more of the stories focus on human interest and relationships.

The male PI created in the 1930s and 1940s set the standard for the American hero. This archetypal hero has pronounced physical ability. He deals out and absorbs great quantities of physical punishment. He is proficient with a gun and seldom travels the streets without one. He works alone and drinks alone, operating outside established social codes. He prefers his own instinctive justice to the "often tarnished justice of civilization." The police are most often portrayed as incompetent, brutal, and corrupt. The subtleties of the deductive method of the cerebral detective are replaced by the PI's sure knowledge of his world and by his keen moral sense. For the hard-boiled PI, social contact is debilitating, and accordingly, he isolates himself from normal human relationships. His toughness and moral convictions conflict with the values of civilization. As a result, he is forced to flee from society whenever he feels his personal integrity and freedom threatened. The hard-boiled private eye acts according to his own understanding of truth, with little regard for the price others have to pay. He is doomed to solitude because he believes himself too good for the rest of society: "While their profession has risks, their selves are never chanced."[22] The private eye perceives beautiful and available women as destructive and manipulative. His quest is more important than love. "Although not a perfect man, he is the best man in his world."[23] He has no past and no family. He appears on the page complete and unchanging. Authors Dashiell Hammett and Raymond Chandler created a new genre in mystery fiction out of this tough, street-talking loner.

Dashiell Hammett's character Sam Spade, in *The Maltese Falcon*, typifies the traditional masculine private eye, who set the standard for the genre. It is in his relationships, or lack thereof, that readers see how Spade delineates, and relates to, his world. In *The Maltese Falcon*, Spade is involved with four liaisons that can loosely be described as relationships. The first is with the wife of his partner, Archer. Spade is having an affair with his partner's wife, the point of which is to get at his partner, a man Spade dislikes. After his partner is killed, Spade quickly distances himself from the affair and the woman. The second encounter is with Spade's new female client. He appears to develop feelings for her, but in the end, those feelings pale in comparison to his sense of his self-preservation and he cuts his ties with her in the face of possible arrest by the police. One of them is going to get caught as a result of the case, and Spade chooses the woman. The third relationship is with his secretary, who he sees as a body to be fondled and a person to run his errands. She is part of Spade's office; she serves his purposes. She gives him her opinion of clients and cases, but in the end, it is his word that matters.

The final relationship is the most important to Spade and has little to do with the actual person involved. Spade does not like his partner, Archer, but when he is killed, Spade fervently involves himself in the case. Spade is obligated to find his partner's killer. It is part of an unwritten masculine code of behavior that guides the hard-boiled private eye. A man must come to the aid of his partner. It is a matter of honor. The people who inhabit Spade's life are caricatures, who exist Spade believes, for his benefit. They have little impact on the meaning of his life, and he does not mature, grow, or develop as a result of his associations and experiences. Spade travels linearly through the pages of the novel, ending when the story ends.[24]

Women authors writing a PI novel with a woman investigator are faced with the task of having to reconcile traditional definitions of "femininity" and their own experiences of womanhood with the conventional marginalized PI character expected in a Spade-type PI novel. Spade was a "lone wolf" observer of society; he was outside the boundaries. Women are socialized by society to pay attention to the feelings of those around them. They are defined by their associations within the community: mother of, wife of, and daughter of. Traditionally shut out of many positions outside the family, such as higher education, careers, and leadership, women have historically learned to build their lives around associations with people. Women learn about their world, where they fit, and how to act through their relationships.[25]

The role of the private eye challenges traditional gender arrangements. Women authors find themselves explaining why their women characters choose such an "untraditional" vocation. Authors and readers both need some type of explanation or justification in the character of the women PIs. The anomaly must be made plausible. By going through the exercise of justifying the woman's choice of career outside the norm, women authors make visible what was taken for granted. They bring attention to the constraints and sometimes damaging consequences of stereotypes on the women, as well as society as a whole. Each of the authors and their detectives takes on the question of attachment and making a hero of the disenfranchised. The women's narratives are part justification, which is necessary within traditional masculine-dominated society, and part critique of such a society and its valorization of the "lone wolf."

Three types of relationships are highlighted in women's PI novels—involving family, lovers, and friends or colleagues—and occupy the center of the novels' plotting and characterization. I have drawn the distinctions between these three groups of relationships for the purposes of this discussion, but the lines are much less clear in the novels. The women authors blur the distinctions between family, lovers, friends and colleagues. The groups are fluid in whom they can include, as well as people being able to move between the groups. The characters in the women's novels are not limited to traditional models or classifications. In novels where the conventional male hero is replaced by a woman, the woman author works to disconnect the bonds between marriage and love and between marriage and motherhood. In contrast, sex and love are portrayed as intimately joined.[26] Creating and maintaining relationships are very important to the woman private eye and her author. The woman PI is created with a past, present, and future that go beyond the pages of the novel. Each person she meets leaves his or her mark. The woman PI may work for herself, be unmarried, or conduct investigations by herself, but she is not solitary. She understands that any feelings of loneliness she experiences are temporary and not of serious consequence. She is part of a community.

Family is key to the woman investigator. Discussions of family often serve as an explanation for why the woman PI strayed from traditional definitions of femininity and became independent, daring, strong, and self-sufficient. She continually interacts with family members, adapting to new situations and reevaluating her own sense of self. Even if the family is no longer living, the PI is constantly reminded of their contributions to her life as new cases bring with them new recollections and new insights.

The families of three of the selected PIs are still living: those of Sharon McCone, Catherine Sayler, and Lauren Laurano. These families continue to contribute and intrude on the investigators' lives. McCone is one of five siblings. Growing up, her brothers and sisters were constantly in trouble. McCone rebelled against this chaos by being independent, rational, and dependable. She comments that she sees herself as the black sheep of the family, looking for peace in their storms of turmoil. As a member of the family, McCone continues to interact with the others after they have left home and made lives for themselves. Each continues to reassess his or her position within the family unit. Over the course of Muller's writing, the family matures, grows, and changes shape. In *Eye of the Storm*, McCone investigates a case for her sister Patsy. She is motivated by her desire to ensure Patsy's continued success for herself and her children after Patsy's troubled teen years.[27] In *Wolf in the Shadows*, McCone's relationship with her older brother, John, changes. The siblings come to experience each other as adults and friends, rather than childhood rivals. The McCone family faces a serious challenge when the parents divorce.[28] In *Where Echoes Live*, McCone and her mother reevaluate their relationship as her mother tries to begin a new life as a single woman. McCone works to redefine the parent/child relationship. Even as an adult, McCone finds it difficult to think of her parents having needs and desires. A parent is defined in relation to power and responsibility. McCone works to understand her parents as interesting people whose companionship and friendship she can enjoy, in addition her feelings toward them as parents. Along the way she must also reinterpret her memories of her childhood and what those images mean.[29] McCone is a product of her family and constantly reevaluates what growing up in her particular family has meant to who she is as she experiences the world as a mature woman.

Linda Grant's Catherine Sayler is also a product of her upbringing. Grant devotes less time than Muller to writing about her protagonist's family, but the family is no less essential to understanding Sayler's motivations and values.

Sayler grew up as her father's child. He is a police captain who raised his daughter as the son he never had. Through her father's work, Sayler was exposed to people's potential for cruelty and viciousness. By the time Sayler becomes a teen, her father has to face the fact that there is no place for the kind of "masculine-skilled" woman he brought up. Sayler later marries a police officer. However, her job as an investigator eventually leads to the breakup of the marriage. Sayler's mother, father, and husband are not happy with her career choice. Her father believes it would have been worse if she had become a police officer, a job he feels is too dangerous for a woman. Male police officers do not accept female officers as equals in the field. Throughout the series, Sayler works hard to stand on her own so that neither her father nor her ex-husband have to bail her out or be embarrassed among their fellow officers. Sayler's parents and husband would have preferred if she had chosen a more "feminine" career. Sayler's mother gives more support to Sayler's sister, who has a more conventional lifestyle. Sayler and her sister, Marion, approached growing up to be a woman with very different strategies. Sayler has little patience with Marion's unquestioning acceptance of the traditional definitions of "femininity." In having to justify her career choice to her family, Sayler is able to make it clear to herself (and the readers) what she finds most satisfying in the career of an investigator. For the women authors, one of the roles of the investigator's family is to make visible the often-hidden constraints and prejudices of gender socialization as traditional perceptions are made visible and forced to contend with contemporary expectations.

Sayler's most complex familial relationship is with her niece, Molly—Marion's daughter. Molly continually runs away from her mother until she becomes part of Sayler's household. Sayler is forced to confront her own adolescent years in light of her new role as parent to a very intelligent, independent, teenage girl. Unsure about the "right" way to handle teenage problems, Sayler remembers her own teen angst and confusion and her mother's struggles with mothering her at that age. Sayler has to discover what kind of mother she wants to be: more traditional like her own mother, mostly absent and preoccupied like her sister, or some idealized model such as she used to imagine for herself when she was a teen. A child in the house also highlights the dangers of being an investigator. Sayler is forced to confront the dangers of her job on herself and those close to her. In *Love nor Money*, Molly is kidnapped and her life is threatened as a direct consequence of Sayler's investigations. Sayler's actions have made Molly vulnerable to whatever actions the killers decide to take. Molly's presence in her life affects how Sayler handles the risks of her job.[30] In *Lethal Genes*, Molly is in trouble with her school. She sees no point to her academic studies and makes a deal to help out in Sayler's office, which she enjoys, in exchange for working harder at school. Sayler reluctantly concedes but continues to protect Molly from the dangers of her job. She will not let her work on anything that is connected to her present case on the chance that the student who died did not do so of natural causes. Nonetheless, it is Molly who provides

Sayler with one of the critical clues in the case.[31] Thus, Linda Grant uses her characters to recreate, redefine, criticize, and reaffirm the strength of family.

Sandra Scoppettone's Lauren Laurano characterizes her mother as a self-involved alcoholic. Her father believes the world to be a dark and dangerous place which admits no fun or joy. Laurano's parent's reluctantly accept the knowledge of Laurano's lesbian lifestyle, which ultimately matters less to them than the other evils in the world or what is happening in their own lives. The relationship between Laurano and her parents is primarily conducted over the phone. Whenever they hear about trouble in Lauren's life, her parents immediately beg her to come home and live in her own room—they even say that her lover can come, too. Evil cannot get to you, according to their worldview, if you live at home or in your hometown. However, Laurano recognizes that life cannot get to you either if you continually retreat into an existence as a child of your parents. Without being a continuous presence in the Laurano series, Lauren's parents are a constant reminder of where and what Laurano does not want to be. Laurano pushes herself to confront and overcome the darkness she sometimes find in life. She refuses to retreat like her parents.

Sue Grafton's Kinsey Millhone and Sara Paretsky's V. I. Warshawski are not encumbered by familial responsibilities as their parents have each died. Nonetheless, both detectives remain a part of their families. In the absence of living parents, Grafton and Paretsky were able to let their characters create themselves. They do not have to answer to a family for their choices and actions. In both cases, too, however, the protagonists carry a great deal from their childhoods into their adult lives. Their freedom to create is not absolute. Memories of childhood and adolescence profoundly affect these women. Each book in the two series is rich with familial anecdotes, memories, emotions, and images. Millhone and Warshawski credit their early life experiences as the source of their career choice and the special skills they possess to perform the job of PI.

Kinsey Millhone's parents died when she was five years old. The story of the tragic auto accident that involved all three of them is often repeated in the series. In the accident, her parents were killed and she was trapped for hours in the car. Her memories of this event are those of herself as a child: hearing her mother cry, holding her father's hand and feeling safe, and the sense of abandonment and loss. Millhone was raised by a maiden aunt who was neither maternal nor emotionally giving. For the first four months in her aunt's house, Millhone lived in a cardboard box. She would only look at picture books, pretend to sail away to new lands, and make sandwiches like her mother had. Her aunt left her alone to work out her feelings. Millhone was taught by her aunt to be independent and self-sufficient. Her aunt taught her how to shoot and gave her her first gun. She also taught her to knit and crochet. "Girl" things, such as fashion and makeup, were a low priority while she was growing up. As a child, Millhone was often taken to the homes of the aunt's friends and told to amuse herself while the adults visited. Millhone learned how to discover people's hidden lives and learned how public appearances do not always correspond to private tastes.

Grafton's tenth mystery, *"J" Is for Judgment*, is pivotal for the character of Kinsey Millhone. She learns that she does have family—a grandmother, aunts, and cousins. They know all about her history. This revelation represents a crisis for Millhone. How she has put together and understands her life is no longer secure. What Millhone used to think of as her own, she learns she shares with others. Her unique ways of doing things come from others. Millhone defines herself as an independent individual, but now she is part of a living family.[32] Grafton leaves much of this dilemma unexplored in the later novels. The character of Kinsey Millhone has to decide if she wants to reevaluate herself as a member of a family or try and return to the way things have always been.

Family is also a very strong force in Paretsky's V. I. Warshawski series. Warshawski strives to fulfill her mother's mission of helping people. Both of Warshawski's parents died when she was a young woman—her mother when she was fifteen and her father when she was twenty-five. Warshawski nursed both parents while they were dying. Her father was Polish and a member of the Chicago police force. While V. I. was growing up, he had made sure she understood guns and cars as potential deadly weapons. She was also exposed to the dangers of the city through her father's job. Her mother was an Italian immigrant who escaped war-torn Italy. She never wanted her daughter to be as helpless or scared as she herself had been while growing up. From her mother, V. I. also learned that she had to take care of herself. It was all right to be pretty, but it was much more important to have a job. V. I. keeps close several possessions that were her mother's—a set of Venetian glasses she carried with her out of Italy and an Olivetti typewriter. These items maintain her mother's presence in her life; they are reminders of what her mother stood for.

Many Warshawski novels involve cases originating with family members. Warshawski takes the case in *Killing Orders* because of a promise she made to her dying mother to always help her mother's sister.[33] *Deadlock* involves an investigation into her cousin's death. He had been her only blood relative after her parents' deaths.[34] In *Blood Shot*, Warshawski tries to discover the identity of the father of her best friend from high school. V. I.'s mother had protected the girl's mother when she was thrown out of her parent's house for getting pregnant out of wedlock.[35] Finally, in *Burn Marks*, Warshawski becomes entangled in the affairs of her father's sister. Warshawski's uncle left the family behind years before and refuses to help in his sister's present crisis. Warshawski does not like or trust her aunt, but she cannot abandon her since she is family.[36] Paretsky's private eye novels are often described as gritty and tough, but the stories are tempered with Warshawski's deep commitment to family.

Women are "supposed" to be family centered. Traditionally, a woman only leaves her parents' side when a suitable man takes her as his wife. Women are first members of their parents' family and then members of their husband's. The transition to marriage is complicated by the conventions of detachment and solitude in the private eye novel. The traditional male PI had little time for a wife and family. Marital status is not an issue for the traditional male investigator. It does not matter to the story if he is married, since either way, he can still move freely to solve his case. However, a woman in the role of private eye confronts social expectations of marriage and a woman's mobility through society. Women are defined by their marital status. Unmarried women must be explained and categorized so that their "problem" can be understood. Women's mysteries tend to spend a lot of time explaining and justifying the woman hero's marital status and how, if single, she can spend so much time away from her primary "job" of looking for a husband.

Three of the PIs in this group have been married but are now divorced—Millhone, Warshawski, and Sayler. None of the five is currently married. Sayler is still in contact with her ex-husband. They remain cautiously friendly towards each other, but he is on better terms with her parents than he is with her. Millhone and Warshawski share antagonistic relations with their ex-spouses. Millhone's ex-husbands make appearances in several books in the series. The women's job as private investigators is a primary cause for the breakups of the marriages and a continued source of conflict for the couples. The excitement of having a smart, independent girlfriend does not translate well when she assumes the role of wife.

Divorced women are exempt from much of the societal pressure to catch a husband faced by never-married single women. They are blamed for the breakup of the marriage, but at least they are approved for having followed through on the marriage track.[37] Divorce itself is a wrenching experience. It contributes to the development of the character and gives her a skeptical eye on the world. What skills and socially defined qualities a male private eye has by virtue of his masculinity, the woman PI gains through the pains of divorce. The divorced woman learns to distrust appearances and pay attention to the small details that give away the truth. The women authors of PI novels create characters that often have traditional expectations, such as marriage. However, divorce is capable of providing a justification for why the PI's time is not devoted to attracting men. The authors provide illustrations of how an independent woman can create economic security and happiness for herself without a husband.

The woman PI does not lead a celibate life, and indeed, the women authors of PI novels are frank about their characters' sexuality. Unlike the traditional male PI, however, the woman PI does not use sexuality to manipulate. Sex is not a weapon of domination. Some encounters are more casual than others. It is not unknown for the PI to be intimate with a suspect. In each encounter, the PI understands the emotional risks. She is also very aware that her career could eventually break up any relationship. It is not a necessary part of her self-definition that she be involved with a man, and celibacy is neither frightening nor a sign that her life as a desirable woman is over. Sharon McCone is involved in several committed relationships over the course of the series. In the later books, one man becomes her companion. Kinsey Millhone falls in love with a man in *"G" Is for Gumshoe*, but they separate when his job takes him out of the country.[38] He reappears in *"M" Is for Malice* and Millhone is confused about her feelings for him and the degree to which she wants to commit to him—or have him commit to her.[39] Warshawski has several lovers over the course of the series. In the last several books, one man is a constant. Sayler is in a committed relationship and navigating the territory between dating and living together. Laurano could be described as the most conventional of the group. She is not legally married, but has been involved with the same woman for fifteen years. Instead of being the most marginal of the five PIs as a lesbian, Laurano is possibly the most traditional.

The women investigators do not define their lovers simply in terms of sex. These are people who inspire the women to learn more about themselves. The reader witnesses the PI's maturation process through her relationships. As she grows through time and experiences, the types of relationships she develops mature as the author instills these characters with more depth and richness. The Sharon McCone series is a good example of how the author and the PI mature in their crafts over time. This progression is reflected in the relationships in which McCone is involved. Muller, for example, originally began her series with McCone feeling attracted to the police lieutenant assigned the case. This type of PI/police pairing often provides the author with a method for plotting the course of the story. The police officer's mistrust of a woman investigator spurs the woman PI to try to beat the man to the solution. McCone and the lieutenant's relationship vacillates between frustration and intimacy, but after it ends (several books later), they develop a very close friendship. McCone's next boyfriend is similarly frustrated by her occupation. He cannot imagine that what McCone does for a living is for real. In *There's Nothing to Be Afraid Of*, he follows her into a hostile situation with the idea of protecting her.[40] In *Pennies on a Dead Woman's Eyes*, McCone's mother suggests that her next boyfriend might not be best suited for her. He is a psychologist developing a new theoretical personality model, and she feels that his character profiles are too stifling to capture the nuances and freedom that McCone requires.[41] McCone's most current relationship is with Hy Rapinsky, a man in a line of work similar to her own. He understands what her job entails, physically and emotionally. In *Wolf in the Shadows*, McCone must come to his rescue, in a reversal of the traditional story of the man coming to the woman's rescue.

It is difficult for the woman PI to develop a lasting relationship. Most people do not understand her job, her unpredictable hours, and, more important for a prospective boyfriend, her inability to focus all of her attentions on the other person. Once involved in a committed relationship, the woman is "supposed" to devote her life to the other: making him happy, making him comfortable, and making his priorities her own. Creating a relationship with someone in a similar profession appears to be the most common answer developed by the women authors. McCone, Millhone, Warshawski, and Sayler have the most satisfying relationships with fellow investigators or police officers. As the authors have matured in their writing, they have added depth to what may have started out as a cliché relationship. In 1978, McCone's relationship with a police lieutenant was little more than a source of motivation for her as an investigator—a tool used by the author to motivate her character to continue investigating. With the addition of Hy Rapinsky to the series, however, Muller has worked to create a complex and mature relationship between the two investigators. In most cases, these men are able to see the women as professionals. They are witness to their skills, and indeed, they see the world through very similar eyes. They understand a reality where violence, death, and the destruction of lives are not uncommon. However, these men are involved in their own investigations and are often gone for extended periods of time. Thus, the women must continue to rely on themselves and cope with their time alone. Independence and intimacy are possible goals for independent and strong women. The pull of traditional definitions of wife, girlfriend, and romance are still not completely absent in these women, however. Moments of concern and confusion do arise as the women reflect on their relationships and how they fail to match traditional arrangements. Involvement with a man who is either on the police force or an investigator gives the women the chance to talk about their fears, victories, and losses with someone who understands. In such a relationship, they need not fear that their emotions will be interpreted as a sign of weakness.

Catherine Sayler and Peter Harman have a relationship illustrative of the demands, pressures, concerns, and rewards that can be achieved in the woman PI novel. Harman has his own investigations firm, but he and Sayler often assist on each other's cases. They have very different styles and philosophies of investigation. Harman devotes his energies to the underdog, while Sayler's office investigates corporate financial crimes. In the first book in the series, *Random Access Murder*, Harman is framed for murder and Sayler becomes involved in the case he was investigating in order to clear him. Harman is reluctant for Sayler to be involved and risk possible danger because she is a woman. Sayler, on the other hand, recognizes Harman's desire to protect her as no different than her desire to protect him. They are the concerns of people who care for each other. Harman must choose between having Sayler involved and at risk or losing her by trying to keep her safe. It is Sayler who, when the pair is held by the criminal, saves them both.[42] Harman and Sayler continually work to balance the tension between a man and a woman who help each other out and the man's "natural" response to protect the woman. The most satisfying relationships portrayed in women's PI novels by women are those where the traditional roles and expectations are continually renegotiated and exposed as social definitions, rather than innate qualities.

Intimate relationships are not the only types of attachments the woman PI creates, nor are they always the most important. The woman PI makes it a point to be connected to her community. She works within a group environment, even if she works out of her own office. The woman PI values friendships and works very hard to maintain them, even when her job pulls in opposition to this goal. The PI does not abandon her friends for the sake of her own security or safety. Even if choosing to help a friend or colleague puts her own life at risk, she most often chooses to help. Close interactions with people of all types fulfill the women's need for attachment. Second, it gives her the opportunity to study human nature at close range. This type of information is critical to her ability to do her job well. Though each operates with differing office arrangements, the five women PIs all illustrate a commitment to connection and responsibility.

Muller's Sharon McCone began her investigatory career at the All Souls Legal Cooperative. Breaking with the male PI tradition, Muller put her character into a group—of very liberal-minded lawyers. "I chose this setting because I wanted Sharon to have more than the traditional, sleazy, private office with a bottle in the desk drawer." While working on her manuscript, Muller attended a symposium entitled, "Women in the Law" and met several women who were part of a law cooperative that provided legal service at a low price for clients who could not otherwise afford quality representation. Muller found the environment attractive for a woman investigator.[43] All Souls Legal Cooperative is very familial in its design. The offices are located in a Victorian house and employees are offered an apartment in the building as part of the employment package to compensate for the relatively low wages at the firm. Meals and activities are often communal. Everyone stops by or pitches in. McCone does not live in the building but regularly shares pizza, wine, and conversation.

McCone's relationship with her boss, Hank Zahn, is typical of the friendships at All Souls. Their friendship goes beyond contact at the office. Zahn is a long-time friend as well as employer. He hired McCone after she finished college and was fired from another investigations firm. To Zahn, McCone is an employee, friend, and little sister. McCone models her relationship with her assistant, Rae, on her experiences with Zahn. Rae and McCone's friendship builds as they help each other cope with Rae's failed marriage, McCone's shooting of a man, Rae's relationship with a former client of the cooperative, and McCone's task of teaching Rae the investigation business. Clients of McCone and the cooperative often reappear in later stories as friends and part of the All Souls extended family. In *Till the Butchers Cut Him Down*, McCone leaves the employment of All Souls to work for herself. Nonetheless, she continues to preserve her longtime friendships.

Grant's Catherine Sayler is another investigator who works for an organization. She owns her own investigations firm and employs a staff. As the boss, Sayler is responsible for making decisions that affect her company and employees. Sayler actively engages her investigators and secretary in discussions about the direction of the firm and progress on a case. She defines her position as owner of the company in terms of both leadership and responsibility. Her decisions affect the economic security of her employees, and thus she feels obligated to consider their feelings and needs.

Grafton's Kinsey Millhone and Paretsky's Warshawski work by themselves, but each maintains close connections with larger organizations. In *Burn Marks*, Warshawski has close working and personal ties with Ajax Insurance and an intimate relationship with an Ajax Insurance Company reinsurance agent. For much of the series, Millhone's office is part of California Fidelity Insurance's offices. In exchange for being available to investigate possible insurance fraud, she is given free office space. Millhone's best friend, Vera, is a California Fidelity supervisor. The two talk about men, relationships, fashion, and fellow employees. The friendship extends beyond polite office small talk. Millhone is a maid of honor at Vera's wedding, for example. The two continue to keep in touch after Millhone's office arrangement with California Fidelity is terminated. Rather than work solely from home or set up a private office, Millhone continues to work in a group setting. She has enough money to find her own office but instead rents office space from the Kingman and Ives law firm. Lonnie Kingman is Millhone's attorney and friend. Millhone reflects:

> I discovered how much I like my current circumstances. The location is good, and it was nice to have people around me to work. One of the few disadvantages of living alone is not having anyone to tell when you're going someplace. At least now at work I had people who were aware of my whereabouts, and I could check in with them if I needed any mothering.[44]

The "lone wolf" is part of the pack in the mysteries of women.

Even with the a preference for working around others, Millhone and Warshawski conduct much of their research and planning from home. The reader is brought into the PI's private life and neighborhood to explore her more private relations. In the case of these two detectives, it brings up the issue of "father" or "father figure" in the lives of contemporary women. Millhone lives on the property of Henry Pitts, a handsome man in his eighties. She looks at Pitts as part father, part friend, part lover (in a different time and place), and part landlord. After an explosion destroys Millhone's apartment in *"E" Is for Evidence*, Pitts takes over the rebuilding and begins to take more of an interest in Millhone's continued well-being. Millhone at first struggles against his concerns. After much internal debate, however, she realizes that she has never really known "fatherliness" and that it would feel good to have Pitts step into the role on occasion.[45] Pitts shows Millhone that it is possible to be concerned, protective, and respectful of another's privacy. Thus they reconstruct the father/daughter relationship. Instead of power and control, the relationship focuses on mutual respect and concern.

Warshawski, too, has attracted a protector and friend. Mr. Contreras is in his late seventies. He is a retired union machinist for a tool and die company who lives downstairs in Warshawski's apartment building. This man comes from a time when divisions between the roles of men and women were very clearly delineated. He occasionally calls Warshawski "Doll" or "Cookie," yet with no disrespect intended. Warshawski is not offended and does not correct his anachronistic language, which she understands as genuine terms of endearment from a kind man. Contreras is quite proud of Warshawski, often commenting that she is better off being unmarried and childless. He takes it upon himself to monitor people going in and out of Warshawski's apartment and to keep an eye on things. Warshawski allows this "meddling" in her life because she likes him and wants him to feel needed. Contreras's own daughter resents Warshawski's presence in her father's life. She accuses her father of wishing that Warshawski was his daughter instead of her. She keeps telling her father to slow down and act his age, whereas Warshawski includes Contreras in some of her investigations, giving him small tasks and responsibilities.

In *Bitter Medicine*, Warshawski asks Contreras to help her protect women entering a clinic besieged by pro-life demonstrators. He is thrilled to be given a job requiring strength and command. In a later novel, Warshawski and Contreras share ownership of a dog whose original owner shot himself after Warshawski and the police exposed his crimes.[46] In *Blood Shot*, Contreras and the dog save Warshawski's life after she is wrapped in a rug and left for dead by a killer. Contreras takes on the role of father, protector, friend, and confidant. Warshawski knows that when her cases get difficult and she does not know whom to trust, Contreras will ask no questions of her and is always ready to help.

Including a "father figure" in the life of the woman PI goes beyond the stereotypical assumption that women need, and seek out, a protective father. Pitts and Contreras are older men who do feel protective toward the young women who are a part of their lives. Their roles do not however, include authority, superior knowledge, or control over the women. Each party works to maintain a relationship based on respect, privacy, care, and concern. These are examples, not just of how contemporary women take on traditional social definitions of gender, but also of how it is possible for older generations to reconfigure their own ideas of gender roles. The old men's own adaptation to living through their senior years appears to include reconsidering accepted views of gender. They are also involved in reinterpreting stereotypes of age. If age does not mean what they were always told by society, there is room to reconsider other social definitions.

In a discussion of relationships, Paretsky's Warshawski and Scoppettone's Laurano appear, at a cursory glance, to operate outside the traditional "feminine" sphere. Paretsky's more hard-edged stories and Scoppettone's lesbian protagonist would appear to be marginal to such qualities as empathy and nurturing. Instead, however, the two have some of the closest and most endearing relationships. According to social mythology, Laurano should not value the same qualities in a relationship as heterosexual women—qualities such as commitment, attachment, and love. Laurano, however, has been involved in a committed relationship with her lover, Kip, for over fifteen years. They share each other's work, doubts, fears, victories, and day-to-day lives. Kip is a therapist with little direct contact in the kind of world in which Laurano has centered her career. She has little understanding for this type of work or the time Laurano spends on her computer for her work or leisure. Theirs is far from an idealized relationship with perfect harmony between partners. They argue, they explain, they debate—but they are also committed to ride out the difficulties. In *Let's Face the Music and Die*, the women agree to separate but their years together keep them from making the break final.[47]

Paretsky is criticized by some readers and critics for writing in a style too close to the model of the traditional hard-boiled male private eye. Warshawski lives on the mean streets of Chicago, surviving death threats and assaults. She also has one of the most enduring and deep-felt friendships of any woman PI. Warshawski's best friend is Dr. Lotty Herschel. They met while involved in an underground abortion ring during a time when abortions in Chicago were illegal. Herschel is an Austrian émigré who escaped Nazi occupation. Warshawski turns to Herschel when she is hurt, wants to get away from the horrors of her work, or she needs a fresh perspective. Their friendship is not always easy for Herschel, who must stand by as Warshawski is hurt, often seriously. Herschel becomes directly involved in several of Warshawski's cases. Herschel's uncle is nearly killed in *Killing Orders*, and the doctor is mistaken for Warshawski and attacked in *Guardian Angel*.[48] Herschel refuses to speak with Warshawski after this attack. For her part, Warshawski is devastated at the possibility of losing someone she loves so much—and reminded of the love lost when her mother died. The quarrels and separations are temporary, however; commitment to their friendship always brings the two women back together. In the friendships between women, the reader will find richness and complexity. The mystery novels of women explore the depth that is possible in friendships, particularly among women. The PI's sense of self is heightened by the friendships she constructs with other women, whereas when dealing with men, women can lose their sense of self to social expectations involving femininity and sexuality.

To put a woman in the role of PI is to uncover an array of complex gender issues. To justify and explain a woman in such a role implicates the men who came before her. The woman PI is not simply a substitute; she is a critique of the "heroic," solitary male figure. She is a part of her community. The woman PI shows that to do the job of investigator well, it is necessary to participate in realistic human interactions. The job of the PI is to find clues, and clues are found in the details of human relationships. At a panel discussion, Paretsky was asked if the new fictional women were too tough: "I've been re-reading all of [Raymond] Chandler. Marlowe is so alone. V. I. has connections. She can be weak and wounded and need help. In our society, tough means you're alone, and when you think about it, that's pretty sick."[49] It is through connections that people gain the strength to act independently.

It is not helpful to label the people in the lives of the women PI's as simply substitute husbands, mothers, or fathers. Just as these PIs are not simply "men in skirts," the people in these fictional narratives are not reproductions of traditional "necessities" in women's lives. Muller, Grafton, Paretsky, Grant, and Scoppettone, as well as the other women writing mystery novels, are reformulating the gender myths. These writers challenge what it means to be "wife," "husband," "mother," and "father" through their narratives of women's lives. The family unit can include different kinds of people and relationships. Most of the detectives' deepest commitments are to their "chosen" families. For a woman to be complete, she does not have to have a traditionally defined husband, mother, or father take care of her.

> [F]or that cherished independence to be preserved, the connections must fall outside the boundaries of those socially sanctioned relationships that have defined and oppressed

women. The women authors portray their heroes freely but carefully choosing important relationships that do not merely replicated traditional ones—essentially inventing new modes of connectedness.[50]

The woman PI highlights the human drive for connection, the potential flexibility of social roles, and the primacy of commitment. The aim of the woman PI is to create egalitarian relationships, as well as put a priority on professionalism and independence.[51]

Feminist literary critic and mystery writer Carolyn Heilbrun notes:

As human beings we all make fictions of our lives, those of us who write books, or read them, and those who tell only ourselves the stories of the lives we shall lead. But that fiction has already been inscribed for women; they are to be married, to be circulated, to mediate between the man and his desire for a son, between male groups.[52]

The traditional story of women in the novel is subservience to men and the consequences should this expectation be subverted. Past writers projected culturally repressed values onto their female characters in order to criticize the established order. The women characters were given the role of disrupting the norms by unmasking their limitations. The sympathetic, and even tragic, treatment of these fictional heroines by their authors signal the authors' recognition of the personal costs of defying social order. Nancy Miller argues that if certain values can only be expressed by their displacement and the ultimate sacrifice of the tragic heroine, then the novelist's intended critique of society may actually be a tacit confirmation of the existing order.[53]

By studying women's literature, feminist literary critics find alternative representations of women and reality. These representations are distanced from the tacit assumptions of the dominant culture. Novels by women are still mediated by their culture. For critics Carolyn Heilbrun and Margaret Higonnet, women-authored works provide evidence of the routines and phases that pattern women's external lives, the psychological affiliations that shape their sense of identity, and the personal ties that give them their social strength.[54] In the novels of Jane Austen, for example, Nancy Miller detects "an unsentimental confrontation of the self in its irreducible dailiness and the trivial excitement of the details of representable experience; the cost of love, of marriage, of property, and the specifics of that worldly intersection." In women's novels, the narrowness of the domestic sphere and its attention to personal relationships and commitments widens the realm of the interesting.[55] One of the most potentially revolutionary features of the woman's private eye novel is its repositioning of the domestic sphere as vital and interesting. Great attention is given to the daily chores of waking, showering, dressing, putting on (or not putting on) makeup, and eating. The mundane of the everyday life is important; in daily life lie the clues to a person. Through her daily activities the woman PI exposes social codes of behavior for women. By the constant attention to the trivialities of everyday life, she focuses the reader's attention on the usually unseen.

The woman PI is very aware of herself as "constructed." Her clothes, makeup, and jewelry all create an image of who she is that is interpreted by those she encounters. Even where it is a matter of personal style, the PI is conscious of how she will be treated by others as a result. Her "external" self (how others define her) is fluid and variable; it changes as she tries to move across social boundaries and investigate her cases. In each book in a PI series, the detective goes to special care to describe herself in detail and draw the readers' attention to how she changes. Lauren Laurano describes herself in the beginning of *Everything You Have Is Mine* as a conservative dresser:

> I'm a conservative dresser, and today I wear a lavender turtleneck under a pink sweater, and jeans. My matching socks are pink, my Reeboks white.
>
> My jewelry is modest, too. I wear my grandmother's gold bracelet, my wedding ring, and a wristwatch with a black leather band.[56]

Laurano's dress is as important for the reader to understand and follow as the clues that she uncovers. Each time the PI changes her wardrobe, she reveals information about herself and the social group of which she is a part. For example, Sara Paretsky goes to lengths to describe Warshawski when she dresses in an evening gown in *Guardian Angel* even though she is not investigating a case at the time. Warshawski observes, first, the crowd's reaction to the robes of a children's choir. "Some PR genius" had decided to dress them in bright dashikis, velvet Afghan jackets, and embroidered white dresses, rather than choir robes. "[I]t was their appearance that brought down the house." Warshawski leaves her seat during intermission to "admire the costumes of the patrons—they were even more colorfully decked than the children." As she walks, she keeps catching her heel in the threads of her skirt. She observes that she is not used to moving in evening clothes and keeps forgetting to shorten her stride. She had bought the skirt for a Christmas party at her husband's law firm during her brief marriage thirteen years ago.

> The sheer black wool, heavily shot with silver, didn't compare with Or's custom-made gown, but it was my own most elegant outfit. With a black silk top and my mother's diamond drops it made respectable concert attire, but it lacked the dramatic flair of most of the ensembles I saw in the foyer.[57]

From this one event, Paretsky has drawn the reader's attention to the complexity of clothing as image: how it is constructed by others to create a response, how it holds history and memories in its fibers, and how different "costumes" require different postures and physical adaptations.

Attention to the details of the everyday can focus on the simple, as in Muller's *Where Echoes Live*, where she describes a cabin as McCone walks through it and surveys her surroundings:

> The small living room has the look of rustic summer places everywhere: a rattan sofa and chairs whose flowered cushions were faded and flattened; a potbellied wood stove in one

corner; a Formica-and-metal dinette set in from of the door leading to the kitchen. The smell was the same, too: musty with dry rot, stale cooking odors, dead fires, and age.[58]

Muller later leaves the cabin to meet her associate and changes clothes, again keeping attention on the details. "I went through the curtained archway to one of the cabin's two bedrooms, pulled my favorite green sweater from my week-end bag, and traded it for the light T-shirt I'd been wearing. After I brushed my hair and refastened it in its ponytail, I grabbed my bag."[59] Muller sets the place and the tone and connects the scene to the readers by evoking their own recollections and memories. A more extreme example of attention to the external as a clue to self is in Sue Grafton's *"H" Is for Homicide*, where Kinsey Millhone takes on a new identity and explores her own feelings as she is about to be able to slip out of herself for a time and thus recreate herself.[60]

The "mean" streets of major U.S. cities define reality in the traditional hard-boiled male private eye novels. New York and Los Angeles, for example, are most often described as full of dark alleys, seedy bars, mysterious shadows, lurking thugs, and secret rendezvous. There are clear lines between the good guys and the bad guys. The villains are corrupt, wealthy men and femmes fatales. The police tend to be either corrupt or stupid; they do little to stem the tide of crime. Readers are swept up in the adventure fantasies situated outside their daily frame of reference.

The world is a much different place for the contemporary woman PI. Life in the United States has changed a great deal from the 1930s and 1940s, but this is not enough to explain the fundamental differences in the fictional worlds created by women private eye authors. The neighborhoods, atmosphere, and locations where the woman PI operates are fundamentally different than those of her male predecessors. Locations are not limited to the urban centers of Los Angeles and New York. The five PIs discussed here work in Santa Teresa (Santa Barbara), Chicago, and Berkeley/San Francisco, as well as New York City. The world is not an unexplained sinister curtain that envelopes the characters and pervades their every move. On the contrary, the streets of the woman PI have a past, present, and future. They are inhabited by people with dreams, expectations, and failures. The PI explains her surroundings to the reader as carefully as she does a new character. She cannot conduct her investigations without critiquing the external factors that created the evil she investigates. It is not enough for the woman PI to just find the bad guy. She goes after criminals with the same zeal as her male counterparts, but she realizes that the criminal seldom works alone. There are institutional and cultural causes that must be investigated. The PI may not be able to radically alter how institutions conduct their business, but she is able to expose the dangers of their impersonal facade. The woman PI concludes her investigations by elucidating the social roots of the crime to the characters in the books and the readers.

Scoppettone is the most specific in her critique of social and political institutions. In *I'll Be Leaving You Always*, Scoppettone's detective, Laurano, remarks on U.S. policy toward homelessness and gays.[61] Her best friends run a specialty bookstore, bringing up topical commentary on the growth of book superstores. Scoppettone's selling of her manuscript to a large publishing house instead of a small feminist press is, itself, a political act. Scoppettone was able to sell the manuscript for more money, but, more important for other "marginal" stories, she also gained entrance to mainstream genre publishing. Other publishers looking for "hot" topics now also look to include a lesbian detective to their list.

Lauren Laurano is rooted in the politics of her day—for just a few examples, she is lesbian, her lover's brother is diagnosed with AIDS and later dies through assisted suicide, and the economic survival of her friends' bookstore depends on the policies of large publishing corporations. For Laurano and the other woman PIs, observations are made about the role that social institutions play in the fabric of people's lives. Society's attempts to maintain the status quo of privilege, unequal distribution of wealth and power, and domination of men over women capture the authors' and detectives' attentions.

Linda Grant's Catherine Sayler specializes in corporate financial investigations because the problems are purportedly neat and the clients well-mannered. However, her cases often fall short of this ideal. Corporate criminals are the result of a society that puts a high priority on acquiring. Society equates being a "good man" with being rich and powerful. The character of Peter Harman is an alternative version of the "good man." He encourages Sayler to question the motives of large institutions. Harman brings the best of the 1960s, including the era's idealism and commitment to building a better world for all, to his investigations. He cautions Sayler, who did not have an intimate connection to the struggles of the 1960s, to be cautious of appearances and institutional motives.

In one of the later Sayler books, *In a Woman's Place*, Grant looks at the social roots of evil as she investigates a case of sexual harassment in the workplace. Her own status as a successful businesswoman is at stake. She realizes that it affects her when other women are harassed in the workplace because of their gender or their degree of success. Grant explores men's and women's different reactions to this issue. Is it a harmless office prank or a serious threat of violence? While investigating the case, Sayler learns that her niece has been confronted by harassment at school. Molly and her female classmates simply moved their desks to get away from the boys bothering them. The girls were casual about the incident and having to move, but Sayler questions why it was the girls who had to make the adjustments and whether this was symptomatic of the consequences of sexual harassment in the community at large.

Sayler is hired by the head of a firm experiencing trouble with a recently acquired "Young Turk" computer firm. He wants to find out who, in this new group, is responsible for harassing women employees—provided it is not someone important to the future of the company. The client does not take the situation seriously. He is just trying to make an example of the offending employee in order to placate the female staff. No one is surprised by the inappropriate behavior of the brilliant young men in the new computer company—they accept a "boys will be boys" justification. It is difficult for Sayler to get the men in charge to take the situation seriously, even after certain women start receiving "snuff-type" photos. When one woman is brutally killed, a few of the men begin to see the connection between physical violence against women and the workplace harassment.[62] Sayler's case does not simply involve finding the man who is responsible, it also means exposing the violent and aggressive underpinnings of sexual harassment. This case makes it clear that the corporate world is not necessarily a neat and well-mannered place.

Marcia Muller, Sue Grafton, and Sara Paretsky put human faces on the despair and evil that is the city, the institution, or the corporation. They look for the social roots of tragedy, not stopping with just the "bad guy." It is not enough to race through the landscape to find the criminal. The causes of the initial rift in the social order must be brought to light if there is to be any chance at resolution. Cities and crimes have pasts, presents, and futures. A simple drive past a neighborhood usually elicits comments by the woman PI about the people who live there and how the area came to be the way she sees it now. McCone explains the ebb and flow of neighborhoods in San Francisco as a process of minorities being treated to the leavings of the ruling class. Buildings are described in terms of who lives or used to live in them, not simply as architecture. The central theme in *There's Nothing to Be Afraid Of*, for example, is housing and urban growth. McCone is struck by the contrast between San Francisco's Tenderloin District, with its immigrant population, and the safety and security she feels in her boyfriend's loft in the warehouse district. She also remarks on the public's fears about the influx of immigrants. McCone recognizes the vitality that the Vietnamese immigrants have brought to the old, dying areas of the city. The immigrants come with their families to build new lives. The McCone series, her cases, and the mission of the All Souls Legal Cooperative all highlight the contrast between a commitment to others and a selfish drive for material profit, which is shown as being most often reached at the expense of others. Immigrants, patients of profit-oriented doctors, and clerical staff are sacrificed for profit in *Where Echoes Live*. In *Pennies on a Dead Woman's Eyes*, the government's paranoia about Communists and groups who zealously defend the "American way of life" are exposed.[63] The threats to Mexican citizens desperate to get into the United States are revealed for their callousness and cruelty in *Wolf in the Shadows*.

Sue Grafton focuses on the interpersonal level—relations between men and women, in particular. Like Muller, Grafton's murderers are not simply corrupt individuals. Violence and hatred have their roots deep in society. Western society's gender mythologies are implicated in the breakdown of the social order witnessed by the woman detective. Greed and power are influential components in the relations between men and women. The murderer in *"I" Is for Innocent* is a husband who had, six years earlier, killed his wife, having decided, in his desperate drive for more money, that she was expendable.[64] The murderer in *"J" Is for Judgment* is a woman who is driven to kill after the man she stood by and helped for five years plans to leave her. She is humiliated by his portrayal of her as just a part of his "midlife crisis." A woman's commitment to her socially dictated role of wife and mother is central to *"A" Is for Alibi*. A man is killed, and Millhone questions his ex-wife to search for clues. Her comments reveal a man who had little regard for his wife as a person. She had adhered to the "dutiful wife" routine and found herself ill-prepared for life after he ultimately left her for another. She took care of their children for the thirteen years of the marriage, but it was he who was ultimately responsible for shaping their lives. Finally, the woman confesses to Millhone that she poisoned her ex-husband because he ruined her life. The realities of life as wife and mother had not come close to meeting what society had promised her if she did what she was supposed to.[65] The gendered nature of Western society is exposed to the reader and implicated in many of the murders in the Millhone series.

The city of Chicago is as much a part of the Warshawski series as any human character. It is a part of Warshawski and her perceptions of the world. She grew up on Chicago's South Side, and it taught her how to be tough. Her fights were about race and ethnicity, issues for which she continues to fight. The case in *Killing Order* revolves around suspicions that Warshawski's aunt is embezzling money from her church, but the novel itself is an indictment of the authority of the Catholic Church. Warshawski argues over church policy prohibiting abortion and homosexuality. She exposes the close ties the church maintains with local politics and how it dictates local policies according to church doctrine. Authority and control inform church policy, according to Warshawski, rather than empathy and compassion. *Indemnity Only* is a critique of labor unions and their connections to organized crime. Paretsky draws the readers' attentions to the contrasts between labor unions' original mission, the lifestyles of its worker members, and the lifestyles of the union leaders.[66] Other institutions implicated in the crimes of individuals are for-profit hospitals (*Bitter Medicine*), chemical companies (*Blood Shot*), national and state policies regarding the homeless as well as the groups trying to help them (*Burn Marks*, *Tunnel Vision*), and gentrification (*Guardian Angel*).[67] Specific companies or industries are not intrinsically evil. Social pressures for control, power, and wealth encourage institutions to weigh such goals for profit much higher than their human costs.

Mystery novels that stop when the bad guy is apprehended stop short of finishing the story. In the mystery novels of women, "[c]rime is shown as a continuum rather than as something entirely 'other' inhabited by an 'enemy' that needs to be destroyed."[68] In a society where large corporate institutions are increasingly granted more rights and privileges than the citizenry by the government, individuals are often overlooked. The woman PI reminds the reader that the urban street is full of the lives of its people. The attention the woman PI pays to a simple drive across town points the reader to reflect on her own streets. Each city and institution encompasses the ebbs and flows of human success and failure. Paretsky believes that:

> any large institution is more concerned with its own survival than the needs of the people it was originally designed to serve. And that any kind of institutionalized man offers a wonderful opportunity for displays of the more venal side of human nature. I don't have

a particular bias against large institutions, but I don't think it matters what the intentions of the founders were by the time they get large.[69]

Even in the worst neighborhoods, people are raising families. Even in the best neighborhoods, disregard for property and life can be found.

Every day, hundreds of people mark us in some way. Many of them make our lives possible, yet most receive no more than a passing glance. In women's mystery novels, these people fill in the story and give it richness and depth. They are the electricians, travel agents, waitresses, bartenders, doctors, and nurses on whom the PIs call for help and information. For the authors, these people provide the chance to play God. In these characters, the authors fantasize, play, and create a society they would like to see. They put faces on the unseen masses. Many of the workers in the PI novels of women are women. It is a woman who fixes Warshawski's front door and security system, a woman who fixes Millhone's broken window, and, a woman who attends Millhone in the hospital after an explosion in her apartment. Police officers on the beat are often women. Most of the time no one remarks on the work being done by women—it is perfectly normal for them to be there.

Assumptions regarding "proper" work for women can still be found in women's mysteries. The PI, herself, is sometimes surprised that a woman is at her door, ready to work. She may refer to a person as "he," only to be reminded that women are often doctors, plumbers, glaziers, and so on. The PI, too, is a victim of such misunderstandings. V. I. Warshawski prefers her initials to her name, Victoria, but many clients and people she questions often expect her to be a man. By continuously putting women in unexpected jobs, women authors fantasize about a time when gender mythologies will have lost much of their foothold on the national psyche. Readers are challenged to pay attention to their own assumptions; particular job descriptions are not innate to the sexes.

If the detective novels of women are about women actively challenging and directing the course of their lives and not merely waiting to be swept along by others, what is the role of the women PIs gender in this adventure? Can femininity and heroism coexist? Carolyn Heilbrun claims that the detective story provides greater momentum away from stereotypical sex roles than any other fictional genre.[70] These stories provide one of the best locations for women to view issues of gender and heroism.

One way of moving away from sexual stereotyping in fiction is through the concept of androgyny, which "seeks to liberate the individual from the confines of the appropriate." A woman does not have to act like a man in order to be androgynous. Instead, androgyny suggests a spirit of reconciliation between the sexes. Human beings choose their place without regard to propriety or custom. A full range of experience is open to individuals.[71] Striving for androgyny means allowing men to be more "feminine"—tender, emotional, passive—and women more "masculine"—forceful, competent, rational. It goes further, to unpack the notions of gender from the very terms applied to it. Heilbrun and the women mystery writers raise questions about the assignation of, for example, emotion to "feminine" and rational to "masculine." They ask why it is that masculine traits are held in higher regard by society.[72] Androgyny is not a science fiction creation of genderless and uniform beings. Rather, it is a concept that focuses discussion on the differences between the sexes, the social meaning of these differences, and the roles played by each sex in society. Sexual stereotyping promotes difference-as-opposition—"male versus female." Androgyny redefines difference to include multiplicity and heterogeneity. Feminist critic Mary Jacobus locates writing, which is the production of meaning, as the site of challenge to both stereotyping and "otherness." Focusing on difference allows for variety and exploration; "otherness" implies a foreignness to be conquered, dismissed, or feared. The play of difference is perpetually enacted within writing.[73]

Male detective novel writers have received fame and recognition for writing "antistereotyping" novels. Dick Francis and Robert Parker are just two examples. Carolyn Heilbrun remarks that such critical attention for women writers has lagged. She suggests that women characters written by men are not as threatening, unfamiliar, or dangerous as the androgynous females being penned by women. "Men may acquire 'feminine' characteristics, but woe unto the woman who becomes 'masculine'—author or character." Society has taught that not only is aggressiveness not feminine, in women, it is frightening.[74]

Heilbrun credits the formulaic conventions of the mystery novel with the form's ability to tackle questions of gender. What makes great novels unconventional is their unacceptance that agreed-upon modes of action and belief are eternal principles.[75] The detective novel's great contribution is its "openness about the prison of gender." The momentum of a mystery and the trajectory of a good story with a solution give the author the freedom to "dabble" in revolutionary thinking.[76] The aggression and violence of the traditional hard-boiled private eye novel is a supreme test of the tensions between androgynous writing and the social pressures regarding gender.

Placing the detective hero in physical danger is a convention of the PI genre. Putting a woman in the shoes of the detective changes the significance of the danger. A male detective is operating well within expectations for his gender role when he uses his fists (or more likely, his gun), to fight his way out of danger, yet a woman who does the same is clearly outside her boundaries. The male detective proves his masculinity by injuring his opponents and emerging victorious; a woman doing the same calls her femininity into question (as well as threatening a male opponent's masculinity). The hard-boiled male detective was created to glory in violence and how naturally it comes to him. The woman PI challenges violence as an accepted part of masculine heroism and also challenges femininity's aversion to confronting danger.

The women characters who have taken over the private eye beat have mixed emotions about violence and evil, as well as their role in how such emotions are played out.[77] Androgyny faces its toughest challenge when confronted by violence and aggression. Fundamental to the social definition of femininity is passivity and nurturing. A "good" woman must work to perfect these qualities, while realizing that these skills rate faint praise when compared to the masculine attributes of action and aggression. The woman authors of the PI novel struggle to address the question of how their protagonists can be feminine and show the value of femininity and yet take action in their world.

The most volatile and controversial aspect of the woman PI mystery novel is the tension between passivity and action. The woman PI confronts the stereotype of passivity since the private investigator must, by definition, put herself at risk. Criminals do not want to have their identities revealed. Having already committed one crime, it is not inconceivable that they will commit another to keep their secret. The PI must, at the least, take personal protection seriously. Even Catherine Sayler, an investigator of financial crimes, has learned to shoot and practices a form of martial arts. Instead of accepting the violence of the form as "conventional," the narratives of the women writers critically evaluate it. They separate defense and protection from offensive aggression. The women's PI novels include a critique of the traditional vigilantism of the form. Hand-in-hand is a celebration of women who are capable of defending their independence.

Shoot-outs and chases are not uncommon in many detective novels by men. The role of the male PI is to identify the criminal in order to exact punishment. The stories are written such that they end with the PI and criminal locked in mortal combat. Theirs is a battle of wills. Women authors define the role of the PI as an investigator who does not take direct action against the criminal, but rather works to lead the police to the offender. Of course, she may have to defend herself in the course of this objective. "Defense" does include possibly having to use a gun, but only if alternative strategies are not available or have not succeeded. Guns are a last resort. Intelligence is more highly prized. Smart women are capable of using the resources at hand or avoiding confrontation. Theirs is a battle of wits. With their training, many of the women PIs can physically take on a male attacker. The women, still, make it a priority to stay out of such dangerous situations. The woman PI is not an aggressor wielding deadly force, nor does she passively accept the role of victim.

Four out of the five women private investigators selected own a gun. All four are explicit in using it for self-defense only. Sayler does not own a gun, but she can shoot and will carry one if the situation is extreme enough to warrant. Besides guns, other precautions are taken to ensure the women's safety. Sayler actively studies aikido as a method of self-defense. Millhone and Warshawski exercise and keep fit in order to be physically able to get out of the way of danger or defend themselves. McCone, too, is physically up to the challenge. Contrary to traditional ideals of femininity, these women accept the risks of their chosen profession and are physically and mentally prepared to protect themselves.

The issue of a woman operating in a nontraditional role that requires her to handle violence, aggression, and action was uppermost in the mind of Linda Grant when she created her protagonist. Catherine Sayler was created, not as a superwoman, but to be "everywoman." She faces the ordinary fears of ordinary people. To create a character with a risky profession meant that Grant had to provide her with a realistic means of defense. Over the course of the novels, aikido has become the philosophical foundation of Sayler's life. Grant finds this style of martial arts compelling and useful for women. Its moves are based on getting out of the way—understanding the energy coming at you and blending with it so as to deflect it. Aikido's philosophy and method of fighting is to redirect the aggression of others. Women are not usually able to overpower a man intent on harming them. Guns can be taken away and used against their owner. Through aikido, Grant has found a way of teaching her protagonist to deal with the dangers of her job and her vulnerabilities as a woman by understanding the risks and dealing with them, rather than letting them overpower her.[78]

Sayler faces threats to her own safety several times during the course of the mystery series, as do the other investigators. She is held at gunpoint, threatened with a knife, beaten, shot at, gassed, and harassed. Millhone, in addition to physical fights and threats of deaths, has been run off the road, injured in two explosions, poisoned, trapped in a fire, hit on the head with a baseball bat, and stunned with an electrical shock taser gun. Muller's McCone continues the theme of physical fights and threats from the enemy at gunpoint. In most situations, the PI emerges without any critical injuries. She deflects most of the danger, keeps her health insurance paid up, and takes advantage of the resources around her to escape or overcome her attacker. In *Random Access Murder*, Sayler pretends to stumble on a step as she and Peter Harman are led into a cellar by gun-carrying thugs. She is able to catch her captors off-guard and gain the advantage. Grafton's Millhone, when facing a killer with a gun and a bomb about to explode (in *"E" Is for Evidence*), tells the man she needs a painkiller from her purse. Finding her gun there, she shoots him through the bottom of the purse and runs into the bathroom. To stop his attempts to get to her, she uses the toilet tank lid to smash his hand and stop a bullet. McCone is held at gunpoint in *There's Nothing to Be Afraid Of* by the killer, a mentally disturbed man. As the situation escalates, he turns the gun on himself, but McCone talks him out of committing suicide by reciting lines from the poetry he had written. In *Wolf in the Shadows*, McCone throws a billiard ball at one of her captors and knocks him out.

Of these women warriors, V. I. Warshawski sustains the most damage to her person at the hands of the villains. The dark side of Chicago and its legendary mob connections are well illustrated by the lengths to which killers go keeping Warshawski out of their way. She is well known in her fictional Chicago as a tough investigator who can deliver criminals. In *Indemnity Only*, the first Warshawski novel, she fights with two mob hit men and is beaten by another as a warning to stay away from the case. *Deadlock* finds her seriously injured in a car accident after her car is tampered with, onboard a cargo ship during an explosion, and nearly drowned after fighting with a killer on his yacht. A gang leader cuts her in *Bitter Medicine*. In *Blood Shot*, she is left for dead; later, she stages an armed rescue of a friend's mother. In *Burn Marks*, an assault leaves her unconscious in a burning building, and later, she is kidnapped. *Guardian Angel* follows her narrow escape from capture by several motor plant employees. Warshawski fires her gun, jumps onto a crane, and dives into a polluted water canal. Her foes try to run her over with a truck as Warshawski drives away. Paretsky fills book after book in the series with the extremely dangerous situations for her heroine. She challenges the reader's assumptions about the connections between violence and gender, going so far as to make some readers uncomfortable. This level of discomfort makes tacitly accepted forms of social stereotyping visible. The reader of women's mysteries is confronted by the contrast between appropriate female behavior and the expected conventions of the private eye novel. The woman PI challenges traditional rules of the genre and gender by taking care of herself and developing alternatives to glorified violence. Where the conventions are stretched, bent, and broken, new discourse is created.

The gun is a standard in the PI novel. In the stereotypic PI novel, the private eye blasts away at thugs, escapes their shots at him, and victoriously walks over their bodies on his way to his next case. The reality of guns is much more complex, however. Guns can go off accidentally, get into the hands of children, and be used against their owners. Ultimately, they destroy life. The novels of women PIs portray a more authentic scenario with guns, however. Here they are not the traditional metaphor for male power, but simply a tool of violence. Guns destroy families, and lives; they can also damage the user's humanity.

The woman PI novel writer spends much time explaining how and where the PI keeps her gun. In some situations it works out for the best that the gun is out of reach. Paretsky's Warshawski stores her Smith and Wesson gun in a safe built into her bedroom closet. The other women keep their guns locked up in their desk drawers, file cabinets, or car glove compartments. Muller's Sharon McCone makes a point of not carrying a gun into most scenarios since it can intensify an already dangerous situation. She never carries it unless she is fully prepared to use it. The McCone book *Eye of the Storm* illustrates how the woman PI weighs the risks of carrying a gun. For the duration of the investigation, McCone keeps her gun locked up in her car glove compartment because she does not want her sister's two children to find it. A killer has committed two murders, but McCone must look for other strategies to reveal the criminal while keeping her family safe.

Guns are also carried in women's purses, which causes women mystery authors to spend a lot of time keeping readers informed of where the purse is at any given moment. For example, in *"G" Is for Gumshoe*, Grafton traces Millhone's gun and purse through a series of events. In one scene, Millhone transfers her .32 pistol from her locked briefcase to her purse. She puts the purse on the passenger seat of her car. Millhone's car is struck by the truck of a hired hit man and the purse flies into Millhone's lap. The truck rams her again, and the purse acts to cushion the impact of the steering wheel. With the next hit, her car goes into a wet ditch. Millhone then has to scramble to locate her purse and gun and prepare to shoot should the truck's driver return for her. However, the driver leaves the scene and Millhone does not have to shoot. The author carefully tracks each move of the purse and gun in this situation. The standard feminine accessory, the purse, takes on a new role as the holder of the gun for the woman

PI. It may not be full of makeup, perfume, and hairbrushes, but it does carry what is important for these women. The purse becomes an "article of the trade" for the woman investigator, who thus endows an artifact traditionally associated with stereotypic "femininity" with renewed vitality. She takes its image and definition back.

To own a gun means being prepared to use it. During her investigations, the woman PI sometimes has to shoot and kill. Lauren Laurano is the most "casual" about having a gun—and in that way, more like the traditional male PI. Laurano does not fire her gun any more than the other women, but she will point it at people who are giving her trouble. It is difficult at times for a woman to be taken seriously or to repel unwanted attention by men. When telling them does not work, Laurano will use her gun to stress the seriousness of her point. As a woman, Laurano has comparatively little power or authority; with the gun, she regains control over the situation. When it comes to actually firing a gun, it is worth restating that the women investigators fire specifically at their attackers, rather than all villains. Unless cornered and without options, they will not fire. The consequences of their actions—the fact that they would be responsible for taking another life—seriously disturbs these women. It takes time for them to put the death into perspective and figure out how they are going to go on with their own lives now knowing that they have become a person who kills. Such inner conflicts are not easily resolved. Killing changes who they are and who they are to their friends and family.

Grant's Catherine Sayler makes a point of directly dealing with her actions. Her aikido training focuses on experiencing the consequences of her actions. Sayler does not carry a gun or have a permit to own one since she does not like them. Guns, however, are still a reality in her job. Her ex-husband, a police officer, made her learn how to shoot. In *Blind Trust*, Peter Harman insists she take a gun when she goes to a remote cabin to confront a murderer, and she eventually shoots and wounds the man.[79] In *Random Access Murder*, Sayler takes a gun away from one of her captors, fires at another, and hits yet another over the head with the gun so that she and Harman can escape. The intensity of these moments masks Sayler's fears; she is trained in self-control. Once the immediate crisis has been resolved, Sayler is left to confront her own mortality and her responsibility in another's death.

Neither Grafton's Millhone nor Muller's McCone takes her role in another's death lightly, even when the person would have killed her otherwise. The Kinsey Millhone series begins with *"A" Is for Alibi*, which opens by informing the reader that Millhone killed someone the day before. She tries to sort out what this means to her, as she had been emotionally involved with the man who was a suspect in her investigation, and this lapse in professionalism almost cost Millhone her life. The man tries to kill her when it becomes clear that she has uncovered his guilt. He chases her along the beach. She hides in a metal trash can, but he finds her and comes at her with a ten-inch blade. Millhone has to shoot him to save her own life. As a "killer," Millhone now compares herself to soldiers and maniacs. She knows she will mentally recover from this episode, but she also knows she will not be the same person she was before the shooting. The act changes how she understands herself.

The consequences of the shooting continue for Millhone in *"B" Is for Burglar*. Millhone keeps trying to push the shooting from her mind. She has always thought of herself as a good person, but she is no longer sure what "good person" means. Millhone knows she would fire her gun again if the same situation presented itself. This does not lessen the emotional impact or guilt for having killed another person. She is tired of feeling helpless and afraid; she does not want to continue being a victim to the situation. Her landlord and friend, Henry Pitts, is instrumental in helping Millhone put the shooting into perspective. He helps her see that she shot in the heat of the moment. It was not something she had contemplated doing. The shooting is not some kind of platform for a political campaign to be bandied about. It is not a turning point in her intellectual life. Millhone killed another person, but the extent to which she is a good person has not changed.[80]

In *"C" Is for Corpse* Millhone is hired by Bobby Callahan to find out who is trying to kill him. Callahan is recovering from an automobile accident that wounded him and killed his close friend. His body and spirit are a metaphor to Millhone for coming close to, but escaping, violent death. Millhone's commitment to Callahan, even after he is killed and she no longer has a client, comes from her own struggles with violent death, and particularly, the role she played in the death of one man.[81]

Muller's Sharon McCone faces a similar test of morality. A nonfatal shooting provokes her to reevaluate her life, her career choice, and her priorities. *Trophies and Dead Things* marks a pivotal moment in her maturation process. McCone is hired to investigate the death of a 1960s peace activist. She learns that his death might be linked to a group of soldiers who served together in the Vietnam War—one of whom is her boss and friend, Hank Zahn. McCone takes the job of protecting Zahn, but he is shot as he and McCone leave the All Souls office. McCone chases down the sniper and gets off two shots as he tries to run away. The first shot goes wild, but the second causes him to stumble and lose his gun. He continues to run, jumping off a set of steps to the sidewalk. As he goes down on one knee on the pavement, McCone gets off another shot, which causes him to fall completely. McCone is able to grab the arms of the sniper and pin him down. He stops struggling when she threatens him by holding her gun to the base of his skull. McCone's rage lessens when she gets a look at the faces around her. She is taken aback as she sees their fear of her. Rather than being some monster, the sniper's face is just that of a panicked young man. McCone blames herself for Zahn's being shot. She failed in her duty to protect him. She suspects that those around her fear her just like they would the murderers she is hired to expose.[82] *Trophies and Dead Things* is a novel about pain, anger, and disillusionment. The mythic charms of the 1960s conceal a legacy of dark, painful secrets. McCone's naïveté and gullibility about herself and society are slowly being stripped away for a more realistic picture of the violent acts of which she and others are capable. McCone's test is to find a way to live with this experience without letting it overwhelm her.

*Where Echoes Live* is next in the McCone series and continues her process of self-discovery. McCone continues to be troubled by almost killing the man who shot Zahn and the distance that has developed between her and her colleagues at All Souls. She is no longer just Sharon McCone who hangs out around the office and shares pizza. Her friends realize now that she really is trained to kill. McCone questions her choice of profession. She is not sure who she is. Her reaction to the gunman scares her. The job of the investigator is to fix things, but McCone does not believe she can "fix" how her friends and colleagues now see her.

The shooting in *Trophies and Dead Things* is a catalyst for changes in McCone's professional and personal life. In *Where Echoes Live*, McCone works with another investigator, Hy Rapinsky. She talks to him about her fears and doubts. Rapinsky reminds McCone that although she has been enraged by the murderers she has faced, she has not killed them. This is the difference between her and the bad guys. McCone admits to Rapinsky that conquering danger and her own fears make her come alive. She is excited by the danger inherent in her job. It is the rush she gets with risk and danger, as well as her anxiousness over the power she has over life and death, that defines who she is. Reconciling such feelings with her own thoughts that such feelings are not appropriate or "normal" for a woman continues through the series.

In her later book, *Pennies on a Dead Woman's Eyes*, McCone recognizes her own maturation. She is no longer the young, idealistic McCone who was shattered as ugly truths were revealed. Her world, she admits, is probably more bad than good. McCone has not become so cynical that she cannot appreciate the good and hold on to special moments. The journey is sometimes wrenching, but part of the woman PI's growth comes from confronting the dangers in herself and others. The world is not necessarily a safe place for women, but there are other choices besides withdrawing, being a perpetual victim, and becoming too hardened to care for anyone. The woman PI struggles to stay out of such traps and forge new narrative alternatives.

Violence, guns, and death take their toll on the people who have to deal with their destructiveness regularly. Physically—headaches, nausea—and psychologically—nightmares, self-doubt—the woman private eye investigates the meaning and impact of violence on the society she inhabits. The woman PI defines the job of private investigator as finding answers that can contribute to life. It is her search for justice. McCone comments that every death diminishes us, but that those deaths that leave differences unresolved and things unsaid are the most painful of all. She perceives herself as out in the middle of the filth, crime, and violence, fighting on a slow, day-to-day basis. She tries to make things go right to the best of her abilities. The woman PI is not out to save the world, just her little corner of it. Paretsky's Warshawski suggests that she is a garbage collector cleaning up little piles here and there. Millhone probes the "murky waters" to gather the artifacts that are washed up like rubble on the shores of the present. She continues to be uneasy about those treasures that are as yet undiscovered or just out of reach.

The five women protagonists of the PI novels were drawn to the profession of investigating by their search for the truth, not the chance to use a gun or fight. Marcia Muller critiques the job description of the traditional male private eye: "Those supermacho types in male private-eye novels set themselves above the law and take it into their own hands. It's that superior attitude that leads to their patronizing treatment of women, as well as their lack of human sympathy for all the people they deal with."[83] As PIs, the women are their own boss. They can afford to search for a sense of justice, rather than strictly focusing on points of law, as with the police. Justice has a very human quality for the women writers of PI novels.

Even though the private investigator sets her own agenda and is solely responsible to her client during an investigation, the ultimate aim of the woman private eye is to turn the criminal over to the police. She generally will have working relations with several members of the local police force. The police do not usually like having private citizens involved in their investigations. Private investigators have no legal jurisdiction in cases being handled by the police. The investigators usually counsel their clients to seek out the help of the police first in criminal or missing persons matters. The police simply have more resources and authority to run a thorough investigation in most situations. It can happen in the PI series that the police consult the private investigator when their cases overlap. Kinsey Millhone goes undercover for the police in an auto insurance fraud ring in *"H" Is for Homicide*. She has a close relationship with the officers in charge of the case, and they trust her ability to act appropriately. Lauren Laurano often talks with a local police detective who thinks of her like a daughter. Catherine Sayler is able to call on police backup through her father and ex-husband. Muller's Sharon McCone is able to count on her ex-boyfriend on the police force (a police lieutenant) to respect her "hunches" during an investigation. A working relationship with the police department complicates the traditional view of the PI as judge, jury, and executioner. The woman PI and police are shown to mostly respect each other and often work as a team to see that justice is carried out.

There are times when the woman PI does cross the line in her pursuit of justice. The woman private investigator does bend quite a few rules in her search for the truth. Breaking and entering, mail tampering, eavesdropping, concealing evidence, and computer hacking are not uncommon. The woman PI justifies these minor infractions of law by believing that no one is really hurt by them. The search for the truth is so great and the crime of murder so terrible that certain laws of evidence should not stand in the way of the private investigator's search for answers. She recognizes a certain thrill in taking risk and facing the danger of discovery—situations not usually part of a women's life. Only information relevant to the crime is turned over to the police. The public—through the courts and police—are not made privy to all the secrets the investigator uncovers. Searching through private lives reveals many very personal secrets that the PI must discover and be trusted to keep confidential. The PI understands that she can lose her license for her illegal acts, but, again, she limits their use to times when legitimate sources have been exhausted. The PI novels of women contain the vicarious thrills of their traditional predecessors. The reader follows as the PI narrowly escapes detection and discovers truths hidden from official eyes. The PI is careful, however, to remind the reader that such procedures are illegal and must be used with discretion. There are costs to having such intimate access to people's lives.

The official judicial system does not always convict the guilty and satisfy the PI or her clients. Knowing that the legal system will not be able to convict a killer serves as a strong temptation for the PI to seek justice outside the system. An unrepentant killer is difficult for the women investigator to let escape. V. I. Warshawski and Kinsey Millhone each call in a mysterious "higher power" to take care of a killer who cannot be brought to justice through legal channels. Warshawski calls in a mob hit on a corrupt Catholic archbishop (in *Killing Orders*), who destroyed many lives in his singular pursuit of power. In his ruthlessness he also tries to kill Warshawski twice, once by hiring someone to throw acid in her face. Warshawski understands what she has done in calling in the hit. At the far-off sound of an explosion, Warshawski knows that the job is complete. She does not question her own motivations.

Millhone makes a call to a mysterious, and obviously well-connected, man who is interested in her case after it becomes clear there is no legal way to get the killer in *"K" Is for Killer*. She immediately regrets her actions and tries to warn the intended victim. Instead, he incapacitates her in the same way he did with his first victim. Her temporary paralysis makes it impossible for her to warn him that his next visitor is going to kill him. He is called away before he can kill her; it is this appointment that is his undoing. Millhone reports her actions to the police as soon as she is able, but without any evidence of foul play, the disappearance of Millhone's would-be killer remains unexplained.[84] Millhone knows what she has done, but without any obvious evidence of trauma or death, her act of calling for a hit loses some of its impact for her. For the reader, the incident is buried in the middle of the alphabet. It is not clear just who Grafton is referring to in the title of the book. I would argue that both of these incidents fall outside the norm for the woman detective—perhaps as a brief play with the traditional history of the PI form. The women authors and their PIs work too hard to celebrate commitment and responsibility for such extreme violence to be the norm.

Calling for a hit puts the PI in very close company with the criminals she works to expose. The line between them becomes confused as the reader's trusted friend and ally is exposed. She is no longer the defender of life. Warshawski's hit in *Killing Orders* is such an example. She accepts a mysterious payment several days after the archbishop is killed in a car bombing. Her grief at the destruction left in the wake of the archbishop's ruthlessness and his exposure through her investigation does not completely exonerate Warshawski. The reader is never quite sure if Warshawski will kill again should another case become too difficult for her to handle. Kinsey Millhone is shown to regret her actions. She tries to make amends, but the death is still hers. To the reader, the illegal acts of breaking and entering or tampering with evidence are shown as mostly innocent. There is no harm in looking for clues in someone's apartment, especially if you know that the person is implicated in a crime. The excitement level is raised, and the reader and PI share the thrill of the danger. The hits called in by Warshawski and Millhone illustrate the potential trap for the PI who believes she is above (or outside) the law. The reader is left to ponder the line between the acceptable and unacceptable.

Those women authors of PI novels whom I interviewed stated that the mission of the woman investigator is "justice," but a more accurate description might be "fair play." In the traditional hard-boiled private eye genre, "justice" includes components of vigilantism. The hard-boiled PI puts a priority on his worldview, to the exclusion of others. The male PI hurtles through the landscape to exact a punishment of his own determining. As Marcia Muller noted, the macho male PI sets himself above the law and takes it into his own hands to deal with the people around him. The woman detective, on the other hand, is more interested in getting along with others.[85] Justice as "fair play" includes this idea. It implies a discussion with others about how everyone can be a part of the game, as well as how the rules should be written and enforced.[86]

The woman PI wants to ensure that the "big kids" (big money, power, authority, and control) cannot take over the game or win at the expense of those with fewer resources. Catherine Sayler illustrates this point in *Love nor Money*. She lets a killer, Kevin Doyle, lock her up so he can escape the country. Doyle had killed a pedophile in a fit of rage. Doyle had been molested as a child by a man who later became a judge. The judge called Doyle, as a reporter and unaware of their past relationship, to hear his side of a current story of abuse with a minor. The drunken judge kept telling him how "his boys" had really been after him; they had wanted sex. Doyle had not planned to kill the man, and he is now frightened of going to prison and what will happen to him there once his story gets out. Sayler allows Doyle to leave the country and the life he has made for himself after he promises to mail back a confession, to ensure that an innocent man is not tried for the crime. Her actions are illegal and unethical, but "[i]n the messy world of real life, moral, legal, and ethical aren't always possible. One out of three isn't so bad—as long as it's the right one."[87] In the worlds of the women PIs, life is messy. There are no hard-and-fast rules or truths. The best that can be achieved is for everyone to be at least given a chance. Justice is rooted in concern for relationships and a life viewed in context. The obligation of the woman private eye is not to an abstract ideal of society, but to the real people who inhabit it.[88]

When asked what kinds of mysteries she read growing up and what authors inspired her to write, Linda Grant remarked that as a kid she liked Nancy Drew, but Nancy Drew did not grow up.[89] The women who began writing women PI novels in the 1980s were looking for the rest of the Nancy Drew story. They wanted to know what happened after she left college and her father's house.

What happened when she had to find her own apartment? What happened when she needed a job to pay the rent? What happened when she faced a world of tough streets and tough answers? Stories by authors like Raymond Chandler and Dashiell Hammett were exciting to women readers for their grit, toughness, and edge, but women characters were routinely excluded from these adventures. It was a "boys only" club. The stories were exciting, but not satisfying for a girl looking to be the hero of her own narrative adventure. The treatment of women as objects in male hard-boiled detective fiction was clear and decisive. According to feminist critic Maureen Reddy, in these novels women were all potentially destructive and predatory, with some women able to be redeemed by their willingness to submit to patriarchal rule. The women who write for the PI novel today make it their own by refusing to encode a simple reversal of this pattern. They do not simply substitute female for male and keep the rest the same. No single pattern has emerged for the portrayals of either men or women. By removing women from the position of "other," these women mystery novelists opened up an enormous range of possibilities for the narratives of women.[90] In the PI novels of women, readers can find excellent models of a woman deciding on the life that suits her and then living it.[91]

What is arguably one of the most conservative and misogynist of the detective novel formats, the hard-boiled private eye novel, has been molded by women into a flexible, revolutionary, and liberating form. Kinsey Millhone ironically notes that the basic characteristics of any good investigator are a plodding nature and infinite patience. She adds that society has been grooming women to this end for years. The woman PI novel, as a popular cultural artifact disseminated through hundreds of readers, perpetuates a view of woman that calls attention to her competence and skills rather than her sexuality. She is not necessarily learning new skills (i.e., how to be a man). Rather, she is relying on skills she has always had and finding a new outlet for them. Lorraine Gamman remarks about women in the role of police officer in the television drama, "Cagney and Lacey":

> The attraction of law enforcement as a site for positive representation of women derives not from any great love of the police force or consensus that women are more ethical or less aggressive and destructive than men, but from the fact that such scenarios permit focus on female *activity* rather than on female *sexuality*. Positioning female characters in the role of detective shows them "thinking" and pursuing "knowledge" without overdetermined reference to their physical competence or conventional "attractiveness."[92]

The woman PI is a character of action—both physically and mentally. A woman in the role of private eye, as depicted in the novelistic form descended from the hard-boiled detective novels of the 1930s and 1940s, is not simply a substitution. She complicates the gender assumptions of both men and women, as well as the prioritization of traditional (masculine) definitions of the heroic. The central quality of the traditional private eye novel was solitude. The heroic male was heroic because he stood alone to fight the enemy.

The quality that most captures the quality of the 1980s and 1990s private eye novels of women is connectedness. To know how she detects and why we must look at the woman PI's deep attachments and commitments to others. Mystery critic Kathy Phillips describes Sharon McCone's style of detection: "[s]he doesn't just detect or discover or find, she compels others to act, to react to her intrusion into their past. And it is in their reactions to her that the truth comes out."[93] Clues are not just bits and pieces to be picked up at a crime scene. For the woman private eye, "detection" is the analysis of human relations. Clues are in how a woman talks about her husband; how a man conducts his business; how secrets are protected; and, how a person defines a life that matters. The woman PI, too, is a part of the picture. Her presence affects the scene. The woman PI is touched by those she meets during her investigations.

In an interview about the role of the PI, Paretsky connects Warshawski's compulsion to be an investigator with her obligation to those who have been oppressed by the prevailing system. Warshawski's job is to share information with those who have been systematically uninformed. Paretsky explains: "Secrets maintain oppression. It is the ultimate patronizing aspect of the patriarchy to say that you can know X amount, and we have the right to decided what's for your own good."[94] Sue Grafton sees Kinsey Millhone and the other women private eye's as a vehicle for social commentary. The PI is literally a "private eye." She is an observer and someone who comments on society, family relationships, and the state of justice.[95] The woman PI is not motivated by an abstract notion of right and wrong. It is her commitment to people's lives that keeps her in the game and gives her a passion about her work. Raymond Chandler summed up the image of the hero in the traditional male hard-boiled detective novel: "The whole point [of genre heroics ] is that the detective exists complete and entire and unchanged."[96] The hero in today's mystery fiction has a more difficult task. The woman PI must find a way to change with the times and still function as a hero. Instead of being static, she values the risks and uncertainty of change, maturity, and growth.

## NOTES

1. Marcia Muller, *Edwin of the Iron Shoes* (New York: Mysterious Press, 1990).

2. Maxine O'Callaghan had published a short story with a female private investigator, Delilah West, a few years previous, but Muller was unaware of this work.

3. Carolyn G. Heilbrun, *Hamlet's Mother and Other Women* (New York: Columbia University Press, 1990), 234.

4. Thomas Chastain, "The Case for the Private Eye," in *The Murder Mystique: Crime Writers on Their Art*, ed. Lucy Freeman (New York: Frederick Ungar Publishing Co., 1982), 27.

5. Jon L. Breen, "Introduction: Private Eye Mysteries," in *The Fine Art of Murder: The Mystery Reader's Indispensable Companion*, ed. Ed Gorman, Martin H. Greenberg, Larry Segriff, and Jon L. Breen (New York: Carroll & Graf Publishers, 1993), 153.

6. Ernest Mandel, *Delightful Murder: A Social History of the Crime Story* (London: Pluto Press, 1984), 35.

7. Marcia Muller, telephone interview, 27 January 1994.

8. Ellen Hawkes, "G Is for Grafton," *Los Angeles Times Magazine*, 18 February 1990, 22–23.

9. Breen, 154–55.

10. Marcia Muller, "In the Tradition of . . . Herself," in *The Fine Art of Murder: The Mystery Reader's Indispensable Companion*, ed. Ed Gorman, Martin H. Greenberg, Larry Segriff, and Jon L. Breen (New York: Carroll & Graf Publishers, 1993), 156.

11. Robin Gee, "Q&A with Marcia Muller," in *Mystery Writer's Marketplace and Sourcebook*, ed. Donna Collingwood (Cincinnati, OH: Writer's Digest Books, 1993), 43.

12. Muller, "In the Tradition," 157.

13. Anne Cranny-Francis, *Feminist Fiction: Feminist Uses of Generic Fiction* (New York: St. Martin's Press, 1990), 157.

14. Muller interview.

15. Rosemary Herbert, "Aiming Higher," *Publishers Weekly* 237.15 (13 April 1990): 32.

16. Hawkes, 22.

17. Sara Paretsky, "The Writing That Got Me Started," in *Mystery Writer's Marketplace and Sourcebook*, ed. Donna Collingwood (Cincinnati, OH: Writer's Digest Books, 1993), 267.

18. "Ladies' Choice," Narrated by Betsy Aaron, *Sunday Morning* (New York: CBS, 29 March 1992).

19. Marilyn Stasio, "Lady Gumshoes Boiled Less Hard," *New York Times Book Review*, 28 April 1985, 39.

20. Linda Grant, telephone interview, 2 February 1994.

21. Sandra Scoppettone, telephone interview, 26 January 1994.

22. Stanley Cavell, *The World Viewed* (Cambridge: Harvard University Press, 1979), 56; Cavell's discussion of "the dandy" is useful for understanding the hero of the hard-boiled private eye novel. Cavell, 55–60.

23. George Grella, "The Hard-Boiled Detective Novel," in *Detective Fiction: A Collection of Critical Essays*, ed. Robin W. Winks (Woodstock, VT: Foul Play Press, 1988), 106.

24. Dashiell Hammett, *The Maltese Falcon* (1929; New York: Vintage Books, 1989).

25. Psychological developmental models for men and women and their implications are more fully elaborated by Carol Gilligan in her book, *In a Different Voice* (Cambridge: Harvard University Press, 1982).

26. Margaret Marshment, "Substantial Women," in *The Female Gaze*, ed. Lorraine Gamman and Margaret Marshment (London: Women's Press, 1988), 40.

27. Marcia Muller, *Eye of the Storm* (New York: Mysterious Press, 1989).

28. Marcia Muller, *Wolf in the Shadows* (New York: Mysterious Press, 1993).

29. Marcia Muller, *Where Echoes Live* (New York: Mysterious Press, 1992).

30. Linda Grant, *Love nor Money* (New York: Charles Scribner's Sons, 1991).

31. Linda Grant, *Lethal Genes* (New York: Scribner, 1996).

32. Sue Grafton, *"J" Is for Judgment* (New York: Henry Holt and Company, 1993).

33. Sara Paretsky, *Killing Orders* (New York: Ballantine Books, 1992).

34. Sara Paretsky, *Deadlock* (New York: Ballantine Books, 1986).

35. Sara Paretsky, *Blood Shot* (New York: Dell Publishing, 1989).

36. Sara Paretsky, *Burn Marks* (New York: Dell Publishing, 1991).

37. Mystery author K. K. Beck followed a different strategy for her detective. Beck created a character who is a young widow, which means that she is assured of public sympathy for her loss, rather than blame for a divorce. She, too, does not have to concentrate all her attentions on finding a husband since she has already complied with that aspect of being a woman. She is young, attractive, and vital, and yet not encumbered by social pressure to find a mate. K. K. Beck, telephone interview, 3 November 1993.

38. Sue Grafton, *"G" Is for Gumshoe* (New York: Fawcett Crest, 1991).

39. Sue Grafton, *"M" Is for Malice* (New York: Henry Holt and Company, 1996).

40. Marcia Muller, *There's Nothing to Be Afraid Of* (New York: Mysterious Press, 1990).

41. Marcia Muller, *Pennies on a Dead Woman's Eyes* (New York: Charles Scribner's Sons, 1992).

42. Linda Grant, *Random Access Murder* (New York: Avon Books, 1988).

43. Muller interview.

44. Grafton, *"J" Is for Judgment*, 2.

45. Sue Grafton, *"E" Is for Evidence* (New York: Bantam Books, 1989.

46. Sara Paretsky, *Bitter Medicine* (New York: Ballantine Books, 1989).

47. Sandra Scoppettone, *Let's Face the Music and Die* (Boston: Little, Brown and Company, 1996).

48. Sara Paretsky, *Guardian Angel* (New York: Dell Publishing, 1993).

49. Charles Champlin, "Women Sleuths and the Rise of the Whydunit," *Los Angeles Times Book Review*, 29 October 1989, 15.

50. Maureen T. Reddy, *Sisters in Crime: Feminism and the Crime Novel* (New York: Continuum Publishing Company, 1988), 105.

51. Reddy, 110.

52. Carolyn G. Heilbrun, "Women, Men, Theories and Literature," in *The Impact of Feminist Research in the Academy*, ed. Christie Farnham (Bloomington: Indiana University Press, 1987), 221.

53. Nancy Miller quoted in Carolyn G. Heilbrun and Margaret R. Higonnet, introduction to, *The Representation of Women in Fiction: Selected Papers from the English Institute, 1981*, ed. Carolyn G. Heilbrun and Margaret R. Higonnet (Baltimore, MD: Johns Hopkins University Press, 1983), xviii.

54. Heilbrun and Higonnet, xv.

55. Nancy Miller, *The Heroine's Text: Readings in the French and English Novel, 1722–1782* (New York: Columbia University Press, 1980), 155.

56. Sandra Scoppettone, *Everything You Have Is Mine* (New York: Ballantine Books, 1992), 2.

57. Paretsky, *Guardian Angel*, 15.

58. Muller, *Echoes*, 4.

59. Muller, *Echoes*, 5.

60. Sue Grafton, *"H" Is for Homicide* (New York: Fawcett Crest, 1992).

61. Sandra Scoppettone, *I'll Be Leaving You Always* (Boston: Little, Brown and Company, 1993).

62. Linda Grant, *A Woman's Place* (New York: Charles Scribner's Sons, 1994).

63. Marcia Muller, *Pennies on a Dead Woman's Eyes* (New York: Charles Scribner's Sons, 1992).

64. Sue Grafton, *"I" Is for Innocent* (New York: Fawcett Crest, 1993).

65. Sue Grafton, *"A" Is for Alibi* (New York: Bantam Books, 1987).

66. Sara Paretsky, *Indemnity Only* (New York: Dell Publishing, 1991).

67. Sara Paretsky, *Tunnel Vision* (New York: Delacorte Press, 1994).

68. Lorraine Gamman, "Watching the Detectives: The Enigma of the Female Gaze," in *The Female Gaze*, ed. Lorraine Gamman and Margaret Marshment (London: Women's Press, 1988), 14.

69. Susan J. Kraus, "Paretsky Spills the Beans," *New Directions for Women* 20.1 (January/February 1991): 16.

70. Heilbrun, *Hamlet's Mother*, 248-49.

71. Carolyn G. Heilbrun, *Toward a Recognition of Androgyny* (New York: W. W. Norton & Company, 1982), x–xi.

72. Heilbrun, *Androgyny*, xiv.

73. Mary Jacobus, "The Difference of View," in *Women Writing and Women Writing about Women*, ed. Mary Jacobus (New York: Barnes & Noble Books, 1979), 12, 20.

74. Heilbrun, *Hamlet's Mother*, 250.

75. Heilbrun, *Androgyny*, 56.

76. Heilbrun, *Hamlet's Mother*, 251.

77. Reddy, 112–13.

78. Grant interview.

79. Linda Grant, *Blind Trust* (New York: Ivy Books, 1991).

80. Sue Grafton, *"B" Is for Burglar* (New York: Bantam Books, 1986).

81. Sue Grafton, *"C" Is for Corpse* (New York: Bantam Books, 1988).

82. Marcia Muller, *Trophies and Dead Things* (New York: Mysterious Press, 1991).

83. Stasio, 39.

84. Sue Grafton, *"K" Is for Killer* (New York: Henry Holt and Company, 1994).

85. Beck interview.

86. Gilligan's *In a Different Voice* discusses in more detail the differences between girls' and boys' play on the school playground. The boys are more interested in the rules and finding a winner, while the girls are more likely to negotiate play so that everyone can participate.

87. Grant, *Love nor Money*, 272.

88. Reddy, 117–18.

89. Grant interview.

90. Reddy, 102.

91. Carolyn G. Heilbrun, "The Women of Mystery," *Ms.* 1.5 (March/April 1991): 62.

92. Gamman, 19.

93. Kathy Phillips, "McCone and the Comic," *Drood Review of Mystery* 10.0 (January 1990): 8.

94. Kraus, 16.

95. Herbert, 32.

96. Raymond Chandler quoted in Marilyn Stasio, "What Happened to Heroes Is a Crime," *New York Times Book Review*, 14 October 1990, 57.

*Chapter 3*

# The Police-Trained Detective

The "police procedural" mystery format was developed as a revolt against the hard-boiled mystery novel of the 1940s and 1950s. Today, women writers use the procedural to focus attention on women who are a part of the official, "masculine," state system. These women have been trained to see crime, evidence, and methods of investigation through the language of law and order. Their training in this "official" language is not unlike girls being socialized to speak, think, and see according to society's worldview. Women learn this "language" and work to make it fit their experiences. They must try to explain or justify inconsistencies. Women strive to fit into the social order, learn the "foreign" language of masculine society, and retain their own sense of identity and language.

The police procedural was originally an attempt to bring realism to the mystery genre. Authors portray "real" police officers solving "real" crimes in the way real crimes get solved.[1] "Detection" for the police consists of rules and regulations. There is no place for the larger-than-life superhero of the traditional private eye novel. The restrictions of the job and the police officer's obligations to society require the hero to be very human and accessible.[2] The fictional police officers work on more than one case at a time alongside several other officers in their team. They juggle the threads of several cases, bringing them together in the end. There is no one "supersleuth" who can dominate the case; it is the team that conducts the investigation and works toward the conclusion. One police officer may be the primary focus of a mystery author, but other members of the team have important roles in the process.[3]

The police are given the authority of the state to maintain order, restore stability, and solve one of the most brutal disruptions of social life—murder. The issue of "state authority" makes the procedural detective stories illustrative for feminist studies. One of the most controversial debates in feminist studies is the question of feminism in an ideologically masculine society. How critical or revolutionary can women be as part of masculine-dominated society? Can women understand the unique experiences of being a woman if the only tool available is androcentric language?

For the purposes of this analysis, I have expanded the traditional definition of "police procedural" to include women characters acting as sleuths under the authority of the state, though not necessarily police officers—"police-trained" detectives. Private investigators, while licensed by the state, are not a part of this category. Their investigations are conducted privately. For a PI, the solution of a case often takes priority over the letter of the law and rules of procedure and evidence. As an officer of the state, the woman "police-trained" detective joins a predominantly male profession. She must work in company with these men on a daily basis. The woman is granted a degree of authority and control by the state that is not usually given to women. The state works to frame her professional behavior, experiences, and attitudes according to its androcentric priorities.

The following is an analysis based on the works of five women authors and their police detective series. Their protagonists and stories highlight the conflicts and conversations women have about themselves as part of masculine-dominated society. The authors and their detectives are: Susan Dunlap, writing about Homicide Detective (and later, Beat Officer) Jill Smith; Margaret Maron's Lt. Sigrid Harald; Dana Stabenow and her investigator, Kate Shugak, (originally part of the Alaskan District Attorney's office); Joan Hess's Police Chief Arly Hanks; and Patricia Cornwell's Dr. Kay Scarpetta, Virginia's chief medical examiner. Other authors write well in this same format, but these particular authors were selected for their popularity and respect within the mystery community. Their stories are well crafted. They cover very diverse territories with a well-developed sense of place and voice. These authors have become very strong writers, with their characters and plots becoming more complex and interesting as the series continue. This sense of maturity is evident in their discussions of women's language and social place.

In her study of three hundred detective novels written with a woman private eye and authored by men and women, critic Kathleen Gregory Klein concludes that the woman heroic mystery character in the PI novel is not allowed to act like one within the confines of the mystery genre. She finds it inherently conservative in that it upholds dominant notions of power, privilege, law, and order.[4] According to Klein, the woman detective is always a spy and sexual object; she is an intruder in the public realm controlled by masculinist, patriarchal power. Because she has abandoned her traditional ("home") sphere for the public ("work") sphere of men, the woman detective is deviant.[5] Female characters are excluded from the role of hero because male behavior is the norm in the mystery. The message of the detective novel is that any changes in social organization that arise from women's active participation in public life can be dismissed by the reader as short-lived and inconsequential.[6] Klein finds feminism and the detective genre incompatible. A licensed investigator is part of the system, which oppresses women—"she is working for the 'bad guys.'"[7]

Rather than dismissing the genre, the purpose of this investigation is to examine how the genre is a part of society—how it used by readers and writers. The norms and expectations of genre fiction are enmeshed with the norms and expectations of society. Focusing on genre fiction exposes how gender enters into, and is constructed by, the form. It illustrates how and why these constructions change over time. As "texts-in-use," women's police detectives represent how women conceptualize themselves, masculine society, and the language of representation.[8] Genre is not static. Indeed, conventions have the potential to change with each new book and reading.

Women's detective stories illustrate their ambivalence toward law and the establishment. For many women, law is something that defends the interests of men and controls the behavior of women. They conclude that in women's mysteries, there is no comfortable way for the law to exist as some kind of embodiment of a shared morality. Women's police novels explore legal contradictions.[9] They illustrate women's position under the law. The conventions of mystery fiction direct the author toward tradition and repetition, individualism, and faith in authority. Women mystery writers pull the genre away from this predictability and toward psychological and social explorations of crime.[10] Their police investigators work to reconcile their experiences as women in masculine society with their commitment to the law. While using the language of the masculine state, these women challenge its methods of representation. They offer critique and revolution from within the confines of the potentially repressive and conservative.

The women who have created the police detectives discussed here came to their writing with similar expectations and concerns. Each wanted to created a woman character and explore her maturation. She was to have a past that set her on a path, but along the way she would meet people and experiences that could potentially change her. They try to answer the question, "Who is the woman in a man's world?" Throughout their series, the women authors include references to family and social pressures. The police detectives all search for answers to how a woman can hear her own voice even while wearing the badge of the state.

The development of a series character most interested author Susan Dunlap.[11] She wanted to create characters with depth who matured over time. Jill Smith, her protagonist, is a member of the Berkeley, California, police force. Her quest is to discover what "justice" means. She asks questions about how society can account for individuals within the institution of the law. She wants to explore how individual justice is served by laws written for a homogenous society. Inequality because of differences of race and gender is unjust, but Dunlap and the other women mystery writers examine where the line should be drawn between the rights of society and the rights of individuals. The authority of the state attracted Dunlap to create a character who is a police officer. In exchange for the loss of mobility and free choice, Smith was created with a degree of power over her environment that is unfamiliar to many women.[12] Jill Smith came to Berkeley with her first husband, Nat. She took the patrol officer's exam to earn money to support them while he went to graduate school and completed his dissertation. Smith found a place for herself on the force and as a part of Berkeley. A police officer was not considered a "proper" wife for an aspiring professor by Nat nor his strict Bostonian family. The couple divorced, which forced Nat to put aside his degree and find work. Smith continues to feel the guilt of being a "failed" wife and inconveniencing her husband's plans for his future. Dunlap writes the Jill Smith series in the first person. Through the character, the reader sees and experiences the people around Smith, the city of Berkeley, the police chases, and more important, the issues that confuse and excite Smith.

Dana Stabenow includes race in her conversations on the mythology of women. The first Kate Shugak mystery came out in 1992. Stabenow wanted to talk about the lives of the Aleuts and their race—and the character of Kate Shugak evolved from there. The edge that Stabenow needed for her series came by giving Shugak a professional police background as an investigator for the office of the district attorney (DA) in Alaska. Her character is intimately involved in the horrors that people inflict on each other. In order to mirror real life, however, it was necessary for Shugak to leave the DA's office. In Alaska, according to Stabenow, there is a high incidence rate of alcohol abuse and burnout for those involved in police work. If Shugak was going to stay in the DA's employ, she would have had to reflect this fact or become corrupt.[13] Shugak left the DA's office after being injured during a case. She confronted a man abusing his son, was attacked, and became so angry that she went after the father with a knife. The naked child she was there to protect then grabbed her and begged her not to hurt his father. Shugak suffered a slashed throat during the confrontation. On recovering from the injury, Shugak resigns her position and returns to her family's homestead in the Alaskan frontier. That child, as well as the pain and suffering she has to confront almost daily, are as much a part of her training as her lessons in law and order. Stabenow thinks that Shugak's broken voice, the result of her injuries, is a symbol of the broken voice of the Aleut people.

Shugak's family's story is similar to that of many native Alaskans. Her father drank too much to fish and would beat her mother. Her mother had to go on welfare. She, too, spent most of her time drinking and left the children to raise themselves. When Shugak was six years old, her mother died of exposure after passing out drunk in a snowbank. Shugak's father drowned two years later. As a result of her own family's suffering and the pain she sees all too often in the Park (a large area of Alaskan wilderness that also incorporates the lands of the Aleuts), Shugak does not drink alcohol. She chooses to live alone on her family's remote homestead with her part-wolf sled dog, Mutt. Shugak's grandmother, Ekaterina, is the matriarch of the family and tries to keep the family and tribe together by observing the traditional ways of their people. Shugak and Ekaterina often clash over how best to serve the family and the Aleut people. Thus, Stabenow has woven together a story of an individual woman that includes both her own unique experiences and those familiar to her readers.

Joan Hess takes a lighter, more humorous approach to handling issues of gender and social constraint. Hess began the Arly Hanks series at the suggestion of her editor. Regional mysteries were "hot" in the market. Hess is from Arkansas, and since no one had "taken" that state yet, her editor thought she might be able to sell an Arkansas series.[14] The Hanks books take place in a broken-down little town in the Ozark Mountains of Arkansas—Maggody, population 755. Arly Hanks was born in Maggody but later moved to Manhattan and married. She moved back to Maggody after her divorce to regroup and recover. Hess thought it was more realistic that the character be female since a man was less likely to come home and seek comfort from family and friends.[15]

The final police detective examined here is Dr. Kay Scarpetta. Patricia Cornwell began the series in the late 1980s. Like the other women authors of the police detective, Cornwell's books illustrate how state authority can be more complicated for women than for men. Along with the job of solving crimes comes the problem of dealing with the social stereotypes about the "proper" role for women. Cornwell highlights this problem by juxtaposing a female protagonist with very explicit and gruesome murders. As with British mystery author P. D. James, for example, reader and critics are often shocked that a "nice" lady is able to imagine, let alone write about, such brutal and graphic crimes.

Cornwell's Scarpetta is an upper-middle-class, middle-aged woman. Her beginnings in Miami were much less auspicious. Her grandfather emigrated to the United States from Italy. Her father owned a small grocery story and died when she was twelve. Since his death, Scarpetta has not been very close to her mother or sister. In medical school and law school she felt out of place, both as a middle-class Italian among the wealthy white students and as a woman in very male surroundings. She was one of a very small handful of women to enter these programs and an even smaller number who finished. It was a very lonely and isolating time for her. Her reaction was to try even harder to succeed. She saw success as her best revenge. Scarpetta married out of law school but was divorced several years later. Her husband was abusive; she does not talk much about this period in her life. Later, when she becomes reacquainted with one of her law professors, he comments that he had been disappointed in her attachment to the young man. She was the one with the gift for law. It was wasted on her attentions to her then boyfriend. As one of the few women medical examiners in the country, Scarpetta faces extreme public scrutiny whenever her office is involved in a case. The public (and reader) pay close attention to her life, trying to find something to explain the anomaly of a woman who seems to enjoy cutting up dead people. How can she have chosen such a macabre job? What is wrong with her?

The author of the police detective novels explores the confrontations between the worldviews of men and women. She examines the complications and contradictions that the women face as part of masculine society—learning its rules and speaking its language as police officers. Feminist literary criticism, too, is interested in exploring masculine texts with a view toward women readers. Everyone, according to literary critic, Judith Fetterly, learns to read like a man—the androcentric perspective that pervades most authoritative texts of a culture adopted by the society. The more a woman reads, the "more extensive her schooling is in seeing it 'his way.'"[16] According to feminist literary critic Patrocinio Schweickart, a literary education may very well induce a kind of schizophrenia in women due to its androcentrism. Women become powerless as a result of the endless division of one self from another. She is called on to identify herself as male while being reminded that to be male ("universal") is to be not female.[17] The question asked in this analysis is Jonathan Culler's:

> If the experience of literature depends upon the qualities of the reading self, one can ask what difference it would make to the experience of literature and thus to the meaning of literature if this self were, for example, female rather than male. If the meaning of the work is the experience of the reader, what difference does it make if the reader is a woman?[18]

For Culler, the female reader is just an example—"if" the reader is a woman, he says. However, it is not just a matter of "if," but also of "when." Women are an important market for fiction. They have played, and continue to play, a critical role in the history and development of the novel.

The relationship of women to language and the difficulties women experience trying to escape its patriarchal structure are central to the work of feminist studies. How do women express their unique experiences through a masculine language system? In *Women and Men Speaking*, Chris Kramarae documents the difficulties women writers can experience in trying to find their own "voice." They try to speak about their own experiences through and "around" the literary language form accepted by men. For women to participate in society, they transform their own models of experience into acceptable masculine forms of expression. Men and women experience the world differently—Kramarae attributes this to society's gendered division of labor—but the masculine system of perception is dominant. Women's alternative models are impeded. Their perceptions are "lost in translation."[19]

Literary critic Elaine Showalter divides the feminist literary project into two areas of investigation. The first, "feminist critique," is an analysis of women as consumers of male-produced texts. The aim of this analysis is to make sexual codes and ideological assumptions more explicit. The second area of analysis concerns the women as writer, or "gynocritics." Critics explore the world of female culture, while constructing a female framework for the analysis of women's literature.[20] The women writing mystery novels of women police investigators are continuing Showalter's program of analysis. Their women police officers confront and reevaluate strong male-produced texts. As women writers, the authors work within patriarchal language and models to name their own experiences.

Literary genres are special systems within language. The norms and expectations of each genre are enmeshed with the norms and expectations of society. They change as social systems and institutions change. Understanding language as a system of constructing arbitrary differences, which has more to do with power relations than absolute meanings, women writers realize that it can be changed and that genres can be reworked.[21] Looking closely at specific themes within the books of the five authors selected, women's conversations about language, patriarchal order, and the validity of women's experiences are detailed. As each new book enters into public discourse, it acts to change social understandings. New conversations (and even arguments) are built from those that came before. Guns, public perceptions (and misperceptions) of the woman investigator, and the social devastation caused by murder are some of the topics discussed by these women mystery writers that give voice to women's experiences and perceptions.

The five women police detectives in this chapter are licensed to carry a gun, but deadly force is not how their cases are typically solved. The women accept that they need to protect themselves since they hold very dangerous jobs. A gun offers a measure of security. Like the private eye, the police detectives do not enjoy using their guns. They do not rely on them to solve their cases nor to get them out of trouble. One of the most marked differences between mysteries written by men and those by women involves the use of guns. Even in some of the "coziest" men's detective novels, a violent shoot-out between the detective and the killer can be expected. The firepower of a gun may even out differences in physical strength between men and women, but women authors' detectives are more likely to rely on brain than brawn. Guns are taken very seriously as weapons of destruction in the fictionalized fantasies of women.

Dr. Scarpetta has the most fire power of this group of detectives. Her job puts her in contact with very dangerous and violent criminals, often serial killers. She owns a Ruger .38 revolver loaded with Silvertips (a destructive exploding-tip type of ammunition). Scarpetta practices several times a month at a shooting range and when home alone, she feels most comfortable when she has the gun close at hand. Nonetheless, in the course of the series (from *Postmortem* to *Cause of Death*), Scarpetta only aims her gun twice. In both cases the murderer is trying to kill her; and in only one of these situations does she fire.

The first incident is in the first book, *Postmortem*. A serial killer brutally murders women who seem to have no connection to one another. The women are raped and their throats are cut—each case is more brutal than the last. With the help of a newspaper reporter (whose sister was one of those killed), Scarpetta plants a story in the paper to make the killer believe that the medical examiner's office is closing in on his identity. The man breaks into Scarpetta's home and, with a knife at her throat, threatens to brutalize her. Scarpetta's niece, Lucy, is in the house as well. Lucy often comes to stay with her aunt. Her mother may look like the perfect mother, writing children's books and always looking to remarry, but in reality, she has little time for her daughter. Scarpetta identifies with this lonely and very smart girl. Scarpetta keeps talking to the intruder in her house so that he will not find out about Lucy. In a moment of distraction, Scarpetta reaches under her pillow for her gun, rolls off the bed, and pulls the trigger. In her mind she shoots the murderer and is able to save herself and Lucy, but it is Lt. Peter Marino of the local police department who fires the fatal shot. Scarpetta had been so worried about Lucy finding her gun that she forgot to load it.[22] Cornwell illustrates the uneasy combination of children and guns. The situation leaves Scarpetta trying to resolve possibly endangering Lucy's life, having been too distracted to load her gun, the man's extreme cruelness at such a relatively young age, and having been able to think her way through her captivity and break free. There is no easy balance between being safe and confronting the cruelty possible in society.

Dr. Scarpetta does pull the trigger in her next book, *Body of Evidence*. One of the central issues of the book is relying on a gun for protection, especially for people not fully trained in its use. A young woman is stalked and killed. In order to solve the case, Scarpetta gets very close to this woman's life. Consequently, after the woman's death, the stalker turns his attentions to her. Lt. Marino offers Scarpetta an automatic-type gun to use instead of her usual Ruger. The automatic has more firepower, but Scarpetta declines. She cites quality over quantity. "More firepower" is no substitute for being informed and practiced. It is defense, rather than offense, that most concerns her. This is best insured by understanding a dangerous situation and being so well practiced with a gun that in a crisis, its use will be second nature.

The original murder victim did not start carrying a gun until the threats against her began. She was not used to carrying it, and the killer was able to catch her off-guard. This is not a justification for why everyone should own a gun, however. Even for the most trained individuals, guns are not a foolproof solution to danger. Scarpetta, too, is caught off-guard by her attacker. The stalker comes to her door representing a courier service returning her lost piece of luggage—he is an "innocent-looking" person. It is not the gun, by itself, that saves Scarpetta. Realizing her error in judgment, Scarpetta hits the man with his clipboard as she runs away. In their struggles she uses the resources at hand—a fire extinguisher and cast iron skillet, for example. When he finally comes at her with a knife, Scarpetta fires her gun and kills him. It is self-defense, but no less overwhelming for Scarpetta. She is not sorry she had to kill the man; he would have killed her. She is sorry that such a man was born.[23] She sees the situation in terms of its societal implications. This man was created somehow out of his family and community. He damaged many lives during his lifetime. Killing is not glorified in the Patricia Cornwell books. The murders are grisly and shown to be perpetrated by very seriously damaged people. Scarpetta and her police colleagues do not take their roles in death lightly. Scarpetta's job is to make sense of death and provide its victims with some degree of dignity. It is only when directly threatened that she uses her gun. It is a serious weapon, which she treats with due seriousness.

Guns play a relatively minor role for Stabenow's Kate Shugak, although they are standard on the Alaskan frontier. She attempts to hold the line against man's cruelty to man. In several cases, Shugak is shot at by people trying to keep her away from investigating. Twice, in *A Cold Day for Murder*, Shugak must dive for cover. Her cousin is responsible for the first shooting. He shoots to keep his sister from sexually throwing herself at a local radio operator, whom Shugak was in the process of interviewing about an unrelated matter. The second set of shots is aimed at Shugak. A man she regards as her surrogate father fires at her to keep her from discovering his role in the deaths of two men. He later appears to threaten her again with his gun, but instead turns it on himself.[24] In *A Fatal Thaw*, Shugak is injured when a bullet grazes her head. The killer was, again, warning her to stay away. Shugak recognizes these shootings as desperate acts by people trapped by their own actions. They are not a motive for her to act and seek revenge. She does not shoot back; rather, she continues to uncover the truth.

In only one case does Shugak use her own gun on a murderer. In *A Fatal Thaw*, she is warned that a sniper is heading in her direction. The man has killed seven or eight people for apparently no reason and must be stopped. When Shugak hears a snowmobile approaching, she takes her shotgun down to the road to intercept him. Still, she shoots at the road in front of the vehicle. No matter what he has done, Shugak does not want his death on her conscience. She loses her gun when she tries to run out of the woods and apprehend the gunman. The killer points his gun at her, but Shugak's dog, Mutt, jumps him. She calls off the dog before Mutt can go for the killer's neck. Everyone in town comments that Shugak should have just killed the man. "He deserved to die anyway," according to the townspeople.[25] Shugak, however, cannot participate so casually in another's death.

When pressed to defend herself, Shugak is more likely to employ her own agility, strength, and intelligence. In *A Cold-Blooded Business*, Shugak and a woman whom Shugak discovers selling drugs and illegal artifacts fight during a blizzard. To hold the woman until authorities arrive, Shugak makes her lick a frozen pipe. Witnesses are horrified that Shugak apparently left the woman to die of exposure, but she knows the storm has run its course and her prisoner is in no real danger.[26] In *Dead in the Water*, Shugak is knocked into the frigid sea while setting a large crab pot. Once back on board, Shugak and Andy (a young man on board who was not involved in killing two men on an earlier crew) push one of the guilty crewmen into the full crab hold of the boat. Shugak hurls a boat hook at one man and kills another of the guilty crewmen after he shoots at her. The DA is concerned that Shugak will be overcome by guilt for causing this man's death. Shugak understands, however, that he was about to kill her. She had to protect herself and the young man, Andy, who was innocent of any crime. The boat hook was the only available means to disable and disarm the attacker.[27] Protecting innocent life is paramount to Kate Shugak, both on and off a case. As an author, Stabenow contrasts the willing disregard for human life that can accompany greed with Shugak's determined effort to preserve life, even under direct personal threat.

For Jill Smith and Sigrid Harald, guns are a part of the police uniform—as is seeing the damage guns can cause. In *Death of a Butterfly*, the second in the Harald series, the reader learns that Lieutenant Harald has not shot at a living target, even though she is a veteran of the force. During target practice she makes it a point to aim at specific nonvital parts of the body.[28] Harald shoots to *not* kill. In the first eight Harald books, the lieutenant only draws her gun twice. The first time is in *The Right Jack*, which begins with an off-duty Harald on the way to the airport with her mother. She notices a man and woman acting suspiciously. Harald then interrupts what proves to have been a mugging and attempted rape by aiming her gun low and shooting the mugger in the leg. He is still able to use his knife and seriously injure Harald in the arm. Harald's mother is taken aback that even when injured, Harald remains very professional. She instructs her mother on how to notify the police and inquires after the suspect's health once the officers arrive. Lieutenant Harald's duty is to preserve the lives of those she serves as an officer of the law, even the guilty ones.

The second situation comes while Harald is on duty. A police officer murders two people in order to hide having taken money from a police drug bust. The case ends when Harald and another police officer, Vaughn (an African-American officer from Brooklyn working with Harald as part of the task force trying to find this killer), chase the murderer, with guns drawn, up to the roof of a tenement hotel. The killer apprehends Harald on the roof and holds her at gunpoint. Vaughn is able to get a clear shot and kill the man. He is then surprised that Harald, as a woman, does not break down as she tells the details of the shooting to the arriving officers. He does recognize that Harald is profoundly affected by the human consequences of the situation. Three people died, the suspect included, because this police officer could not resist the temptation of "easy" money. A woman lost her husband; three children lost their father. Harald and Vaughn are survivors, but they are left to wonder if they could have handled the case differently and prevented at least one death.[29] This case, like most of those handled by Harald, stresses the human cost of murder. For Harald, murder is comprised of the killer, the victims, and the countless lives touched by the event.

Guns play a conspicuously minor role in the Jill Smith series. Smith is a police officer for the city of Berkeley; she is responsible to the whole community. Smith is aware that firing a gun is often too dangerous to justify its use. The risk of hitting innocent bystanders is too great. A confrontation with a suspect in *As a Favor* becomes a physical fight instead when Smith realizes that she cannot fire her weapon without hitting the nearby house windows.[30] In *Death and Taxes*, Smith and several other officers set up a sting operation to catch a killer. When he runs from the scene, Smith chases him, but she cannot fire her weapon into the crowded streets. The killer is ultimately apprehended when Smith pushes over the portable toilet in which he is hiding.[31]

Smith's strength as a police officer does not come from playing the "tough guy." She sees it as coming from her skills as an interrogator and listener. She deals with suspects and witnesses by slicing away at their statements and keeping at it until they realize she has the information she needs—more than they may have intended to give. Author Susan Dunlap reinforces the link between police department actions and the community the department serves. The safety of the community must be considered before firing a weapon. Guns are a part of the police uniform, but so is the ability to use wits and intelligence.

Joan Hess takes the caution of the other women mystery writers one step further. She mocks the macho gunplay of stereotypic masculine mystery novels. As chief of police, Arly Hanks is issued a gun as part of her uniform. She is not, however, issued the necessary ammunition for that gun. The town council will not approve the expenditure. Hanks takes the situation lightly and jokes about rearranging the three bullets in their foam case when she is bored. If Hanks got into a gun battle, it would be a very short one. It is a good thing, then, that she only has to draw her gun once in the series.

In *Malice in Maggody*, Sergeant Plover, of the state police, reluctantly teams up with Hanks to check out reports of an escaped fugitive hiding in a local cabin. The two officers arrive and stake out the cabin with their guns drawn. The owner of the cabin, Robin Buchanon, has already taken charge of the situation. Robin is a small, filthy, illiterate, poor woman. She is the one who subdues the fugitive and captures the missing Environmental Protection Agency (EPA) official, who had escaped after being abducted by the town council.[32] Hank and Plover's drawn guns look rather foolish at the sight of Robin taking control.

"Light" mysteries are often discounted by critics on the grounds that as humorous stories, they are unable to contribute anything of substance or consequence to the genre. Hess shows how humor can highlight the conventions of the genre, as well as larger topics such as gender mythologies. For Hanks, the gun is a rather forgotten part of the uniform. Her role is to work with the citizens of Maggody—to protect them, defend them, and help them see the error of their ways. The stories told by women mystery writers have much to say about the issues in women's lives. There is more to the purpose of the narrative than to just move the story to the next shoot-out.

"Crime fiction is especially relevant for women with its exploration of the whole area of victimization, which is so much more significant to women than men." Women's mysteries are a psychological investigation of crime.[33] They are a venue for women to expose and confront their persecution at the hands of men and society. Men use money, position, authority, power, and control to manipulate women. Women's powerlessness and isolation have been common themes throughout their history in the mystery genre. The similarities in theme between the works of early women crime writers, like those of the Golden Era, and their contemporary counterparts highlights women's continued struggles against powerlessness, vulnerability, and a sense of society's general disregard.[34] One lesson women have learned is that there is no glamour in being the victim. Women mystery writers work hard to stay away from such simple labels; they expand the traditional (masculine) definition of culpability. They find strengths in their women protagonists and put faces on the casualties often left unnoticed by the killer and society.

Carol Gilligan's *In a Different Voice* explains the differences between men's and women's points of view, in particular with regard to "responsibility." According to Gilligan, in the male context, responsibility is associated with liability and the ability to exercise one's rights without impinging on the rights of others, whereas in female discourse, it is defined in a context of responsiveness to the needs of others. Women try to work out compromises that minimize pain and preserve relationships.[35] Morality, for women, is a problem of inclusion rather than of balancing claims. Morality comes from attachment. Female identity is defined in the context of relationships. It is judged by a standard of responsibility and care. The male "I" is defined in separation and with the confidence of certain truth.[36] The moral dilemma for men involves exercising one's rights without interfering with the rights of others. For women, the dilemma involves leading a moral life that includes obligations to self, family, and others.[37]

The contrast between the "rights" of men and the "obligations" of women is central to the police mysteries written by women. The laws of the state are written in the language of rights, certain truth, and individual separation. How are women able to work under such a system in the company of men? How can a woman succeed in such an environment? What does it mean to be a good police officer if you are a woman? Can you still believe in obligation and responsibility and carry out the duties of the state? The five authors selected here confront these questions by imagining how their protagonists are viewed by their male colleagues and how the public responds to them when confronted by their authority. These women detectives work to balance understanding and carrying out the rules of the state with what they feel to be their higher purpose—their responsibility to their community. The law must take into account the people it is supposed to serve.

Kate Shugak has the most difficult time reconciling her own experiences, as a woman and an Aleut, with being in the employ of the state. The white world has a long and painful history of oppressing women and Native Americans, as well as destroying the wilderness of Alaska. Kate had been the DA's star investigator. The Federal Bureau of Investigation (FBI), at one time tried to recruit her. Because of her expertise, her boss continues to contact her to work independently on cases that involve the Park. The weight of the DA's office ensures Shugak entry to a variety of places and situations. She can talk to the necessary people and operate with a degree of authority not often afforded to women or Aleuts. Shugak accepts the jobs and money of the DA's office, but she makes the DA understand that she conducts investigations her own way. Her first loyalty is to the people of the Park. In *A Fatal Thaw*, Shugak suspects early in her investigation that Lottie killed her sister Lisa, and not the sniper who had been shooting in the area. Kate continues her investigation, hoping to find another explanation for the death. Lottie later kills a park ranger, and Shugak realizes that she made an error in judgment by waiting to apprehend Lottie. She blames herself for the ranger's death since she had the power to stop Lottie before it happened. Lottie escapes into the Alaskan mountains with Shugak chasing her. During an earthquake, the two women are separated. Shugak reports Lottie's death to the police, thereby ending the investigation and closing the case, even though she knows that Lottie has the skills necessary to have survived the quake and continue hiking further into the wilderness. Kate also knows that the killings destroyed Lottie. Without her sister, she has no identity. She may have hated Lisa, but as her sister, Lisa made her whole. Lottie is punishing herself psychologically far worse than the state could by simply locking her up. Alone in the wilderness, Lottie is no longer a danger to anyone but herself. Kate took her investigation and pursuit as far as she could—and farther than anyone else could have done—and must be satisfied with the less-than-satisfactory resolution.

While investigating Lisa's life, Shugak discovers that she was trafficking in contraband and finds her stash of bear bladders and walrus tusks. Shugak illegally sells the bladders, which would have been thrown away by the authorities, because she needs the money for winter supplies. Shugak gives the tusks to a local artisan to carve. In this way, the money will stay in the Park, and a traditional art form will be encouraged. Shugak operates within her own code of justice and morality. Rather than the code that typified the traditional male "lone wolf" detective, Shugak does not set herself up as better than those around her. She does not believe that she must survive at the cost of others. She makes decisions based on empathy, particularly for the Native Americans of Alaska, and on meeting her own basic needs provided others are not harmed.

Shugak's credibility as an investigator is questioned in one case, when she is recommended to RPetCo Oil to investigate illegal drugs found on the North Slope area of Alaska. Most other times she is simply working for the DA or making inquiries for her own information. The chief executive officer (CEO) and security chief of RPetCo object to hiring Shugak on the grounds that she is a Native American—a recent RPetCo spill affected a great deal of the Alaskan wilderness and many people—and a woman. What can Shugak accomplish that the security chief, a man, cannot? Only after several recommendations by men, including the FBI, is Shugak hired. Shugak does not beg for the job or attempt to justify herself as the right choice. She is confident in her abilities and knows that if hired, she will do the job. She only works on cases of her choice; if they do not want her for this case, she will go on to something else. During her investigation on the North Slope, Shugak witnesses an incredible display of greed and stupidity as a result of drugs. At its conclusion, Shugak informs the DA that she will no longer work on drug-related cases. The excesses are too great. Drug buyers and sellers contribute to their own demise, and Shugak has no sympathy for them.

For the women of Maggody, Arkansas, there is a very limited definition of success. The lines are drawn very clearly between men's and women's appropriate places. Ruby Bee, Arly Hanks's mother, and her friend, Estelle, both own their own businesses. Estelle runs a beauty shop out of her home, and Ruby owns a grill and motel. Each of these businesses is an extension of appropriate female duties and priorities. Women are supposed to be focused on grooming, beauty, food, housekeeping, and service. Hanks is often criticized by Ruby Bee and Estelle for not trying to be attractive and sociable in order to find a nice husband. (Arly's first husband does not count because he was an "outsider" from New York.) The women of Maggody are expected to do as the church and their husbands tell them. Hanks is pressured by both the men and women of her community to be a more traditionally defined "lady."

The men of Maggody, the mayor, other town officials and police officers, doubt Hanks's ability to perform her job as chief of police. Arly Hanks was appointed chief of police by the town council. She was the only candidate for the job with any police experience (this "experience" remains unspecified in the series). Had any man been qualified for the job, Hanks would certainly have not been appointed. Once Hanks has been given the job, the men who run the town learn that she has also been given the authority to stand up to them. It is a very uncomfortable and relatively unknown situation for most of these men. Hanks is often ridiculed by them for her efforts. Although she was appointed chief of police by the town council, conversations with the mayor tend to include his threats of firing her. Hanks never does her job the way the mayor would like. His wife, whom Hanks calls Mrs. Jim Bob or Her Honor, is of the same opinion. She chastises Hanks for not taking the moral high ground that Mrs. Jim Bob points out to her. If Hanks were a true woman, according to the mayor's wife, she would not be doing the job of a man. Since she does have the job, she is obligated by her sex to stamp out sin and provide a moral example to the community.

Like Kate Shugak, Arly Hanks is an outsider in her own community. As a strong, independent woman—and one who left for the big city—she is unlike the women of her community. The women have to accept her, however, since she was born and grew up there. Hanks both protects the town from outsiders and gently pushes them to expand their views of the world. Hess uses the humor of the backwards and naïve town, as well as the "fish out of water" Hanks, to poke and pick at the inconsistencies of sex-based stereotypes and mythologies.

In *Malice in Maggody*, Hanks must work with Sergeant Plover of the state police. An EPA agent is missing after last being seen in Maggody, and a prison inmate has escaped and is reported to be in the area. Both state and local police officers join forces to investigate. At their first meeting, Plover adopts an intimidating posture. His request for cooperation is little more than a formality. Plover is sure that a woman, especially one from such a small, "backwater" town, cannot handle anything as dangerous as an escaped convict nor have the police skills necessary to track down the missing agent. His attitude toward Hanks is dismissive as he takes over her small office for his command post. Plover does not expect Hanks and her deputy to contribute anything of importance to the case. He does not want her to worry about the escaped felon since he and his men will take care of him. In the face of Plover's condescending attitude, Hanks reacts with sarcasm. She is not intimidated by his authority. She is determined to do her job. If the crime takes place in her town, she is the best person to handle the investigation.

Arly Hanks uncovers the details of the agent's kidnapping, solves the murder of a local young woman, and, by the end of the book, rounds up the suspects. She does not have to kowtow to the mayor, his wife, or Sergeant Plover, since they cannot fire her. The town council will not fire her; there are no qualified (male) candidates for the job. Hanks is unmoved by male authority for its own sake. Within the Maggody series, author Joan Hess illustrates how positions of power do not necessarily mean that the men holding them are morally, ethically, or intellectually superior to women. Hanks is shown as confident in her own abilities. She can see through the veneer of male superiority. In Hess's fictional narrative, gender stereotypes are exposed as ridiculous and inappropriate.

For women who are part of much larger police systems—Smith, Harald, and Scarpetta—interaction with male colleagues, witnesses, suspects, and the general public is an everyday obstacle. These women are responsible for defending their gender while performing their jobs at least twice as well as their male counterparts. For Jill Smith and Sigrid Harald, dedication to duty and years on the job grant them a grudging acceptance by most male police officers. They have proven their worth to their superiors and are able to conduct their own investigations. Situations do arise that remind these police detectives that they are still not "one of the boys." Women police officers have to perform their jobs while being both defender and representative of their gender.

Susan Dunlap's Jill Smith started out as a beat officer working almost any case that occurred within her jurisdiction with the help of her fellow beat officers. Smith is granted a degree of acceptance by the public because of this time she spent on the streets. She makes a point of treating people with respect and avoiding preconceived ideas. This goes for the street people, local artisans, and 1960s "dropouts," as well as the working or wealthy citizens of Berkeley. She is trusted to give suspects, witnesses, and informants a fair deal within the system. This attention to establishing relationships gains the homicide detective the respect she needs to investigate and solve cases.

Gender is a factor for Smith within the police department. She and fellow beat officer Seth Howard both try for promotion to Homicide after the department is created. Both, ultimately, have their sights set on the chief of police seat. Smith gains the advantage when she solves the murder of a Buddhist guru, in *Karma*.[38] Howard is Smith's closest friend. She is saddened by her promotion over him. Rather than seeing it as a victory for herself, it is more like a loss for Howard. Howard joins Special Investigations (Vice and Substance Abuse), a less prestigious post than Homicide but one for which he is well suited. The relationship between the two becomes unstable as a result of their new jobs. Howard does not like resenting his friend for her promotion, nor is he pleased by his suspicion that Smith's gender was an important part of the decision. Smith's new superior officer, Inspector Doyle, questions whether a woman detective will be too soft or too emotionally involved with the widows to ask the tough questions. Her superior as a beat officer, Lieutenant. Davis, pushed for her promotion, having been impressed by her work on the street. His word convinces Doyle. Both Howard and Doyle come to accept Smith as a competent homicide detective, but the situation is still not the same as if a male officer were in the position. Smith is not a homicide detective who happens to be a woman. She is a *woman* homicide detective.

*Too Close to the Edge* concludes with Smith crashing into San Francisco Bay in a helicopter while trying to apprehend a suspect. Smith then goes to Florida to convalesce at her parent's house.[39] She returns to work in *A Dinner to Die For*, in which she is put in charge of a high-profile homicide investigation. A celebrity restaurateur is poisoned to death and while in he death throes, he impales himself on a metal sculpture of a bird of paradise in front of his restaurant. The case also involves working with a crime scene supervisor who had been up for Smith's homicide detective position. He is very resentful and claims that sexual bias lost him the job. Smith is concerned that if she cannot perform her duties, Inspector Doyle will change his mind about a woman's ability to work homicide. She takes the upper hand with Sergeant Grayson, the scene supervisor, by exerting her authority and ensuring he understands that she will handle the investigation and that he, too, is expected to do his job by the book.

The situation with Doyle is more complicated. Smith initially believes that he doubts her abilities as an officer. However, she later learns that it is more a case of fatherly overprotectiveness. Throughout the case, Doyle checks on Smith's health and how she is handling the investigation. Doyle would never do this to Howard or any other male officer. Smith tries to talk to Howard about her frustrations, but he does not understand. He fails to be angered by Doyle's actions. Howard recognizes that Doyle is concerned about Smith and that he would not act similarly to some other male officer, but Howard does not see this as problematic. Smith's only recourse is to recognize Doyle's attitude and continue to work on solving the case. She respects Doyle and hopes that he, in turn, respects the job she does.[40] The fact that Smith is a woman doing potentially dangerous and important "men's work" does not completely disappear for him and the other men of the force. Men are supposed to protect women from the evils of life outside the home. By nature, the myth goes, women are more vulnerable, delicate, and sensitive. Doyle and Howard cannot completely reconcile gender mythology with the person of Jill Smith.

Seth Howard occupies an important place in Smith's life. He starts out as a fellow beat officer and friend who listens while Smith goes through a difficult divorce. They help each other through cases and relationships, and eventually, they become lovers in a committed relationship. As close as they are, Howard cannot understand what Smith has to go through as a woman in masculine society. Howard is a white male who is very secure in his privileged position. In *Death and Taxes*, Smith tries to explain to Howard what it is like to be a woman. Dunlap created the character of Jill Smith with a history not unlike the experiences of many of her women readers. As a girl, Smith was taught to be afraid of the outside world. She learned to be a passive spectator of life. For example, while growing up, Smith was often left at her grandmother's house while her parents and brother went on to set up housekeeping in a new city. Smith's grandmother vigilantly kept her inside the house for "her own protection." Smith once tried to plan a camping trip just like her brother did, but her mother told her she could not go because it would be inappropriate for a girl.

Smith spent her childhood and teenage years being careful and afraid—always on the inside looking out.

Seth Howard has no idea that such limits exist or that society is not always a safe place for women. Women are taught to be afraid, dependent, and insecure. Howard does not want to feel like this; it is a weakness for him even to think about it. Smith, however, is affected by these feelings every day. They are a part of who she is and do not go away just because she is a police officer. To give Howard a small taste of her life, Smith sabotages a prize plant of his in *Death and Taxes*. Howard becomes frantic about protecting it, imagining a conspiracy and lurking figures ready to harm his plant as soon as he relaxes his vigilance. Thus he gets a look, albeit limited, at some of the feelings and constraints with which women have to live. For Smith to share her life with Howard, she has to know he will not merely echo social conventions. Howard needs to understand the fears that are a very real part of Smith's life. He cannot protect her from them by ignoring their existence or locking Smith away. This only adds to their strength. Howard will never have to face these fears himself, but they are real to the woman with whom he wants to spend his life. It is Smith's professional duty to make the community safe, but she has to overcome her own fears in order to step out into the dangerous world and do so.

Sigrid Harald is also committed to the job of defeating the dangers in society. Harald is very professional about how she performs her police duties. The series begins with Harald as a veteran police officer in *One Coffee With* (published in 1982).[41] She is single and shares a household with an older man who was originally a friend of her mother. Besides learning the details of Harald's professional and private life, the reader is drawn to pay attention to simple details, such as what Harald wears. Maron devotes much time to what Harald wears and how others react to her as a result of her wardrobe. What clothes a woman wears sets the standard for how she is judged by society—how "good" she is at being a woman.

Lieutenant Harald conducts her business through most of the series in very serviceable, neutral-colored clothes that serve more function than form. She owns a more colorful wardrobe, but it is reserved for visits to her family. Her mother is responsible for selecting the clothes on this side of Harald's closet. The women on Harald's mother's side of the family are known for being southern beauties. Harald's grandmother often accuses Sigrid of not even trying to look attractive—meaning that she is not trying to find a husband. In comparison to her mother, Harald sees herself as gawky, too tall, and homely. She avoids mirrors and has resigned herself to a strictly functional look.

Harald has a great deal of confidence in her skills as a police officer, but her mastery of "femininity" is uncertain. Her clothes, mannerisms, attention to detail, and rational deductions are all part of her police persona. Outwardly, Harald does not concern herself with pretty clothes or makeup. Her clothes and look are pragmatic. A male officer is respected because of his badge, but a female officer must continually work to gain respect—and a responsible-looking wardrobe is one part of the strategy. Respect is not guaranteed. While the citizens with whom she comes in contact see Harald's wardrobe as professional, they are often confused by her lack of "female-appropriate" clothes. It is sometimes difficult for them to reconcile professionalism and police authority with their ideas of appropriate femaleness.

Authority and control are antithetical to traditionally defined female qualities. Witnesses, suspects, and colleagues often comment on how they imagine Harald's private life to be based on the fact that she looks so drab. In *Death of a Butterfly*, the woman who is later revealed to be the killer remarks to herself that Harald must live a sad life. Based on her observation of Harald's clothes, she feels sorry for her. The murderer understands dress as an appropriate measure of "femininity"—and a woman finds fulfillment by leading a "feminine" life. Harald uses external appearances to mask who and what she is inside, rather than as a sign announcing herself. One such example of how she hides her herself is found beneath her uniform-type clothes—where Harald likes to wear lacy lingerie. Like the main character in another mystery by a woman author, *Love Bytes*, it is not uncommon for Sigrid Harald to keep a piece of herself secret, while outwardly working to be a part of "the group": "We all have pieces of our hearts that get buried every day by the rigors of our jobs, but to maintain sanity we let our real selves peek out in small, subtle ways."[42] It is not uncommon for female detectives in mystery novels by women to regard their clothing as costume. They evaluate their surroundings and make a conscious decision about what the prevailing group will feel is appropriate for a woman to wear. The job of the detective is to blend in so that she can gather information without anyone becoming suspicious. Societal definitions of femininity are shown to be imprecise measures of the quality of a woman's life, and each detective finds small ways of trying to break free.

Most of the police officers who work with Harald believe her to be cold and unforgiving. This includes the female and male officers alike. Her coldness is a misinterpretation of how women officers in positions of authority must conduct themselves, or at least feel they must conduct themselves. As a woman she is supposed to be more focused on the emotional consequences of her job. This would leave her, ironically, unable to perform the job. This is a common theme for women writers of police series. Susan Dunlap's Jill Smith series highlights the same issue. Smith comments that if a woman officer shows any emotion, reaction, or nausea at the sight of a dead body, she will feel the contempt of the other officers toward her. There is a mistrust of women officers. A man is thought more human if he sheds a few tears for the victim, but a woman will never be trusted again if she shows any emotion at the murder scene. Lieutenant Harald is overwhelmed by the violence and destruction that often surround her. She is overcome by the lives touched by the crime of murder, not the sight of blood. Harald is forced to hide these feelings by the nature of her position and job, and subsequently continues to be misunderstood by those for whom and with whom she works.

Lieutenant Harald is very clear in her own mind that being able to do a job has nothing to do with gender. Her brains and stamina are responsible for her position in the police force. She is not a passionate supporter of the Equal Rights Amendment, but she does recognize that she moved more quickly through the police force because of the women's movement. When promoted to lieutenant and the Detective's Bureau, Harald stressed to her captain that she would not be the token female, but rather would pull her own weight. He knows she can handle the requisite violence of the job, but he is still more comfortable assigning her "easy" murders—straightforward cases of murder between family and friends.

In *One Coffee With*, Harald is assigned the case of a university campus poisoning. Her captain is relieved that the case is not an apparently dangerous one since Harald is the available officer. The investigation goes on to illustrate how job title does not necessarily translate into respect for a woman's position. Harald, as the detective in charge of the investigation, takes her position in the front of the room and says nothing for a few minutes. She waits for the witnesses to get used to a woman in command.[43] The case in *Past Imperfect* also highlights conceptions (and misconceptions) of gender. The male police officer who has been identified as the killer holds Harald at gunpoint. He claims he did nothing wrong, although he took money from a police drug bust, killed a police officer and a civilian clerk, and tried to kill a homeless man who was a witness to his crimes. According to him, "bitches and niggers" were to blame for his downfall. Harald is devastated by the hatred felt by this fellow police officer, as well as the destruction he has left in his wake.[44] For women, success in a man's world, does not just mean doing the job as well as a man. Doing a "man's job" does not necessarily come with the same rewards as those accruing to men. According to the killer, Harald is not allowed to do the job traditionally held by men. Gender comes before the uniform in determining the public's attitude toward women in authority.

Patricia Cornwell's Kay is under the jurisdiction of elected and appointed officials, men who are guided by their need to stay in office and retain the favor of the electorate public. Besides the job of examining bodies, Scarpetta must play politics with the men who control her job. In *Postmortem*, her job is in on the line because information allegedly coming from her office about a case has leaked to the press. She is penalized by being frozen out of the information loop by her government superiors. She cannot get the police information necessary to her investigation. A male friend of Scarpetta's, a forensic psychiatrist, gives her some advice: make sure the boys know you have some teeth so you are not considered an easy mark.

In *Cruel and Unusual*, Scarpetta is implicated in the murder of her morgue supervisor. Her job and credibility are, once again, on the line. She is called to a meeting in the governor's office. He cannot fire Scarpetta, but he does try to use the clout of his office to force her resignation. The conversation between them is more about what is not said. Each player tries to gain authority over the problem and its eventual solution. At the resolution of the case, the governor is forced to resign. Ten years previous, he had had an affair with a woman who was killed. He did not want the affair to come to light in the subsequent investigation and so paid to have a briefcase he had left at her house returned to him. This resulted in a prisoner's early release and his subsequent series of murders.[45] The men of the establishment are both fascinated and threatened by Dr. Scarpetta. Instead of focusing on her ability to do her job, her superiors in city and state government look for opportunities to criticize her work and force her from her job. A woman whose actions they cannot control threatens their well-ordered ideology of men's innate superiority over women. Scarpetta is a woman in a man's world, and in order to keep her job, she has to at least play by a few of their rules. It is necessary for her to define her job in terms of crime investigation as well as political power and control.

Scarpetta is a valued member of the crime enforcement community, who has been able to gain respect based on her expertise in the field. She most often works with police lieutenant Peter Marino and Benton Wesley of the FBI. All three are members of the FBI's Violent Criminal Apprehension Program. Wesley's relationship with Scarpetta as a professional is never put in question. He is both a friend and colleague. Later, their private life is complicated by an affair. At the end of *Cruel and Unusual*, Wesley offers Scarpetta a consultant's job at the FBI's Behavioral Science Unit.

Scarpetta's relationship with Marino is more complex, and develops and changes over time. Their first meeting is not congenial. She sees him as a stereotypic street cop, ill-mannered, opinionated, and poorly dressed. Their conversations reveal his low opinion of women. His upbringing is largely responsible for his prejudices. He had an impoverished childhood in the "wrong part" of New Jersey. Marino distrusts anyone who has had it better. Scarpetta's Mercedes and big house belie the fact that she grew up in a middle-class Italian immigrant family, always feeling out of place with her wealthier neighbors. Marino has never had to confront his prejudices about women nor deal with them as equals. In *Postmortem*, Scarpetta describes Marino as crude and unreachable, a social misfit. In the next book, *Body of Evidence*, they develop a closer working relationship and a degree of respect for each other. The two come to work very closely on a number of cases, and they talk about their work. They are both deeply affected by the tragedy of murder. It is Scarpetta's ability to do her job well and with compassion, as well as her up-front attitude with Marino, that force him to reevaluate his views. They both value order and justice and work to see those ends met. Cornwell develops more of an interest in the character of Marino over the course of the series, and he begins to talk with a much stronger, more confident voice. His character becomes more complex and interesting as he moves beyond the stereotypes of a street cop to a participant in the narrative. He comes to develop a very close relationship with Scarpetta's niece. They banter, argue, and annoy each other, but with a great degree of respect. Their relationship always remains strong, even after Lucy reveals that she is a lesbian. From Marino, the reader hears change in the male voice.

Scarpetta sets out to succeed in her chosen, and very male-dominated, profession to revenge herself on all the men who stood in her way and did not take her seriously. Her isolation by their hands fuels her desire to be the best. Making it to the office of chief medical examiner does not mean the end of such unfair treatment. Scarpetta plays the game of gender politics to keep her superiors from taking away her job. She knows that she is not following a traditional feminine path. She confronts the expectations of the men she comes up against and shows them that she can be just as determined and focused as a man. She also has another, private, side that she saves for her patients. Scarpetta defines one of the most important tasks of her job as reclaiming the dignity in the lives of the victims lost to their killers. She treats their bodies with respect and uses them to find clues to the identity of their killers. In this way she can ensure that justice is served. Scarpetta illustrates how success can come from bringing passion, outrage, personal history and experiences, and skills to bear on each case. She is not trying to be more masculine then the men for whom she works. She strives to bring together skills and resources often relegated to only one sex or the other.

The question that originally sparked my interest in studying women's mystery novels, and has been a concern for many critics of the genre, is how women can do such a good job in a field that focuses on violence, murder, and mayhem. Murder is a brutal act that "nice women" should both avoid and remain ignorant about. More realistically, women have been taught to avoid danger and risk since they are a vulnerable and an often sought-out target. In the mysteries of women, however, you can find some of the most heinous crimes described. What you will usually not find is gratuitous violence. Women authors work to draw a line between the two and make it clear to readers that they do not glorify or revel in violence toward others. Most women writers are serious about their crimes and use them to make a point about the treatment of certain people or the consequences of feelings, policies, or relationships. To say that women's mysteries are about murder is too simplistic. They do contain death, but these are stories really about people. In the five police detective series selected, the authors highlight what murder means to them and why their detectives have gotten into the field of police work to confront it. These detectives come across dead bodies on a regular basis, but they are more concerned with finding some sense of justice than simply putting away killers. Murder highlights relations among people trying to live together in society. The conventional wisdom in the mystery story is that while many people may not like you, family and friends may hate you enough to kill you.

One of the conventional rules for writing a detective story is that someone has to be murdered. This rule has begun to break down in the contemporary mystery. Joan Hess's *Mischief in Maggody*, *Madness in Maggody*, and *O Little Town of Maggody* do not contain deaths by murder.[46] The deaths in each are accidental. Hess does not want to talk about the crimes. People's reactions to the crimes are much more interesting. Murder and death are incredible situations for people to find themselves involved in. Everything is more intense; everyone is at attention. The humor of Hess's Maggody series is always backed by serious thoughts about what social tragedies have concluded in death.

Arly Hanks lived in New York City, but she has not been hardened to murder by city life. She is affected by the violence and death with which she (infrequently) has to deal in her job. As she observes, in New York, a corpse is a corpse, but in Maggody, it has a name and a family. Hanks is most affected by two particular cases, the accidental deaths in *Mischief in Maggody* and *Madness in Maggody*. "Guilt" cannot be pinned on any one person, but is instead shared by the town. Hanks, as representative of the town, takes on much of this burden.

The introduction of Robin Buchanon, in *Malice in Maggody*, presented Hess with a difficult dilemma. The character is interesting and funny, but she is also the mother of five children. Robin lives in a remote part of the woods surrounding Maggody. She makes moonshine whiskey and has sex with the men who come to buy her liquor. She is illiterate, poor, dirty, and rude. Her children do not go to school and will inevitably follow in their mother's footsteps. Hess explained that although she likes the character, she did not feel she could leave the children in such a situation (even fictional children).[47]

Robin is killed when she stumbles into a sabotaged marijuana patch, in *Mischief in Maggody*. The orphaned children get a second chance at life when they reveal their respective fathers—the local preacher, Brother Verber; and Mayor Jim Bob Buchanon. The father of the fifth child, Hammet, is from out of town. Hammet attaches himself to Hanks until his father can be found and arrangements can be made. In investigating the case of Robin's death, Hanks is struck by the degree of poverty in which Robin and her children lived. Robin may have chosen this lifestyle, but her children did not. They need an education in order to escape a fate of poverty. The people who mocked and chastised Robin now have to provide for her (and their) children. Some good results from Robin's death, but Hanks does not lose sight of the fact that Robin was killed in a scheme to make easy money. Two men had set in motion a plan to grow, harvest, and sell marijuana. Three people had ended up dead and Hanks was wounded because of the men's greed and selfishness.

A wave of poisonings masks a much larger crime in *Madness in Maggody*. While the town is captivated by the opening of a new supermarket and an ensuing wave of nausea, a boy poisons his father and grandmother in order to save his sister from the father's sexual abuse. The grandmother is killed and the father taken seriously ill as a result. It is not clear if the boy knew his grandmother would share the father's poisoned food, but Hanks chooses not to pursue this line of inquiry. The story lines in this book—Jim Bob's new store, his conniving partner, and a contest between a boy's baseball team and a coed team—are mere asides to the tragedy of a young boy trying to save his sister. Brother Verber and Mrs. Jim Bob are sure that girls playing with boys on the same baseball team will ruin the moral fiber of the town. As a result, they miss the bigger tragedy taking place and draw attention away from the boy's cries for help. The boy feels that he has to take matters into his own hands after he can find no one who will take him seriously.

Maggody has an active gossip grapevine. Everyone knows what everyone else is up to, but in the case of the boy and his family, the messages coming through are dismissed. The general feeling is that such abuses cannot possibly be true since they are too horrible to think about. Hanks is upset with herself for missing the signs that these children were in trouble. She does not charge the boy with murder nor make the situation public. Hanks contacts social services to take care of the children, but she does not tell them about the poisoning. The children have faced enough pain and suffering. Hanks can at least do something to help them heal. It is not girls playing baseball with the boys that hurts the moral fiber of the town. It is ignoring the children's pleas for help.

In *Maggody in Manhattan*, Hanks travels to New York City to get her mother out of trouble. She arrives to find a situation beyond her scope of understanding. A cooking contest is a front for illegal drug smuggling. The undercover agent assigned to infiltrate the contest explains to Hanks why he killed two of the men involved. Sometimes the government finds itself frustrated in its attempts to indict people who have murdered government agents. The end justifies the means in the drug war. This is very upsetting to Hanks. Her sense of morality is more suited to the "real" people of Maggody, not the full-scale, often impersonal, war she glimpses in the big city.[48] Hess returns the series to its Maggody location, leaving behind the big city's faceless dilemmas. The contrast between *Maggody in Manhattan* and the rest of the series is striking. Through Hanks, the reader views how human lives are dismissed by the enormous power, control, and money wielded, for example, by individuals in the illegal drug trade.

Dana Stabenow concurs that mysteries are more about lives than murders. Authors and their readers are more interested in the characters' lives. Murder is the "hook" to bring readers in and showing how people react to critical situations. Kate Shugak defines her job as preserving life. "Life" also includes one's cultural heritage. Murder is one person willfully taking the life of another, as well as the destruction of habitat by people for commercial gain, the selling off of a person's heritage, and the killing of animals through human exploitation of the environment. Two pivotal books, with regard to the issues of murder and heritage, in the Shugak series are *A Cold-Blooded Business* and *Dead in the Water*. The murders in these stories are the result of greed inspired by the incredible amounts of money possible in illegal drug sales. More important than the murders, however, are Shugak's efforts to preserve native Alaskan culture and heritage.

Shugak is hired to find out what happened to two members of a crab boat crew in *Dead in the Water*. The harbor where the fishing and cargo boats dock is populated by sailors on leave with large sums of money. Large quantities of cocaine are also easily obtained. Shugak is furious at the incredible amounts of drugs present in the town. She is quickly informed that there is nothing the police can do. They are understaffed and underpaid. The young men just off the boats have lots of money and few obligations; they can buy whatever form of escape they want. Shugak is forced to look away and focus on her job.

During her time off the crab boat, Shugak travels to a nearby island from which her family originated. The U.S. military moved the native populations off and resettled them away from strategic harbors during the war. Shugak finds a group of girls on the beach listening to a story told by a young crippled girl, Sasha, with a native story knife. The girl tells her story by cutting figures into the sand. The knife has been passed down through the generations of women in the family. This group of girls has, too, learned to weave traditional baskets from native grasses by Sasha's mother, Olga. The girls use the money from their baskets to buy the usual kinds of teen music and entertainment. Shugak is fascinated by the prospect of modern conveniences helping to preserve a piece of traditional life. In this small community, traditional and modern life have found a way to coexist.

During one of the girls' trips to collect grasses, Sasha witnesses the murder of the two missing crewmen. Shugak knows she cannot have Sasha testify about what she saw. Shugak will not subject her to the pressures of the white legal system. She also cannot go against Olga's wishes to keep Sasha out of the situation; the Aleut way of respecting elders is very strong in Shugak. Her visits to the island rekindle in Shugak a desire to understand more about herself and her history. Investigating a murder among white men has led Shugak to her own Aleut roots. During her last visit, Sasha tells Shugak a new story, about a woman who tricks a bad man. He dies and his body is carried away by the thunderbird to feed its children. The good woman goes on her way. Shugak is the good woman. Now she is a part of Sasha's history and traditions.

*A Cold-Blooded Business* continues the theme of cultural heritage. Shugak takes a job with RPetCo Oil to stop the illegal drug flow to its North Slope operation. On the slope, people live an unreal life of money, drugs, alcohol, and no personal responsibility. For half of the year, workers are isolated on the slope. They have no responsibilities to their families during this time and do not have to do anything for themselves. They are also very well paid. Drugs and alcohol are readily available. Shugak finds an archeological dig in progress in close proximity to the RPetCo operation. The people being studied are not Shugak's ancestors, but she is fascinated by their lives. They used the environment responsibly for their own survival and benefit, giving back to it what they took. Shugak discovers that several people have been smuggling artifacts out of the area and selling them on the black market in order to finance their illegal drug business. Shugak is enraged by this callousness toward the native peoples. Illegal drugs take second place to Shugak's concern for the artifacts. Drugs make people greedy and stupid, but selling off the history of these ancient people is equivalent to committing murder.

Equating murder with the loss of cultural heritage continues through *A Cold-Blooded Business* in a secondary storyline. While in Anchorage on leave, Shugak meets an old man who is trying to sell his collection of carved amulets to a local "native crafts" art dealer for enough money to buy his next drink. The dealer will not buy from the dirty, alcoholic old man. Shugak tries to help him, but he dies from exposure before she can get him the necessary assistance. Shugak asks her grandmother to return the amulets to the man's family on St. Lawrence Island. It is the old man ready to trade his family history for a drink whom Shugak remembers when she faces the drug smugglers on the slope. The experiences of these novels culminate in a later novel, *Blood Will Tell*, where Shugak is asked by her grandmother, a tribal elder, to investigate suspicious tribal business. Her reticence turns to pride when, after her grandmother dies, Shugak moves to take her place among the tribal elders.[49] She experiences a deep fulfillment that comes from seeing herself as part of her people's past, present, and future.

The crime of murder in the Jill Smith series, too, is shown to be associated with relationships between people. Murder is a metaphor for more interesting questions of how people live together in society. Susan Dunlap's books each focus on a specific theme or concern. Secondary story lines help draw attention to other angles of the issue. Society is very complicated; the mystery novel is able to give voice to a few of these complications. Reading clues from human behavior and the small details of everyday life is essential for the police detective to find a sense of justice.

In *Death and Taxes*, while Smith is giving Howard a small taste of the imprisonment women feel in masculine society, an Internal Revenue Service (IRS) auditor is killed. The man was an obsessive character who mercilessly hounded his taxpayer "victims." He was obsessive, too, with his wife. She had been injured several years back in an accident at her artists' studio, in which her immune system was destroyed. She now must spend the rest of her life confined to a sterile apartment. The IRS agent, Drem, took over her illness—making it more about him than her—and leaving his wife with no life for herself. Drem's killer turns out to be a man who had had tax problems in the past and was terrified of going to prison. He and Drem had made a deal that would have kept him out of jail, but Drem went back on his word and reneged on their arrangement. Drem is killed for not following the rules of the deal. At each turn in the story, the issue of imprisonment is examined, twisted, and exposed. It has many different faces and consequences. Women are imprisoned everyday by masculine society and their own fears. Drem's wife is imprisoned by her illness, and even more confined by her husband's obsessive treatment. Drem is trapped by his own selfishness and focus on the letter of the tax law. The killer and Drem are both prisoners to the killer's expectations of fair play and his fears. Dunlap shows how people become trapped by their own ambitions and actions. There is no "solution" to the problem in this book. Solving the case is not the same as solving the problem. Women's mysteries do not involve finding a single answer. They highlight the problems that go unnoticed in everyday life, showing the consequences of such oversights.

Dunlap's theme in *Time Expired* is society's obligation to the individual. She focuses on how society and individuals tend to dismiss people's lives too casually. The question asked repeatedly in this book is: "During which moments is human life important enough to deserve respect?" During a sweep of a Berkeley canyon neighborhood after a hostage situation hoax (the police find no hostage or hostage taker), Smith interviews a tenant of a seniors' residence home on the canyon rim. The resident, Madeleine Riordan, is well known to the police department as a tough defense attorney who never failed to comment on police errors. Smith met her while the former was a young beat officer called to testify during the trial of civil protester, Coco Arnero, who had been hit by a deputy sheriff with a baton in the course of a protest. When asked how it felt to be hit, Arnero testified that he had "left his body" and so did not know how it felt. On the stand, Smith replied that it did not make sense for the police to guard the body when Arnero was not even in residence, and Riordan then asked her to define a life that would deserve such respect. Smith continues to be haunted by this question long after the trial. It challenges her choice of career as well as her own values as a person and a police officer. While Smith never again judges a suspect so automatically, she does not like Riordan any better for having challenged her.

Since their first encounter, Riordan has become an emaciated, bald woman, often clothed in a nightshirt, who suffers the consequences of cancer. While her body has betrayed its owner, Riordan's mind and tongue are still sharp. Smith arranges to meet Riordan a second time, the next day, but the older woman is killed before their meeting. Smith feels a connection with Riordan because of their history and takes her murder very personally. Madeleine Riordan is killed by someone who puts a pillow over her face, knowing she lacks the strength to fight back. It was not enough for her killer that cancer was already violating her body. Smith has to think like, and in many ways be like, Riordan in order to find out who hated her so much to be so cruel. Why didn't her life deserve respect?

The medical system did not put a priority on Riordan's life because she was a woman. She had been responsible; she did what she was told. She got check-ups, did self-exams, and got mammograms at the right times. One year, the doctor had told her everything was fine and to come back next year, which was the standard response. The following year, however, the doctor found an inoperable metastasis. Madeleine was furious at her doctor, the lab, and the government—a government, she claims, that spends more money looking for a cure for baldness than for breast cancer. She resents society for saying that people will be safe if they follow all the rules, yet in the end, lets you wind up in a retirement home in a hospital gown slit up the back and exposed to whoever comes in.

The medical establishment also failed Riordan's mother. Years before, while Riordan recovered from a car accident, her mother had a stroke and was placed in a nursing home. It was a place too busy to see that patients did not go to the bathroom alone and too busy to check that everyone took their medication. Her mother's condition was fragile, and it deteriorated before Riordan was well enough to get to her. Riordan's mother died because no one noticed her.

Riordan dies for the same question she asked Smith at the Arnero trial. Riordan believes we cannot have people choosing which moments of our lives are important enough to deserve respect. She came to stay at the retirement home even though she did not need special attention and could have stayed at home with her husband. She came to help her neighbor at the home, Claire. Riordan does not like Claire very much as a person, but as a human being, she feels that Claire deserves respect. Claire cannot keep a male orderly from harassing her. Riordan witnesses his crimes as she hides in Claire's room. She cannot guarantee to Claire that the police will take Riordan's accusations of abuse seriously because she has humiliated most of the police force in court or at review hearings. Smith is to be their witness to the abuse when she returns to speak with Riordan the day after the hostage situation. Riordan has faith that if something does happen to her, Smith will pursue the case until she has the answer. Smith is late for their meeting, however, and Riordan is killed for her meddling.

Claire is a fastidious woman of the "old school," who plays by all the rules of propriety for women. Everyone, including Smith, dismisses Claire for her outmoded prissiness and modesty. Riordan has no more affection for Claire than does Smith, but she protects Claire and the other older women like her when necessary. Smith follows Riordan's lead, hides in Claire's room, and discovers the crime that drew Riordan to protect Claire. Michael, an orderly at the home, comes into Claire's room and torments her by licking and drinking out of her glass before he gives her her medication. He puts his hand through the opening of her gown and slides down the top. The man does not look at her body; he is not after sex. Michael wants power and control. When he unzips his pants, Smith confronts Michael about Riordan's death. She is in a rage as she holds her gun on Michael. He was sponsored by Riordan in his medical career so that he could help the elderly—but Riordan canceled his chances at being a doctor when she found out about Claire. Michael escapes from Smith into the canyon, but she finds him and holds him at gunpoint. Smith wants to let herself forget about restraint, decency, and responsibility; she wants to kill him. Killing him would be exact revenge for all hostages in life, particularly women. However, in tribute to Riordan, Smith does not shoot him. Riordan would have insisted on justice, even for him. Michael does not understand Riordan's commitment to humanity, but to make him remember something of the evening, Smith has him crawl in some nearby poison oak. This gives some satisfaction to Smith in honor of Riordan and Claire. Michael will be properly represented through the court system, but he will at least remember the pain of that night.[50] No one deserves to have his or her life discarded, but just as important, no one has the right to arbitrate whose life is unworthy of society's attention.

Catching the killer, for Smith, is often a bittersweet experience. The ruin of another human being at her hands is not something in which she rejoices, even if the person did commit a crime. She has her job to do, but she realizes that sometimes, people are forced into very difficult situations. Each case gives Smith another chance to reflect on her own life and choices. In *A Dinner to Die For*, Laura Biekma poisons her husband, Mitch. Smith does not condone the poisoning, but she understands what pushed Laura to this extreme. Mitch had taken everything Laura had to give and then tossed it all aside. She had given up a lot for him, as she believed a wife should, but Mitch took her sacrifice for granted and dismissed her contributions. In *Karma*, a good woman reaches her breaking point and kills to revenge the death of her son. She kills her ex-husband for his role in their son's death and for his attempt to take away her job as commune housemother, a position in which she was competent and happy. These women did what society demanded of them, yet society then failed to reward them, as promised, with a devoted husband, happy family, and contentment for a job well done. The case in *Karma*, too, is also personally difficult for Smith since it gives her an advantage over her friend and fellow officer, Seth Howard, for promotion to the Homicide Division. In *Time Expired*, there is no celebrating at the resolution of the case. The investigation was too personal. Smith catches the killer, but a good woman has been murdered. Madeleine Riordan had an impact on Smith's life. She made a lot of enemies, but Riordan's contributions to the community will be missed. These women, including Smith, reveal the complications women face confronting society's expectations for women—"good wife," selflessness, passivity—and reaching their own conclusions about the definition of personal and career success. Dunlap's police detective is a member of her community. She works with the people around her to arrive at the best possible solutions for all involved. She struggles with the causes and effects of murder. The killer is not an obviously evil, and the victim has a name, family, friends, and a life that will be missed.

Lieutenant Sigrid Harald appears to her colleagues as rational, logical, calculating, and without emotion, but it is with deep concern for human life that she, like Smith and the other women police detectives, looks to restore a sense of order and justice. The resolutions of Lieutenant Harald's cases do not always include an arrest. In pursuit of the killer, Harald often witnesses other crimes requiring a more forgiving hand. She takes her job of being responsible to the people to include responsibility to victims, suspects, and those doing the best they can to make a life for themselves.

*Death of a Butterfly* does not end with the killer's arrest. A young woman is killed in her apartment, and her son is subsequently left orphaned. The woman, Julie Redmond, and the boy's father were divorced, and she had encouraged the boy's estrangement from his father. Redmond was not a very nice woman. She blackmailed people and arranged for the death of her father-in-law for the gems he was carrying. In the divorce, Redmond nearly bankrupted her ex-husband. Harald discovers that a neighbor, Mrs. Cavatori, killed Julie. Mrs. Cavatori often took care of the boy, Timmy, and was angry with Julie's physical, emotional, and mental abuse of her son. Mrs. Cavatori could not have children of her own. She had raised a nephew, but he had died of polio. Mrs. Cavatori claims she murdered Julie murder to reunite Timmy with his father. Mrs. Cavatori had had no noble thoughts, however, when she killed the woman. Harald has no hard evidence to make a case against Mrs. Cavatori, and the judicial system has no way to punish her. During the course of the investigation, Harald witnesses Mrs. Cavatori's commitment to her marriage and her husband. The pain that Mrs. Cavatori causes her husband when he asks if she killed Julie is her punishment. Julie Redmond's justice is Mrs. Cavatori having to face the selfishness that led her to murder. The act was not to save Timmy. Rather, it gave Mrs. Cavatori a chance to once again have a child share her life.

The shortcomings of the state trying to handle very human situations are highlighted again in *Death in Blue Folders*. Neither a full disclosure of the facts nor an arrest come with the end of the case. Harald and her investigating team discover that a murdered lawyer was blackmailing several of his clients, and the officers work through the group to find the killer. Justin Trent was blackmailed for accidentally drowning his grandson and then claiming the boy had been kidnapped in order to cover up his crime. Trent paid an investigator to find a convincing substitute child. Trent kills himself when Harald confronts him with her conclusions. In his suicide note he confesses to the murder of the lawyer and several other people involved in the scheme. Trent does not reveal the true identity of the boy "found" by his investigator. A "deathbed" confession carries a great deal of weight in the courts. Harald's case is therefore closed, and the child's true parentage is unquestioned by the system.

Harald was uncomfortable with what she knew about Trent's actions and the consequences they would have for the child now believed to be his grandson after she confronted him with her information. The boy would have had to be returned to the aunt who had been raising him, and who does not love him. Indeed, she had hated his mother before she died and considers the child a burden. With Trent's subsequent confession, the case is closed and Trent's daughter, who dearly loves the boy as her own son, becomes his legal mother. This version of the truth meets the needs of the legal system, and also gives the child a chance to grow up in a loving home. Harald does not reveal her "truth" to anyone.[51] In this situation, the shortcomings of the legal system help rather than hurt the child involved. Harald, however, recognizes the high price paid by this family and those associated with them for this "happy ending." Several people were killed because Trent could not face his own guilt in killing his grandson or the pain this would cause his daughter.

In the Harald books there are often secondary cases being handled by the police officers. In *Death in Blue Folders* and *Corpus Christmas*, Lieutenant Harald solves these other cases without finding it necessary to make any arrests.[52] In *Death in Blue Folders*, a blackmailing lawyer was also taking money from a group of elderly sisters. An old-time movie actress had had an annuity that would die with her, but her sisters needed the money to survive. Before her death, she switched identities with one of her sisters so that the annuity would continue to benefit the family. Harald deduces that the woman she questions about the lawyer's murder is not really the famous actress she pretends to be, but she does not arrest the woman for fraud or theft, nor does she report the sisters' deception to the necessary authorities. The sisters did not kill the lawyer. The annuity was unfair to the actress's family. They were trying to survive, and no one was hurt. Since Harald's murderer is not among the sisters, she leaves them to their own lives.

*Corpus Christmas* presents a similarly ambiguous situation to the lieutenant. While investigating the death of art historian Dr. Roger Shambley, Harald's team is also assigned the task of unraveling the mystery surrounding several human baby skeletons found in the attic of an old house. The house is traced back to a woman who, now age eighty-seven, lives in a nursing home, having suffered a series of debilitating strokes. Harald talks to this woman, Barbara Zajdowicz, about the babies and learns that they were her sister's. Her sister, Angelika, had been unmarried, while Barbara and her husband were unable to have children of their own. Harald speculates that Barbara's husband was the father of the children. The sisters' brother had also lived with them. He would have killed Angelika if he had known she was pregnant. Therefore, Barbara killed the children, and told her sister they had died in childbirth. Harald turns her report of the highly publicized case over to the District Attorney's office. She knows that this woman, in her confused and fragile state, will never go to trial. Harald also puts a newspaper reporter who was hot on the story's trail on the wrong track to protect Barbara. Harald is very touched by the human drama that has haunted this family for decades. Barbara has lived her life knowing what she did, but also not seeing any way she could have done things differently. After her strokes, and having lost her family, her actions have come back to haunt her. Barbara has become a very religious person in her last years and has tried to find a degree of solace for her sins. Having heard her story and been touched by this woman, Harald lets the story become a part of her life as well.

Dr. Kay Scarpetta's relationship with violence and death is more intimate than for the other police investigators. Police investigators work at solving a case once there is a dead body. This is usually their last contact with the victim. They talk to living people to learn about the life of the victim. Scarpetta, too, is called to work once there is a corpse, but this is where she concentrates her efforts. She learns about life through death by paying attention to the details of the body. The clues of the body help her find justice.

In *Body of Evidence*, Scarpetta talks about what attracted her to medicine and the study of death. She realizes that she has, in effect, taken death apart and put it back together a thousand times. Her father's death began her fascination with the subject. Scarpetta cannot bring her father back, but she learns a few of death's secrets and a little bit more about life in the process of studying the subject. A woman in the role of medical examiner is difficult to comprehend, but Scarpetta relies heavily on attributes traditionally associated with women. A very strong sense of compassion, responsibility for others, and empathy drive her investigations.

Scarpetta comments on the treatment victims receive at the hands of the killer and the public during the case of a serial rapist and killer in *Postmortem*. The killer brutalizes and taunts his female victims before killing them, and each succeeding case is more savage as his hunger for control and power over the women increases. The privacy of a person's life is turned into public spectacle by their violent death. Scarpetta knows that the police tell witnesses and family that they will preserve the dignity of their loved ones, but, in reality, the dead are defenseless. Murder victims are photographed in detail. These photos are displayed for everyone associated with the case—police, press, court officials, and so on. Every aspect of the victim's life is scrutinized, questioned, and commented on. Scarpetta's job is to assist the police investigation and find some degree of dignity for the victim. Doing her job well means that a killer will be punished for violating another human being. It is not just bodies that are brought to Scarpetta. It is people who had distinct families and lives. Scarpetta's predecessor, Dr. Cagney, never saw the lives for which he was responsible. Indeed, his office contained several trophies taken from the corpses. To him, the bodies were just part of the equipment necessary to do his job.

Crimes are not just committed on "the other." Murder is not entirely remote for Dr. Scarpetta. She imagines how the murder took place and "sees" it when she examines the body. The story is there for her to read. Her job is to make it come alive in order for the police to apprehend the murderer. In *Postmortem*, the crime hits very close to home, as one of the victims is a young female doctor. Scarpetta believes she may even have seen the woman at the hospital. She knows what this young doctor's life was like, as a woman trying to make it in the male-dominated profession. Scarpetta knows what this woman went through at the hands of her killer; it could have just as easily been Scarpetta herself.

Empathy for the victim is a theme that repeats itself in *Body of Evidence*, in which a young woman, Beryl, is stalked and killed. Scarpetta gets involved in the investigation and drawn into Beryl's life. Beryl's killer becomes interested in her, and Scarpetta begins to repeat Beryl's reactions to being stalked after she becomes a target and goes to Key West Florida to escape. Scarpetta gains the trust of Beryl's wary friends because of her commitment to the woman. The police had treated these local gay men with disgust and suspicion; Scarpetta is sympathetic and respectful of both their lifestyle and their dedication to Beryl's memory. She is working to find justice for Beryl, not just to complete a job. Before her death, Beryl began the process of reclaiming her life. She wrote an autobiography, which included mention of being sexually abused by her mentor, another well-known author. Scarpetta is able to finish Beryl's project by finding her killer.

Patricia Cornwell continues the theme of making the horror of violent death intimate in two of the later books in the series, *All That Remains* and *Cruel and Unusual*. In *Cruel and Unusual*, Scarpetta goes before the grand jury for the alleged murder of an employee. To save herself and her career, Scarpetta must make the members of the jury empathize with her. They have to see her as human, even though she is a woman who works with dead bodies. She has to help them understand her view of her job as preserving the dignity of life, not just cutting up corpses. One piece of "evidence" suggesting Scarpetta's involvement in a conspiracy to murder her employee is a large withdrawal from her bank account. She explains to the jurors that the money was for a man in England. Scarpetta's lover had been killed in a London bombing, and one man had been with him in the end. To ease her grief and repay this man in some way, Scarpetta sends him and his wife money. The couple had been trying to have a baby, and Scarpetta's money covered the expenses of fertilization. The man was there to ease the pain of death for Scarpetta's lover, as she is for the murder victims who come in to her office. Life and death are not mutually exclusive in the Scarpetta series.

In *All That Remains*, the reader confronts the emotional toll of losing a loved one. A prominent Washington official's daughter is killed by a serial killer, who has murdered six couples in six years. This official's loss is expressed as something very real and human to the readers, not just something that "other" people have to experience. The official tells Scarpetta that fearing for the pain and death of a loved one is worse than fearing for your own life. When someone close dies, you do not know what you are doing most of the time. You feel isolated; people avoid you. They whisper to each other about you. It is like living in a cave and being afraid of being with others or alone, being awake or asleep—you are always half crazy. The woman is unable to cope with her grief since the legal system will ultimately have to set the killer free without the necessary evidence. She goes to his house to kill him herself. Scarpetta and the police arrive at the house and find the killer and a friend of the woman both dead. The woman then turns the gun on herself. The killer murdered twelve people, and the pain and grief caused by these deaths killed three more. Each death is a profound and tragic loss to the community.

Susan Glaspell's short story, "A Jury of Her Peers," is used by feminist literary critic Judith Fetterly to illustrate the differences between men's and women's texts. It is also illustrative for analyzing women's mysteries and the disharmonies between men's and women's language. In the story, a woman kills her husband. The officers of the state who are men suspect the wife's guilt but cannot find any evidence. Two women accompany the men to the couple's house as the men search for clues. In the kitchen, the women find a text that is rich with clues about the wife's life and crime. However, the men pass by the kitchen, pausing only to comment on the woman's poor housekeeping. The men cannot read the text before them. They do not even recognize it as a text because they cannot imagine women having texts. They are looking for clues to murder and not clues to the lives of the couple. The women see evidence of a crime that has gone unreported. A wife killed her husband, but there has also been another crime. In effect, the husband's cruel treatment of his wife over the years is the cause of his own death. The women are not limited by legal statutes in their definition of crime and murder. The husband's crimes are just important, according to the women, and should be recognized.

One of the women brought to the scene comments to the other: "We all go through the same things—it's all just a different kind of the same thing! If it weren't—why do you and I *understand*? Why do we know—what we know this very minute?" These visitors to the scene recognize themselves in it. The men are foreigners; they do not see women's texts or understand their language.[53] The strength of the woman police detective is her ability to read the texts before her. These are the details that translate into human lives. The woman detective recognizes the everyday. She sees women's "poor housekeeping" as text. Similarly, women readers find in the stories of women mystery writers narratives that inform their own lives—they recognize themselves in the narratives of the novels.[54]

Feminist literary studies reevaluate literature's place in society. The novel cannot be understood through linguistic analysis alone. Literature is a social institution. Art does not just mirror life; it has a normative impact on life. Popular art, such as the novel and genre fiction, creates myths and exerts influence. Art helps people to order, interpret, mythologize, and/or dispose of their own experiences.[55] Bakhtin calls for a "translinguistic science" to understand the novel, which would enable the reader, writer, and critic to understand the novel's intertextual relationships, social values, and moral messages.[56]

Women writers use the language of masculine-dominated society, and in the process, they revitalize it. Within the narrative of the novel, according to Bakhtin, a writer can use another's words, giving it new meaning while retaining its previous meaning as well. The result is an "ambivalent" word, full of society and history. The joining of two sign systems revitalizes the text and makes it something wholly new.[57] Language is a system constructed of arbitrary differences. It has more to do with power relations in society than absolute meanings. By reworking language, women rework genre and act on social conventions and norms.[58] The novel is "ever questing, ever examining itself and subjecting its established forms to review."[59]

The novel as a form is never completely finished. It is always young, reforming itself, and alive. Its possibilities are never exhausted. Because it continues to develop, it is a literary form well suited to reflect reality and its unfolding. Reality is expressed sensitively, deeply, and rapidly in the novel.[60] The novel provides a mode of access to the social understandings of past, present, and possible future. It explores the "meeting places" of self and society, and inner desires and external constraints. The novel encapsulates stories of individual lives: how individuals take in the world, how the world shapes them, how individuals perceive the world (with relative degrees of accuracy), and how the world presents them with choices and constraints. In the same moment we see how individual choices, desires, and fears impact the lives of others and the moral fabric of society. Writers and readers are part of a community of shared meanings. The novel is not just about an author's views. It implicates the perceptions of the audience to whom she writes.[61]

The mysteries of women that focus on the police detective are conversations, debates, dialogues, and arguments about women's access to language, and therefore, to their own experiences. The women writers work within genre conventions to talk about violence, death, order, community, responsibility, justice, and morality. They challenge dominant masculine definitions of these concepts through revitalized ("ambivalent") language. The authors, readers, and characters participate in the conversations. The aim of the police detective is not to come up with the answers for all of society's ills. The aim is to allow for a multiplicity of voices. Women's narratives are not about finding where *the* answer is located. The feminist story is a form of "praxis." Women interact with literature. They do so with an understanding that literature acts on the world by acting on its readers.

The woman police detective is a metaphor for all women, as they are all part of a masculine-dominated society. Women police detectives are officers of the state. They must learn its language—the law. They are expected to experience the world through a masculine frame. Their actions are guided by the dictates of the state. No other views or types of experience are legitimate. The state expects all of its officers to be the same in action and belief. There is a certain degree of latitude for individual styles of operation, but officers must still work within approved guidelines.

Lt. Jill Smith, Police Chief Arly Hanks, Lt. Sigrid Harald, Kate Shugak, and Dr. Kay Scarpetta have all learned the language of the state. They are successful officers of the law. They also experience conflict about the disparities between the language of the state and their own experiences. Masculine society does not recognize their priorities as legitimate or important. Ironically, these are the priorities that society has told these women to accept. They have developed their ideas and attitudes by growing up in an androcentric society. As women, they are held responsible for the care of others, especially people who are weak or vulnerable. Women are supposed to focus on the details of everyday life, making sure that everyone is accounted for and taken care of. What they are not supposed to do is take these skills into a masculine-dominated profession. Here, these skills turn into "hunches," and "women's intuition," the subject of jokes by the male officers.

The woman police detective illustrates the tension between women's and men's languages and show how women struggle to find balance between their perceptions of the world and the language they need to express them. There are two basic types of murder in the police detective novel: murder for individual gain and murder as a result of being trapped by social conventions and pressures. The women mystery authors have little patience or sympathy with the former, which involves putting oneself above all others. Gain is made more important than another's life. Prioritizing the self above all else in masculine society has deadly consequences for those who are unable to defend themselves. The weak are victimized by the strong for the sake of money, power, and prestige—and the weak are often women.

Women authors and their protagonists go to great lengths to inform the reader about the lives of the victims and killers in the second category of murder. Society is implicated in these crimes. The murderers feel trapped by choices they felt they had to make. The choices often simply involve following social expectations (being a "good" mother or wife) and discovering that the promise of reward was a false one. The author of the woman police detective novel is most interested in this type of investigation. Officers of the law must arrest perpetrators of crimes, but the women mystery authors are committed to reflecting on the social causes and implications. Murder is not just one individual killing another; we must all recognize ourselves in the texts.

Just as important as illustrating the societal roots of crime and murder is documenting the conversations and debates women have about their place in society. Women have important comments to make about society's priorities.

Genre fiction is widely considered an "unimportant" form of literature. "Serious" study and critics turn their attentions to "great" literature and dismiss popular fiction as uninspired fluff. This lack of attention has inspired many women authors to take the genre seriously. Writers are therefore relatively free to create and experiment. Conventions are twisted, mocked, and combined in new ways. The heroic finds a new face. Ordinary women are shown as heroic in their everyday efforts. The attributes that women have been socialized to take as their own are important in the world of the mystery. Attention to detail, focusing on human relations, empathy, and the commitment to stay on a case because of an obligation to others make the women skilled detectives. To this they have added independence, intelligence, and a strong sense of self-worth. The women assemble what they find to be important qualities, regardless of gender typing.

According to the women police detectives, order and justice are not just a matter of removing the one who disrupted the status quo. The status quo is not a safe or equitable place for women. Most women detectives work within a moral code. The traditional male detective had his moral code, too, but for him this meant preserving his own supremacy. Other people were sacrificed if he was under threat. The consequences of his actions on others were not part of his consideration. The moral code of the woman police detective, however, is based on her commitment to others. The law needs to take into consideration the human lives it is supposed to protect. The spirit of the law, and not just the letter of the law, must be remembered. Lessons are learned from each situation in order to keep the transgression from happening again. In the small scale of the detective novel, these ideals work very well. It is possible to let a murderer go and ensure that a just punishment has been reached. The world of the mystery novel is a safe place: killers are known, suspects are limited, and evidence is available if it is read right. Wholesale, the ideals of the mystery novel cannot be transplanted onto society. As fiction, this was never the purpose. What is possible is a rethinking or questioning of accepted social practices and standards. Other voices have to be included in social debate.

Order and justice are very complex ideas that require more than just removing one bad element from the community. The answer is not in these stories. The point of conversation, debate, dialogue, and argument is to build on each other's ideas and include many different points of view. Women's experiences have traditionally been silenced by masculine priorities on individual strength, individual rights, and individual success. The woman police detective confronts the language of the state, as women in society often find themselves doing, and she works each day to find a place for herself and her community within it.

## NOTES

1. Patricia Craig and Mary Cadogan chronicle the historical sleuth and her development in *The Lady Investigates: Women Detectives and Spies in Fiction* (London: Victor Gollancz, 1981).

2. Hillary Waugh, "The Human Rather Than Superhuman Sleuth," in *The Murder Mystique: Crime Writers on Their Art*, ed. Lucy Freeman (New York: Frederick Ungar Publishing Co., 1982), 33–35, 42.

3. Jon L. Breen, "Introduction, Police Procedurals," in *The Fine Art of Murder: The Mystery Readers' Indispensable Companion*, ed. Ed Gorman, Martin H. Greenberg, Larry Segriff, and Jon L. Breen (New York: Carroll & Graf Publishers, 1993), 212–13.

4. Kathleen Gregory Klein, *The Woman Detective: Gender and Genre* (Urbana: University of Illinois Press, 1988), 1.

5. Klein, 174.

6. Klein, 225–26.

7. Klein, 201–2.

8. On "texts-in-use," see Helen Carr, "Introduction: Genre and Women's Writing in the Postmodern World," in *From My Guy to Sci-Fi: Genre and Women's Writing in the Postmodern World*, ed. Helen Carr (London: Pandora, 1989), 7.

9. Rosalind Coward and Linda Semple, "Tracking Down the Past: Women and Detective Fiction," in *From My Guy to Sci-Fi: Genre and Women's Writing in the Postmodern World*, ed. Helen Carr (London: Pandora, 1989), 51–52.

10. Coward and Semple, 54.

11. Susan Dunlap, telephone interview, 11 November 1993.

12. Dunlap also writes a second series, whose protagonist is a woman private investigator, Kiernan O'Shaughnessy. O'Shaughnessy, for example, has few attachments or obligations. She is free to move around and investigate cases she finds interesting.

13. Dana Stabenow, telephone interview, 25 January 1994.

14. Hess also writes another mystery series, which focuses on Claire Malloy, the single mother of a teenaged daughter. Malloy owns a bookstore in a small college town and works hard to keep her business and family afloat.

15. Joan Hess, telephone interview, 20 December 1993.

16. Judith Fetterly and Kathryn Shevelow quoted in Patrocinio P. Schweickart and Elizabeth A. Flynn, introduction to *Gender and Reading: Essays on Readers, Texts, and Contexts*, ed. Elizabeth A. Flynn and Patrocinio P. Schweickart (Baltimore, MD: Johns Hopkins University Press, 1992), xv, xvii.

17. Patrocinio P. Schweickart, "Reading Ourselves: Toward a Feminist Theory of Reading," in *Gender and Reading: Essays on Readers, Texts, and Contexts*, ed. Elizabeth A. Flynn and Patrocinio P. Schweickart (Baltimore, MD: Johns Hopkins University Press, 1992), 40–42.

18. Jonathan Culler quoted in Schweickart, 36.

19. Mary Crawford and Roger Chaffin further explore this phenomenon in their work on "Muted Group Theory" in "The Reader's Construction of Meaning: Cognitive Research on Gender and Comprehension," in *Gender and Reading: Essays on Readers, Texts, and Contexts*, ed. Elizabeth A. Flynn and Patrocinio P. Schweickart (Baltimore, MD: Johns Hopkins University Press, 1992), 3–30.

20. Elaine Showalter, "Toward a Feminist Poetics," in *The New Feminist Criticism: Essays on Women, Literature, and Theory*, ed. Elaine Showalter (New York: Pantheon Books, 1985), 128, 131.

21. Carr, 7–8.

22. Patricia Cornwell, *Postmortem* (New York: Avon Books, 1991).

23. Patricia Cornwell, *Body of Evidence* (New York: Avon Books, 1992).

24. Dana Stabenow, *A Cold Day for Murder* (New York: Berkley Books, 1992).

25. Dana Stabenow, *A Fatal Thaw* (New York: Berkley Books, 1993).

26. Dana Stabenow, *A Cold-Blooded Business* (New York: Berkley Prime Crime, 1994).

27. Dana Stabenow, *Dead in the Water* (New York: Berkley Books, 1993).

28. Margaret Maron, *Death of a Butterfly* (New York: Bantam Books, 1991).

29. Margaret Maron, *The Right Jack* (New York: Bantam Books, 1992).

30. Susan Dunlap, *As a Favor* (New York: Dell Publishing, 1984).

31. Susan Dunlap, *Death and Taxes* (New York: Dell Publishing, 1992).

32. Joan Hess, *Malice in Maggody* (New York: Onyx, 1991).

33. Coward and Semple, 49.

34. Coward and Semple, 47–48.

35. Schweickart and Flynn, xx.

36. Carol Gilligan, *In A Different Voice* (Cambridge: Harvard University Press, 1982), 160–61.

37. Gilligan, 21.

38. Susan Dunlap, *Karma* (New York: Dell Publishing, 1991).

39. Susan Dunlap, *Too Close to the Edge* (New York: Dell Publishing, 1989).

40. Susan Dunlap, *A Dinner to Die For* (New York: Dell Publishing, 1990).

41. Maron has also begun a new series. Staying in the "legal" vein, she centers the stories around a North Carolina lawyer, Deborah Knott, who is appointed to the judicial bench.

42. Sally Chapman, *Love Bytes* (New York: St. Martin's Press, 1994), 33.

43. Margaret Maron, *One Coffee With* (New York: Mysterious Press, 1995).

44. Margaret Maron, *Past Imperfect* (New York: Bantam Books, 1992).

45. Patricia Cornwell, *Cruel and Unusual* (New York: Charles Scribner's Sons, 1993).

46. Joan Hess, *Mischief in Maggody* (New York: Onyx, 1991); *Madness in Maggody* (New York: Onyx, 1992); *O Little Town of Maggody* (New York: Dutton, 1993).

47. Hess interview.

48. Joan Hess, *Maggody in Manhattan* (New York: Onyx, 1993).

49. Dana Stabenow, *Blood Will Tell* (New York: Berkley Books, 1996).

50. Susan Dunlap, *Time Expired* (New York: Delacorte Press, 1993).

51. Margaret Maron, *Death in Blue Folders* (New York: Bantam Books, 1992).

52. Margaret Maron, *Corpus Christmas* (New York: Bantam Books, 1992).

53. Susan Glaspell's "A Jury of Her Peers" described in Judith Fetterly, "Reading about Reading: 'A Jury of Her Peers,' 'The Murders in the Rue Morgue,' and 'The Yellow Wallpaper,'" in *Gender and Reading: Essays on Readers, Texts, and Contexts*, ed. Elizabeth A. Flynn and Patrocinio P. Schweickart (Baltimore, MD: Johns Hopkins University Press, 1992) 147–64.

54. This is not to say that some men do not, and cannot, understand women's texts. Men can learn to read women's narratives. The women in "A Jury of Her Peers" clean up the kitchen in order to "erase" the story and prevent the men from learning to recognize their language.

55. Annette Kolodny, "Dancing through the Minefield: Some Observations on the Theory, Practice, and Politics of a Feminist Literary Criticism," in *The New Feminist Criticism: Essays on Women, Literature, and Theory*, ed. Elaine Showalter (New York: Pantheon Books, 1985), 147–48.

56. Julia Kristeva, "Word, Dialogue and Novel," in *The Kristeva Reader*, ed. Toril Moi (New York: Columbia University Press, 1986), 39–40.

57. Kristeva, 43.

58. Carr, 8.

59. M. M. Bakhtin, *The Dialogic Imagination*, ed. Michael Holquist (Austin: University of Texas Press, 1987), 39.

60. Bakhtin, 3, 7.

61. Elizabeth Long, *The American Dream and the Popular Novel* (Boston: Routledge & Kegan Paul, 1985), 3–5.

## *Chapter 4*

# The Amateur Sleuth Revolution

The women writing female private eye novels in this most recent Golden Age of the mystery have received most of the media attention and focus. The woman PI is the herald of the "new woman": independent, brave, self-reliant, intelligent, and (most often) single and without children. She moves easily through society to wherever a case takes her. While she blazes through the masculine landscape, it is the woman amateur sleuth, I would argue, who is the greater force behind mystery's Second Golden Age. The incredible proliferation of mystery books by women in this category and their variety of women heroes is truly revolutionary. The numbers of fictional women PIs and policewomen are few, but the number of amateurs, for whom sleuthing is secondary to their primary occupation, are booming. According to Pocket Books senior editor, Jane Chelius: "They don't have the ghost of Dashiell Hammett hovering over them." Ironically, according to *Publishers Weekly*, most women writing in this category "toiled in relative obscurity" until 1982, when two women PIs appeared on the mystery scene—Sara Paretsky's V. I. Warshawski and Sue Grafton's Kinsey Millhone.[1] The woman amateur sleuth can be anyone, in any circumstance, and in any time or place. She can even be married and have children. Her influence and importance to the genre and reading public are often overlooked by critics because she appears to typify the "normal" and unquestioned qualities of woman. One of the earliest and most critically acclaimed mysteries, though one largely lost to history, was written by a woman and featured a woman amateur sleuth—Anna Katharine Green and her sleuth, Miss Amelia Butterworth.[2] The amateur sleuth and her author take a page from this earlier work and continue the amateur sleuth's role in the forefront of the genre.

The category of "amateur sleuth" in the mystery genre is unusually open to new authors and new characters. Finding a niche in the market can be a matter of locating the story in a state or city that currently does not seem to have much competition. Developing a character with a new background or experience is another way of marketing toward an untapped niche. Prospective authors do not have to have an extensive background in criminal procedures or law enforcement, and indeed, "writing what you know best" can profitably include years spent as a housewife and mother. Most mystery authors cannot make a living just from their mystery books, but they do offer them the chance to earn money from their own creativity. Their words become part of the social lexicon; they join other voices to become part of a community of authors and women.

As a venue for critical analysis, the amateur sleuth mystery novels of women provide a way of looking at women who appear to have adopted traditional feminist values and principles. Critic, Lois A. Marchino, in a piece written about fictional women sleuths in academe, writes that one of the most striking current developments in genre fiction is the use of the mystery novel to challenge the traditional roles of women. Earlier female sleuths tended to reflect the prejudices of the day. They were curiosities to intrigue the audience. Today, women authors draw the distinction between writing to amuse and writing to involve.[3] As mothers, daughter, sisters, and wives, these women are not outcasts or marginalized observers of society, such as the woman PI. They are also not intimately associated with the dominant masculine hierarchy, as are the women police-trained detectives. They operate within the confines of "femininity" and its implications of home, marriage, and children. Thus, their observations are those of the "insider." I do not use the term to mean one who is privy to the workings of the dominant order or shares in its advantages. The woman amateur sleuth represents the women who, like most women in Western society, live their lives according to the rules. She is "inside" the ideology. The woman amateur sleuth works to find a place for the "feminine" within masculine-dominated society. She illustrates how it is possible to protest against gender stereotypes and constraints while remaining a part of the community. She illustrates for the reader many of women's shared experiences and concerns, as well as the strains of juxtaposing expectations of career, marriage, and motherhood with life's realities.

The mystery series selected for discussion in this chapter represent the variety of authors and sleuths common to this category of mystery. The authors come from a wide variety of backgrounds and experiences. They write mystery novels that are each very different from each others' works, yet they are connected in their central concerns and themes. Each woman had a life complete with a career and family prior to taking up fiction writing. She had put off her dreams of writing fiction for many years in favor of her obligations to others. For example, Carolyn Heilbrun's life, at age thirty seven, was consumed with university teaching, trying to obtain tenure, husband, and caring for three young children. "I felt I had very little time of my own." Looking back on this time and her creation of the Amanda Cross persona with which she writes the Kate

Fansler series, Heilbrun sees her mystery writing as a way of creating a space of her own. Marriage and children came first, but once the children were in school and the family became financially stable, many of these women thought of creating a space for themselves through fiction.

Heilbrun explains what Kate Fansler means to her: "I sought to create an individual whose destiny offered more possibility than I could comfortably imagine for myself."[4] As Amanda Cross, Heilbrun has been writing mysteries since the mid-1960s, when she began the series to please herself. "I had no more English mysteries to read. The American mysteries were totally male, macho and brutal. I like intelligent people who have intelligent conversations. I wanted to be in the presence of such characters. Kate became a person to me, around whom narratives could be woven."[5] Heilbrun kept her "alter ego" a secret for many years for fear that her university colleagues would no longer take her academic work seriously, thereby jeopardizing her security and chance for tenure. Her protagonist, Kate Fansler, is a university professor of English teaching at a large university in New York City. Kate has remained unmarried for most of her life, but finally agrees to marry (late according to traditional dictates of appropriate female behavior). What is striking to critics and readers is how Cross moved from the relatively simple mysteries in the early books to complex and rich discussion of gender, age, and relationships throughout the later books. Kate worries about the issues of women and justice, as seen, for example, through the disparity in salaries between men and women at the university. She was created, however, with a sophisticated background and independent wealth. Compared to her colleagues, she is less vulnerable to any threats of unemployment as she seeks justice in the university.[6] Heilbrun admits that when she published her first mystery novel in 1964, it was hardly "feminist," but that it went as far as she dared at the time.[7] As a fictional character, however, Kate has always set out to show the possibilities of what a woman can be.[8] Marchino notes that the eight novels from 1964 to 1986 show a progression in feminist consciousness. The early novels feature murders associated with research on male authors and include quotations from mainstream male literature, but increasingly, however, Kate has become immersed in women's issues and the status of women in the professional world.[9]

Each of the other women authors in this chapter took on the amateur detective format in order to create a fictional space for herself. Like Amanda Cross/Carolyn Heilbrun, these women have come to explore the boundaries for women in society and alternative narratives. Nancy Pickard and P. M. Carlson have each been writing mysteries since the late 1970s. Carlson wrote the Maggie Ryan series, which has since ended, while the others in this category have continued to the present. Carlson reached what she felt was the conclusion of her examination of the protagonist's life. The character was followed through college, adulthood, marriage, and motherhood. Carlson wanted to created an unusual detective. A working mother with toddlers had not been used as a mystery protagonist before, as far as Carlson was aware. She set out to answer the question: "Where did this woman come from?" The first books take place before the children are born, but set the stage for the kind of women, wife, and mother, Maggie Ryan becomes. Carlson illustrates how even though sad and even tragic things can happen to people, they still cope and become good human beings with feelings for others.[10] Even while investigating and involving herself in danger, Maggie Ryan puts the well-being of her children first.

Pickard's series, following the character of Jenny Cain, also, puts a priority on family. Cain has a prestigious career in her small New England town, as well as a family history in the town. She begins the series as a single woman, but later marries a man who attended her high school several years ahead of her. He has returned to the town as a police detective. Cain struggles with issues of identity: as wife (in her case, a third wife), as daughter of the family responsible for nearly bankrupting the town, as sister to a woman who is angry that Jenny did not have to bear more of the family's humiliation since she was away at college, and as career woman who is now responsible to many of the same men who played a part in her family's demise.

Ellen Hart and Barbara Neely entered the mainstream mystery publishing market in the 1980s. Hart originally published her mystery series with a feminist press, but has since sold the rights to Ballantine Books, a mainstream publisher. It was Ballantine that approached Hart about selling the rights to her series to a mainstream press.[11] Hart writes the Jane Lawless series, which concerns a middle-aged white woman, a lesbian whose long-time lover recently died. Lawless owns a popular and critically well-received Minneapolis restaurant. She maintains very close ties with a woman she has known for many years, who is also a lesbian. Her father is a lawyer, giving Jane a realistic excuse for being involved in the legal process and investigations. Hart also created a brother for Jane. Hart wanted Jane to have a family and people that she loved around her. She also wanted to make clear that Jane loves men and regards them as people, too. One part of Jane's life is her lesbianism, but that is only one of many facets. Hart was originally concerned when Ballantine questioned whether the word "lesbian" should be on the book covers, for example. When a person is identified by her sexuality, according to Hart, it sexualizes everything associated with her. Hart created Jane Lawless as a caring person struggling with being human.[12] In her analysis of women's detective novels, Maureen Reddy points out a concern that applies here as well. Reddy's (and my own) reading of lesbian crime novels is necessarily the reading of a heterosexual woman. Lesbian feminist analysis is different than her own analysis. Reddy concludes that this does not mean she cannot continue. It is far more important to include the narratives of lesbian women than to continue to contribute to the traditional silence of these authors.[13]

Neely writes for a very different protagonist. White and middle class would describe the largest proportion of characters and authors in the mystery genre. Even in today's "new" and "open" era, this is still largely the case. Neely's character, Blanche White, is a black woman who is a housekeeper. Neely wanted to develop a working-class feminist, who lives a feminist life even though she does not understand the theory. She brings to the mystery genre the sensibilities of the everyday black woman. Popular social mythology in the United States believes poor black women to be stupid. The stereotype is that these women have no inner life. Besides offering mainstream readers an alternative view of black society, Neely also uses the character of Blanche White to bring the mystery to the African-American reader.[14] At the conclusion of the first book, Blanche has the chance to leave her job as a domestic, but she likes the work for its sense of independence. She is self-employed, does her job well, and is largely left alone to work. Neely created Blanche as a housekeeper to create a metaphor for all service workers and low-income women who suffer through numerous hassles and types of disrespect, no matter the job. Blanche understands that she, in fact, has the most power and control in the households in which she works because she controls the food. In her matriarchal view, housework is important. Neely thus redeems the domestic work that many black women have had to do, and still continue to do. It is the work that sent many young people to college. There is nothing wrong with it, except that the pay is low and these women are treated poorly.[15]

The amateur sleuth presents its author with very interesting dynamics. She must first explain, or justify, why a "normal" person keeps coming across so many dead bodies. Many authors choose to write for a police or PI-type detective in order to avoid this "unrealistic" situation. For most people, exposure to death is the exception rather than the rule. However, in order to give life to a series of mysteries, the protagonists must keep finding bodies and still manage to avoid being arrested as the cause of such an extraordinary chain of events. In *The Collected Stories*, Amanda Cross draws the distinction between her amateur mystery stories, the Kate Fansler series, and such detective dramas on television as "Murder She Wrote." In the television show, Jessica Fletcher is constantly followed by brutal murders. Her presence seems to invite the murders she solves. Kate, on the other hand, solves mysteries where "her sympathies, her knowledge of literature and the academic world, and her sense of rightness are caught." It is the puzzle, the human mystery, on which she hopes to shed a little light, rather than wishing to discover the deed.[16] Author Judith Greber notes that she would have liked to write a professional detective novel but was more attracted to the morality of the amateur. She wanted her character to be outraged, not burned out. The amateur detective allows her to pay close attention to the psychology of what makes people feel so desperate that they destroy another and what this means to the characters and society.[17]

The second complication that arises from this type of series of mystery novels is the unsettling relationship that must be created by the author in order to make a sleuth out of her protagonist. The woman amateur sleuth must, by definition of investigating a murder, bring the threat of violence and death into the home, a place that popular gender mythology has constructed to be a haven of nurturing, peace, and love. It is the woman who is primarily responsible for creating this environment. In the amateur sleuth mystery novel, she is also the one now responsible for threatening the safety of the family. She both seeks out danger through her "snooping" and brings the danger into the family environment by associating with a world of death, violence, and criminality. Most of the time, this threat of danger is an unspoken presence in the novels. The reader is allowed to "forget" about the sleuth's role in bringing danger into the home. When it does arrive, as in several instances in these novels when another member of the family is threatened or injured because of the sleuth's investigating, its brutality is jarring and unsettling. The woman sleuth, too, is shaken. She has a very difficult time reconciling her role as mother with that of one who does harm. Nonetheless, these women do not subsequently give up the search for truth. Instead, they renew their efforts to fight against anyone who would harm a child or family member. Fighting for the truth is a task these women take very seriously, but family is just as vehemently protected.

The archetype for the amateur sleuth is Agatha Christie's Jane Marple, who set the standard for the "busybody" protagonist. Marple relied on intuition and her experiences with human nature to solve crimes and the peculiarities of life presented to her, starting in the 1930s and continuing until 1976. This elderly spinster could be counted on to see through the words and actions of the suspects to the real story of what they were trying to hide or protect. As an elderly woman who appeared "grandmotherly," she was asexual and therefore no threat to other woman and no temptation to any of the men involved. She was able to move through English society to discover its secrets because she cut such an unassuming and largely invisible figure, with both her age and her sex making her unobtrusive. Christie and Marple came to epitomize the "traditional" or "cozy" mystery to modern readers and authors. Mystery author Judith Greber, who writes the Amanda Pepper series under the name of Gillian Roberts, thinks of Jane Marple as her "godmother." Christie was a smart woman who took the limits of her life and applied them, according to Greber. It is this idea of having a set of rules and seeing how much an author and character can do to expand them while still staying within their bounds that attracted Greber to the genre.[18] The traditional mystery avoids graphic violence and impersonal crimes. The books are usually set in familiar, noncriminal settings. To Christie, the traditional mystery was the equivalent of the medieval morality play, in which audiences watched actors represent the seven deadly sins. Those whose lives were ruled by such sin could only expect terrible consequences.[19] Evil was a reality in Marple's world; she found its consequences in how people spoke of their lives and the lives those around them, as well as how they constructed their lives.

In the chapters on private investigators and police detectives, the areas of discussion were relationships (familial and otherwise), violence (and clarifying the differences between defensive and offensive actions), and how justice was defined in relation to responsibility and commitment. These same categories are important to understanding the amateur detective novels of women. For the PI and the police detective, debates over a woman's ability to defend herself and fit into masculine society tended to be arguments concerning the sleuth versus the criminal or the masculine institution in which she works. Even where the sleuth is involved in a relationship, she defines her life through her independence. The man she chooses to be involved with knows to wait until she calls for help and to let her conduct her own investigations according to her methods and skills. These investigators expand traditional definitions of family and commitment since most have not been able to rely on a familiar family structure. "Family" comes to mean those who are chosen to be a part of the investigator's life, and who may or may not have traditional familial ties. In the amateur detective novels of women, the definition of the woman is intimately linked with that of the traditional family. The amateur sleuth, as an "inside observer," faces strong objections, from society and herself, to creating an independent space for herself. Society persists in defining her in relation to her role within the family. The amateur sleuth works to create herself in addition to those roles, and not because of them. Her perceptions of murder, violence, justice, and morality are in part derived from how she is able to create herself and her family.

"Marriage, in fiction even more than in life, has been the woman's adventure, the object of her quest, her journey's end." This is the traditional model in fiction, according to Carolyn Heilbrun. Contemporary women, she concludes, have largely altered this. The abandonment of marriage rather than its achievement is now the goal. In contemporary fiction, she sees women detesting marriage, but it is not clear what it is they desire in its place.[20] Traditional models, in life as in fiction, relied on very clear models of behavior and roles for men and women. The husband was the one who needed someone to "take care of his domestic, cooking, cleaning, sexual, breeding needs while he was out attending to civilization and their own appreciation of life."[21] The wife must abandon her sense of self to perform her duties. To be both a wife and a person was largely impossible. Women were to be "rooted in one dear perpetual place."[22] Traditional novelists proclaimed in their work that "[t]o portray female destiny without examining marriage was like portraying male consciousness and not examining work and sex: impossible, unlikely, and dull."[23] The life, hopes, dreams, and future of a woman are in rooms and houses. Heilbrun quotes a study of children's series books that found that while boys acted out their fantasies in the outside world, girls retreated from their regular roles in the kitchen and parlor and contemplated their secret longings. The girl's sense of self is formed inside, where the safety is, not outside, in the world.[24]

In 1963, Betty Friedan published *The Feminine Mystique*. The work proved to be a watershed for contemporary American women in the 1960s and 1970s—an era many of the contemporary women mystery novelists refer to as having been very influential in their own development as authors and feminists. It continues to act on the debate over marriage and the roles and obligations for both men and women. Friedan gave voice to the frustrations women felt regarding the gap between the rhetoric of the wife-companion and a reality that was often empty and frustrating. The "feminine mystique" gave a name to women's frustrations.

> The suburban housewife was the dream image of the young American woman and the envy . . . of women all over the world. . . . She was healthy, beautiful, educated, concerned only about her husband, her children, and her home. She had found true feminine

fulfillment. As a housewife and mother, she was respected as a full and equal partner to man in his world.

Friedan found the image to be a sham. Translating the ideals into practice often had tragic consequences. Suburban housewives often became more like prisoners in their own homes, rather than "full and equal partners." It was not privacy that the suburbs and marriage offered, but the torture of solitary confinement.[25]

In her study of changing attitudes and roles for women, Sheila Rothman credits the Industrial Revolution with the beginnings of what Friedan recognized as the feminine mystique. The Industrial Revolution diminished the father's control over his property by making the family into a unit of consumption and reduced his control over the family by encouraging wives and children to pursue their own interests. The sociologists of the era foresaw a new kind of family that was bound, not by financial ties and the father's autocratic rule, but by affection—romantic love and sexuality. The "highest personal happiness" found through romance and sexuality were the only way of expressing individuality in industrial society. The primary responsibility for keeping the romance alive in the romantic marriage fell to women. Advertising, cosmetics, and beauty parlors all boomed as women were redefined according to their sexuality and ability to attract and keep a husband.[26]

The Great Depression and World War II created problems for the wife-companion since many women were driven into the job market. In 1945, however, normality returned and the concepts of femininity from the 1920s re-emerged and found new life.[27] The creation and boom of the suburbs after 1945 further solidified the ideology of the wife-companion. The appeal of suburbia was intimately linked with the feminine mystique. In the suburbs, the family found comfort, roominess, and—essential to the role of the wife-companion—seclusion and privacy. The suburban housewife was isolated from the problems of urban life and able to concentrate her attentions on the quality of her family's life, in particular that of her husband. Her day was organized around her home and family. The suburban homes looked inward. Spacious master bedrooms, where the woman could devote her time to her husband, were separated from the children's rooms—with each child having his or her own space.[28] The ideal wife-companion had little time left for anything but her marital relationship.[29]

The scientific literature and psychologists of the 1960s and 1970s offered little hope for the family. Contemporary family life was viewed as a battleground among members, with each trying to gain his or her own personal victory. Contemporary critics, too, predict the demise of the family. They are uncertain as to how to rescue it or if it is even worth rescuing. Earlier predictions of the end of the family called on family members to return to the proper duties and thus enhance the fulfillment of their maternal, paternal, and filial responsibilities. The contemporary family is viewed by some of its critics as a zero-sum game, in which the interests of some must be sacrificed for the others.[30]

For the women amateur sleuths, there has to be another solution besides calling for the end of the family. While it may not be necessary to sacrifice the interests of some family members, they do find it a struggle to reconcile their own images of marriage as confining and limiting. These women understand that marriage can mean a loss in identity for the wife. When children are added to the equation, women can lose even more ground as motherhood further limits their mobility and sense of self as an independent being. I have divided this analysis of women amateur sleuths and the issue of relationships into two sections. The first looks at how these women view the role of wife. How do they see themselves as wives? Is this a choice or destiny? The family is often the locus of women's oppression. Traditional family relationships mirror social arrangements under patriarchy and make the continuation of these social arrangements possible.[31] Marriage and sexuality are central facets of all feminist novels, according to Judi Roller's analysis in *The Politics of the Feminist Novel.* Society's rules, duties, and regulations regarding marriage and sexuality, rather than, necessarily, specific individuals, highlight the feminist novel.[32] Three of the five women sleuths in this group are married. Jane Lawless cannot legally marry her same-sex partner, though she considers her relationship with Christine a "marriage." Blanche White declines an offer of marriage and what she views as its implications for confinement. Regardless of their marital status, however, each sleuth is confronted by society's dictates and shares with the reader her own debates and questions.

The second area of discussion centers on woman as "mother." Four of the women have made the decision not to have children. Two of these women, however, come to include children who are not their own into their families. One of the five sleuths chooses to have children and later readjusts her definition of family when a child she had given up for adoption finds her. These women confront issues of identity and appropriate "female" expectations when they consider having children. How does a woman, when defined as someone's mother, maintain her own identity? How do children restrict a woman's behavior and expectations? Is it "normal" to decide not to have children? In the amateur sleuth mysteries of women, marriage and children are not a "natural" part of being a woman. Instead, women work to create a self that balances duty and responsibility with independence and personal identity.

The woman amateur sleuth discussed here puts a lot of thought into the institution of marriage: what it means for her identity as a person, how two lives can join without one (hers) being lost in the process, and how stereotypic expectations and demands pervade the institution without the people involved fully realizing. Nancy Pickard's Jenny Cain, for example, contemplates marriage to police detective Geoffrey Bushfield over the course of several books. This would be her first marriage, but his third. Jenny would be trying to make a success out of something that had already failed for her husband. She would also face the specter of the earlier wives while trying not to duplicate their failings. The marriage itself takes place in *Marriage Is Murder*, a novel that centers around spousal abuse and a graphic portrayal of marriages gone horribly wrong. Days that Jenny and Geof had planned to spend preparing for their wedding are instead spent on the case of a husband who has been shot, apparently by the wife many believe he abused. Geof's own feelings of desolation and defeat at such tragedies infect Jenny. He drives her around normal-looking houses and neighborhoods pointing out those in which families are falling apart—husbands beat wives, wives forgive husbands, and children witness the screaming and violence.

> I gazed out the windshield and spoke to an imaginary person seated on the hood of the car: "And what did you and your fiancé do to get ready for your wedding day, Jenny? You probably had a lot of fun going to parties and picking out china and planning your honeymoon. Oh, no, actually we interviewed a woman who'd just killed her husband, and we met another couple of abused women, and then we drove around town and watched marriages disintegrate. It's fun, really, it ought to be required of very young couple, like a blood test."[33]

Jenny is witness to the pain, as well as Geof's own feelings of worthlessness and desolation at his inability to have an effect on these families.

Jenny's sister, Sherry, contributes to the image of marriage that is created in the story with her own "homespun" advice on what marriage is all about. She is married to a man who is devoted to her, so she does not consider what she tells Jenny to be applicable to her own situation. On hearing from their father that Jenny is getting married, Sherry calls Jenny and insists on throwing a shower for the couple. In the course of their conversation, Sherry informs her sister about marriage and the rituals of the wedding process:

> "What do you think marriage is, Sis? I'll tell you what it is—some man wraps love around your eyes like a blindfold, he binds your hands with sex, then he leads you to the altar to sacrifice your brains to his ambition and your abilities to his convenience. You don't think he's going to cook after you marry him, do you?"

When Jenny balks at the offer of the party, Sherry continues on, telling her:

> "This isn't for you, Jenny. These parties are never for the bride, they're for the married friends of the bride who want to push you into that great sticky vat of marriage in which they're already mired."[34]

Taking a second look at the list she develops for the party, Jenny realizes that she has put together an expert panel on the subject of domestic abuse. On the way to the party, Geof is paged and must report on a possible homicide. Jenny accompanies him to the site of a second apparent killing of an abusive husband by his wife. From the start of the "wedding ritual," spousal abuse frames the marriage.

In the epilogue, Pickard intersperses Jenny and Geof's wedding vows with the details of the case and its solution. Following the question, "Do you, Geoffrey Allen, take Jennifer Lynn to be your lawful wedded wife?" the reader learns that the killer, a social scientist who had studied abusive families, knew the first victim from his interviews with the couple. He walked into their home, picked up the gun he knew they had, and shot the husband.[35] The vows continue as more of the story unfolds, with each killing penetrating the ceremony. The killer had come from an abusive home. His wife had married him in the hopes that she could save him from the pain of his childhood. He hated the men who hurt their wives and, more important, hurt the children through the destruction of the family. He also hated the women for letting the men abuse them and allowing the family to fall apart and suffer.

Jenny is able to use the wedding ceremony to also heal her own thoughts about her family. She has seen firsthand the tragedies that can befall a family, and that involve its most private and intimate secrets. She learns about the women and their pain, but she also learns how large and complicated the problem is. There is no "solution" to domestic violence in this mystery novel. The one element that does become clear is that women must be listened to. Police, social services, and even Jenny, fail to hear the wives when they proclaim their innocence and state that someone else has committed the crimes. Jenny's brother-in-law almost becomes the killer's latest victim because no one will believe Sherry when she tells them that he is not abusing her. No one expects these women to tell the truth or to understand how best to handle their lives. Jenny and the reader are exposed to the societal pressures that threaten marriage and the family. More must continue to be done, but for Jenny, the backdrop of family tragedy is fitting for her wedding. She puts her own family troubles in perspective. Her father bankrupted the Cain family fish cannery business and in the process devastated their small town, contributed to his wife's own mental collapse, and created an environment that led to Jenny's estrangement from her sister. Jenny's father and new wife are at the wedding, as well as her sister. By wearing her mother's wedding dress, Jenny also feels her presence at this family gathering of new beginnings. Whatever else Sherry claims marriage to be, Jenny sees renewal.

Jenny's marriage to Geof comes after much deliberation on her part. Geof first appears in *Generous Death* when he comes to talk with Jenny about the death of an elderly patron of the Port Frederick Foundation, which Jenny administers. They had known each other in high school (he was a senior when she was a freshman), but had gone their separate ways. Geof, as a teen, was rebellious. He did not fit in. He ran with a crowd of fellow misfits. At their first meeting, it is apparent to Geof that Jenny is surprised to find that "crazy Bushfield" became a police officer rather than ending up behind bars. Jenny remains skeptical of him until she later learns his family background. He grew up in wealth as a member of the Bushfield family, owners of the third or fourth largest hardware and plumbing supply company in the Northeast.[36] He is the "black sheep" of the family, who has traded the family business for a job where he makes a difference. The two share very similar backgrounds and experiences. As adults, both are comfortable financially. Each has a family trust fund to ensure that even without working, they could have a comfortable life. Each is free from the threat of poverty in the case of unemployment. For investigating, each is free to do and say as they see fit, rather than worry about the dictates of the power structures in which they work. They both come from families where position and money were expected and normal. They are comfortable in a variety of social settings, moving freely through social classes and situations.

The possibility of being Geof's third wife is difficult for Jenny to accept. When he first proposes that they find a house to share, Jenny balks. Jenny's house—she had been living in the family home that belonged to her mother after the divorce—was violently ransacked in *Generous Death*. Geof was living in the home selected by his second wife before their divorce. Its size and modern style, as well as the fact that it was her house, do not fit with Geof's current situation. Jenny is not ready to be the third of anything, but proposes that they live together without benefit of marriage. For both of them, this arrangement would be a first. Marriage, however, continues to haunt their relationship. It is important for Geof that they commit to each other as husband and wife. Jenny explains her doubts in *Say No to Murder*:

> [T]he safety of conventionality lay all around us, winking and blinking like an old friend of the family with whom we might fell comfortable—while ahead lay territory that held more risk by virtue of being less well charted. Though not noticeably successful at it, Geof like being married. But I had no family model upon which to base any hope for marital bliss. And while I certainly had faith in him as a person, I wasn't sure I'd bet the rent on his prospects as a husband. Still, we could not drift forever, like teenagers, in that foggy, foolish world of not-quite-committed. It was fish-or-cut-bait time, and I was scared. I don't want to lose him.
>
> And yet . . .[37]

She is scared to confront the question of marriage, having remained single by "choice and circumstance," but marriage represents a transition to a new stage of adulthood she has long been outside. Jenny and Geof are without successful models for defining the roles and identities of husband and wife. Jenny finally agrees to Geof's proposal at the end of the case in *Say No to Murder* after helping the police apprehend a killer.

Amanda Cross kept her character, Kate Fansler, single for many years and many books in the Fansler series. The character enjoyed her life as a single woman and the relationships she built with men. "I did not want her to get married, but she got into this relationship and relationships have momentum. . . . But she'll never have children, I promise you that."[38] Children were not a reason to marry, since Kate did not want to have children. Instead, the marriage of Reed Amhearst and Kate Fansler is constructed out of privacy, independence, and commitment. They enjoy each other's company, they have similar interests, and yet they do not need to spend all their time together. Each has friends and interests outside the marriage. Like Geof Bushfield, Reed is connected to the legal system. He is with the district attorney's office. It is through him that Kate gains entry to police investigations, though her investigations are often associated with the university or her associations. The reader experiences the details of their relationship through many conversations, cocktails, and denouements.

They are comfortable with themselves, and therefore are able to construct a marriage rather than accept the traditional expectations and behaviors. Kate's niece, Leighton Fansler, comments, "Reed is now Kate's husband, a word she loathes, but after all a fact is a fact."[39]

In *Sweet Death, Kind Death*, Kate works to solve the mystery of an apparent suicide. The woman was a scholar who profoundly touched the people she met. Through exploring this woman's life, Kate reflects on the lives of women as wives, mothers, and scholars. Marriage, for example, cannot succeed, according to Kate, unless it offers both partners solitude and independence as a matter of course. To investigate, Kate spends time at the woman's university and away from her husband while he goes through a career transition—from employment in the DA's office to law professor.[40] While she is not strictly limited to associating with people only when Reed is present, she misses having him there to share her thoughts and experiences. They have developed a closeness of minds that helps her find peace in dealing with the strains of her work and investigation.

In *Death in a Tenured Position*, Reed is out of town, leaving Kate to investigate without his police experience and companionship. Kate is asked by a friend how she is doing without Reed there with her:

> Reed always knew I had to have times without him. I always knew that he never bored me when I was with him. He's a male strangely composed: the pomposity was omitted. Though I miss him, I don't pine for him when we're apart, nor pine for solitude when we're together. Greater tribute hath no woman.[41]

As the book begins, Amanda Cross includes a quick sketch of Kate for the reader, including her background and relations as well as career and marriage. She describes Kate's path to marriage: "Late in life—at least as these things go—she had married a man who offered companionship rather than dizzy rapture; they had neither of them chosen to view marriage as an unending alternation between lush and dinner in the best restaurants."[42]

Reed is introduced in the novel *In the Last Analysis* (originally published in 1964), as Kate enlists his help in clearing friends of murder. The marriage does not take place until *Poetic Justice*, published in 1970. At their meeting in *In the Last Analysis*, Cross informs the reader that the two have been friends for several years. If either needs a partner for a social engagement, they call the other. It is a relationship of laughs and no real sense of attachment. Neither has ever married, and at this point, marrying each other is a "completely outrageous idea." She needs Reed's help to save her friends from possible prosecution, but the case moves their relationship beyond simple friendship.[43]

*Poetic Justice* is a difficult book to understand in terms of how it contributes to a "new understanding" in marriage and feminism. Kate entertains the reader with witty and insightful commentary on the institution of marriage, but the investigation itself reveals an uncertain picture of what kind of marriage the two can possibly create. Reed solves the case, while Kate spends much of the time during the investigatory process in the dark about the intrigue surrounding her. Indeed, the murder takes place in front of Kate without her seeing it.

Reed asks Kate several times to marry him before she accepts. At one point, she suggests that they live together. She explains that they could: "Occupy the same premises, have the same address. Pretend to be married."[44] She does not believe in marriage at her age, but neither does she want to spend her life without Reed. She wants to be a partner; she wants to have a man. She does not see that these desires should be grounds for marriage. Reed understands her reluctance. Difficulties at the university during *Poetic Justice* leave Kate seeking a sense of belonging. She recognizes this feeling as a weakness and does not want to "give in" to marriage at such a moment, after she has refused Reed in times of strength. Reed will not share an address with Kate unless they are married. He wants to marry her with a ring, a judge, and a license because he is in love with her.[45] He sets the date for Thanksgiving so they will not have to remember a date. Instead, they will just celebrate the anniversary on the last Thursday in November, which will be a holiday, anyway. It is not the ceremony of marriage that is important to Reed. To him, marriage is defined through its commitment of love, not white wedding dresses, tuxedos, church ceremonies, or elaborate anniversaries.

To the secretaries in the English Department, marriage is more important than revolution, according to Kate. They take it upon themselves to plan a party to celebrate Kate and Reed's engagement.

> "You," Kate said to Reed, "are my greatest accomplishment. I have achieved the apotheosis of womanhood. To have earned a Ph.D., taught reasonably well, written books, traveled, been a friend and lover—these are mere evasions of my appointed role in life: to lead a man to the altar. You are my sacrifice to the goddess of middle-class morality, as Iphigenia was Agamemnon's sacrifice to Artemis."[46]

Kate is amused by the fuss surrounding her decision to marry. Amanda Cross points out to the reader that the party is held in the English Department offices, making it a semiofficial function and "obviating the necessity of asking wives." Reed is whisked away by the secretaries upon his arrival, which he likens to being some "unique specimen miraculously caught in the nets of matrimony." The predominantly male department showers Kate with condescending comments about marriage: "A wedding is destiny, and hanging likewise"; "All women should be married. An unmarried woman is an offense against nature."[47] Most of the men in the English Department are very conservative and chauvinistic in their ideas. Women, like Kate, who have remained unmarried and insist on making a career in male-dominated professions are never fully accepted and most often are shunned or ignored. The marriage, to the men in attendance, is evidence of their "right-thinking" that women are meant to be married. They do not see the specific relationship being built by Kate and Reed, only the designation of marriage.

While Kate is talking with one of her colleagues at her engagement party, he is killed, having been poisoned by aspirin, to which he is allergic. She sees the crime take place, but does not recognize it or the killer. Reed is the primary investigator for this case. This is Kate's university, her colleagues, and her university politics, but she cannot see the crime. In their final conversation with the killer, he, Kate, and Reed discuss the case over drinks at her apartment. Reed knows what is going to be revealed, but Kate is caught completely by surprise when she learns that the crime took place front of her eyes. Reed restores order to Kate's university. The wedding itself is an epilogue to the murder investigation. In one paragraph, the reader learns that the wedding took place on Thanksgiving and that the couple spent their four-day honeymoon (Kate was scheduled to teach class on Monday) in Reed's apartment.

It is difficult to reconcile the investigation in *Poetic Justice* with a marriage of equal partners. Reed investigates the murder, solves the crime, and understands the complications of Kate's university. One way of possibly understanding Kate's move to the background is to see this case as a chance for Reed to develop a voice and strength of character not possible when Kate is the primary investigator. Cross allows Kate to be the "weaker" of the two without jeopardizing her position of equality with Reed. Kate needs help bringing order to her life and her career. Reed takes up this role without it lessening his affections for her or her own sense of self in the relationship. He is able to become a partner in the investigations and marriage. She is not the investigator and he the husband; instead, they are the investigators as a team of husband and wife. The roles of husband and wife are not decided by the ceremony or the license. The couple must work to distinguish the roles and each person's sense of place.

Marriage is not an easy decision for the amateur sleuth. Most of the women discussed here have reservations about getting married, and it is only after much debate and reassurance by the prospective husband that the women agree. The reader is not told about the early days of Jane Lawless's relationship with Christine, but it appears that she is the only one of the five women in this category who wanted to marry her partner. Before Christine's death from cancer, she and Jane were together for ten years. It is the power of this relationship that keeps Jane from seriously becoming attached to anyone else for quite a while. Christine remains a part of how she understands and constructs her life. Ellen Hart included Christine in her series but had her die before the first book in order to make Jane human, but unencumbered. Jane understands about relationships, but the plots of the books are not slowed down by romance. Hart was concerned about including a romance that did not contribute to the plot. For authors of women amateur sleuths, romance can create problems. A mystery novel must move on the strength of its plotting, as seen through the investigation. A romance can slow down a novel and detract from the mystery. Ellen Hart's Jane Lawless will continue to have relationships. For her to be "real" and "human," she needs these connections. The books are also very committed to the relationship between Jane and her friend, Cordelia—who often occupies the "sidekick" role in the novels. Hart expressed uncertainty as to how a lover would work within this dynamic.[48]

Barbara Neely's Blanche White decides to remain unmarried. She has a longtime boyfriend, Leo, who is introduced in the first book of the series. By the second book, Blanche has refused his proposal of marriage. He soon marries another woman, and Blanche is left to wonder if she made the right choice by refusing him. She knows that she does not want to marry him, but his marriage to another woman gets her thinking about where the man had fit in her life and if she had expected him to stay there for her even without a marriage license. In *Blanche on the Lam*, Leo is described as an old boyfriend who, friends insist, is the man for her. He continues to be a presence in her life by staying close to her children—the children she is raising after her sister's death. Blanche comments that if the way to a man's heart is through his stomach, then the way to a woman's is through her children. It is his unsolicited advice on how she should live her life and raise her children that causes the most problems. Blanche does not want anyone else minding her business. Leo thinks that his decency and kindness will wear her down, but Blanche defines his attention as a belief that she needs a keeper.[49]

Blanche's models for marriage come from the women around her. Every married woman she knows works in someone else's house, field, or plant and then must come home to take care of her husband and children, who seem to think "her labor [i]s their due." This was never Blanche's plan for her life. She enjoyed Leo's company and having sex with him: "It was always extra-good to have sex with a man you trusted as much as she trusted Leo." For Blanche, however, sex and marriage are not connected. Marriage represents confinement—"someday he might throw her down and hogtie her"—and claustrophobia. It is not that Blanche refuses to marry Leo, but that she cannot at all. She is comfortable with her decision to remain single for the rest of her life, but Leo misunderstands her rejection of marriage as a rejection of him.

With Leo's marriage to another woman, Blanche faces the pain of an ended relationship. She does not understand how Leo could marry someone so unlike herself. The only explanation for the marriage is that Leo wanted a wife, and not the kind of attraction and relationship he had with Blanche. Blanche never rejected Leo, but only his proposals of marriage. He was the one who said "no" to her and their relationship when he married. Blanche feels the pain of her loss and of being misunderstood by the man she loved for her decision to remain single.[50] She does not, however, reconsider her choice of life as a single woman. The loss of a man does not scare her into changing her ways and wanting to marry. Her pain at the close of this relationship is the pain of losing someone who has shared much of her life. It is also the pain of realizing that for most people marriage and sex are too intimately connected to be experienced apart. Marriage is seen as a "natural" part of being an adult. Most men Blanche meets look at her in terms of marriage and the creation of a family. Becoming involved in a relationship for companionship or sexual pleasure is often viewed by society as immoral or "loose." For a woman raising two children, Blanche is in the very difficult position of creating a satisfying life for herself and providing a model for her children. The conflict between social expectations and her own ideals creates the sorrow and pain Blanche feels as she heads off to a new investigation.

Marriage and family traditionally focus a woman inward. Her primary location is supposed to be the home. The women protagonists in the amateur sleuth mysteries written by women look to redefine the roles of wives and husbands in marriage. Traditional models of marriage recognize that kinship and marriage rules ensure the exchange of women between groups, just as economic rules ensure the circulation of goods. In the mysteries of women, the women who have been the objects that were circulated now become subjects. They are able to use circulation, rather than be circulated.

> As human beings we all make fictions of our lives, those of us who write books, or read them, and those who tell only ourselves the stories of the lives we shall lead. But that fiction has already been inscribed for women; they are to be married, to be circulated, to mediate between the man and his desire for a son, between male groups. [51]

Those who choose to marry have found men who want to be partners and share their lives. While the books are marketed under the woman sleuth's name (i.e., a "Jenny Cain Mystery"), the husband occupies a major role in the story. He offers encouragement, comfort, incentives, and help as needed. The men have a voice in the narratives, which neither overshadows the women nor fades into the background. The reader both follows the investigation and shares times with the couple as they create their lives. The amateur sleuths who choose not to marry are not shown as lesser or "defective" characters, but rather as strong women who have made a different choice. They create a life for themselves without husbands, but not necessarily without children, companionship, or sexual fulfillment. Each sleuth we have examined makes her thoughts and questions about marriage visible to the reader. She questions what is usually considered unquestionable, and thus points to what it usually unable to be located.

Children play a relatively minor role in the private eye and police mysteries of women. Only two of the detectives examined in the previous chapters brought up the subject, and then only in relatively limited ways. Both had chosen not to have children of their own but play a large role in the lives of their nieces. Linda Grant's Catherine Sayler lives in a household composed of her lover and her sister's high school-aged daughter. Patricia Cornwell's Kay Scarpetta remains in very close contact with her niece, Lucy. The series follows their relationship as Lucy grows from a young girl to a woman who joins the FBI. The amateur sleuth adds complexity and depth to this area of discussion. Children are much more common in this type of mystery. The sleuths selected for this category cover the gamut of family arrangements with regard to children. There are sleuths who have chosen not to have children of their own (Kate Fansler, Jenny Cain, Blanche White, and Jane Lawless), as well as those who find themselves responsible for children who are not their own (Blanche White and

Jenny Cain). Maggie Ryan is the most "conventional," with two young toddlers, but in a later book it is revealed that as a teen, Maggie also gave up a child for adoption. This young woman finds Maggie, and both must recreate the image of "family" on which they have come to depend. Whether they have children or not, the women sleuths in this category highlight the social constraints faced by women in this regard. For the male sleuth, it is unlikely that the issue of children will ever come up. For women, however, society demands that it be confronted.

Amanda Cross's Kate Fansler is very clear in her decision not to have any children.

> "I don't much like children," she admitted. "I know it's an eccentric attitude, but not a dangerous one. The worst fate I've ever inflicted on any child is to avoid it. As it happens, however," she added, "I did once more or less solve a case for a child. Do you think that will serve to redeem me in the eyes of those with maternal instincts?"[52]

Kate prefers the role of aunt to that of mother. She develops very strong relations with her niece, Leighton Fansler, and her nephew, Leo Fansler. Leighton is given the role of recorder in *The Collected Stories*. It is through her eyes that the reader follows Kate and her investigations. Leo spends a summer with Kate and her husband, Reed Amhearst, in *The James Joyce Murder* (and later comes to stay with them again in *The Question of Max*).[53] As a young boy in this novel, Leo comes to live with his aunt over the summer because he has been having trouble at school and with his parents. She originally rejects the idea of him staying with her while she rents a house in the country in order to organize the papers collected there. Leo, however, runs away to Kate's house. Her brother is upset that his son has chosen Kate over him but lets the decision stand. What attracts Leo to Kate is her ability to treat him like anyone else she knows. She has a manner with children that states, "I take you for granted and like you just as you are."[54] While residing in the country, Leo attends a day camp and has a live-in tutor for the summer. Kate does not take on the role of "mother" with Leo, but serves more as an adult presence who can set a few boundaries. Leo is one of the household, not a child to be protected and coddled. This is illustrative of Kate's relationship with Leo and Leighton as they reach adulthood.

Blanche White comes to motherhood rather unexpectedly. Neely created her to be a "typical" black women, though she admits that such a thing does not really exist. Most women of Blanche's age have their own children. Neely did not want Blanche to be a "loner detective," but neither does not believe that motherhood is a woman's "natural" profession. The African-American culture, according to Neely, is very family bound. Family is required, almost regardless of what the individual wants. Blanche takes on the responsibility of her sister's children after the latter's death from cancer. She takes on her duty grudgingly, but proudly.[55] She initially runs away for a year, leaving the children with their grandmother. She then returns and takes the children from her mother to live in New York City, later returning to her hometown in North Carolina after a man tries to entice the kids into his van. Blanche's mother insists that if Blanche goes off again or otherwise fails in regard to the children, she will take them back. Blanche finds it unsettling that having first resisted the children, she now works hard to keep them with her. Before her sister's death, Blanche had made the decision not to have children. Her sister had thought this decision selfish and unwomanly. For a year after her sister's death, Blanche hated her sister for proscribing her life, but now she fights for the children even when running from the law, in *Blanche on the Lam*. At the end of this book, Blanche is paid a great deal of money (for almost getting killed), which she puts aside for the children's education. The consequences of this education and the role that Blanche still needs to play in the children's formative years form part of the story in *Blanche among the Talented Tenth.*

Barbara Neely emphasizes in *Blanche among the Talented Tenth* how a strong, independent black woman in the United States has still to confront issues of race and prejudice with her children. With the money from *Blanche on the Lam*, Blanche enrolls the children into an exclusive private school, but she then becomes worried about its effect on their attitudes about their own culture and ethnicity. She visits the children in an exclusive all-black resort in Maine and watches them interact with their new, wealthy friends. Even in an all-black community, such as the Amber Cove resort, Blanche finds racism and prejudice. The children have all that money can provide for them and live away at school for most of the year, yet Blanche finds that she retains a vital role in ensuring that they believe in themselves and their cultural identity. Blanche remembers her own struggles growing up and wants to be sure that her children have the strength of character to face similar obstacles. The community's social divisions between rich and poor and dark-skinned and light-skinned are compelling to the children. Blanche is frustrated with how easy it is for them to be swayed to think less of her, both as a housekeeper and as a dark-skinned woman, and try to hide their own differences. Blanche is very strong in her attachment to the children. Her job is to get the very best for them. Money helps for some of those things, but the situation in Amber Cove proves that Blanche has a very important role, too. It is her strength of character that the children need most.

Jenny Cain, too, is faced with the responsibilities of a child who is not her own. Creating and rethinking the concept of family can include bringing into the family children who are not necessarily biologically related to both parents. Jenny is surprised one afternoon when a boy appears on her doorstep claiming to be Geof's son. She then has to confront her feelings for her husband and any prior relationship that he did or did not have, as well as how she can create space for this child in her home. The boy, David, demands that Geof solve the murder of his mother and "real" (adoptive) father, since Geof is obligated by virtue of his biological parentage. This story, *Confession*, is a murder mystery, but even more, it is an exploration of motherhood, responsibility, parenthood, and how women often expect, by virtue of women's socialization, that marriage is synonymous with the birth of a child.

Early in the book, Pickard sets out the basic details of the characters of the series and their relationship. She does this by inviting the reader into Jenny's head as she reflects on the lazy Sunday she is spending with Geof, "a lovely, quiet, community sort of Sunday." She explains that it is just the two of them in this relationship—no pets and no children. He wants children, but she does not. The is no real sense of urgency; it is just that they have not had children yet and are still talking about it. She explains the kind of marriage they have created for each other:

> And so we remain two, very two, blending, merging, weaving our separate egos into a strand of long, long twine, the kind whose threads area so inextricably connected you cannot easily pick them apart, not even with your fingernails or even by sticking a pin between them and trying to lift them apart from each other. He remains exceedingly who he is. . . . I remain absolutely who I am. . . . But who we are is altered by the presence of the other, our molecules rearranged to accommodate each other's DNA, so that it feels as if I form one-half of that strand and he is the other, twisting upward, tighter, closer, as if we could adhere so fast to one another there would be no room for error, for surprise, for fate.[56]

It is into this quiet perfection that fate arrives and calls into question conversations that have not been spoken, either by Jenny and Geof as a couple or by Jenny to herself.

Several issues confuse Jenny and complicate her attempts to understand her life and the life she has created with Geof. One is Geof's apparent lack of responsibility as a teen when he had sex with a girl named Judy. At a lunch with several of her girlfriends, Jenny talks about David (the alleged offspring) and his relation to Geof. The women are sympathetic toward Jenny for the chaos this brings to her life, but they are also angry with Geof for his teenage carelessness. They are angry with him, too, for the problems he is creating for Jenny. He may not have known about Judy's pregnancy, but, according to the woman, he should have used a condom in order to prevent such a problem from occurring in the first place.[57] Jenny later relates her conversations with Geof. He does not understand why they are angry at him, but she explains: "You got a girl pregnant. Knocked her up. Left her with a kid. Landed me with a kid years later. That's how they see it." He is struck by the "gender dividing line" suddenly being exhibited. Jenny tells him that the women think he should have used a condom. He returns that he was just a typical teenage boy. Jenny responds, with the question, "And she [Judy] was the typical easy lay?" Geof wants to claim that things were different then, but Jenny counters that boys are still looking for easy girls, easy girls are still looking for love, and couples are still getting pregnant and passing sexually transmitted diseases. Geof complains that it always comes down to being the guy's fault. Is it fair to blame him, when the girl was there, too? She should have being doing something about birth control, too.

This one situation becomes an argument over the changing roles and responsibilities of the sexes. What do women want? What can men expect? Geof argues that women want independence but define it as meaning having their own condo, their own car, their own money, and their own job. Women do not understand about real autonomy, according to Geof. Women—and he clarifies this to mean women in general, and not Jenny—really "still want to grab some man who'll work for them, so they can quit and stay home if they want to." Jenny takes his comments to mean that he is resentful over her staying at home and no longer working for the Port Frederick Foundation.[58] The appearance of the boy at their door sparks conversations and arguments about topics the couple had previously left unexpressed. The "perfect" marriage is challenged by these struggles. The changing and complicated gender roles and responsibilities have not been completely resolved, if they ever can be.

David appears on their doorstep on page 5 of *Confession*, but it is not until page 199 that Jenny is able to deal with her true feelings about the "new arrival." It has been very difficult for her to face her anger, resentment, and confusion. Much of this is due to how many of her expectations for the role of wife are enmeshed with the role of mother. She is supposed to want children; to "give" her husband a child as a way of proving or expressing her love for him and her commitment to the relationship. The reader learns that a week before the boy arrived, Jenny had decided that they should have a child. She explains that since Geof is turning forty, she had thought that if they were going to get pregnant, they should do it soon. She was going to tell him that she wanted to stop using birth control so that by his next birthday, or soon thereafter, they would have a child. This is described by Jenny as "giving" Geof what he wants more than anything else. Now, with the arrival of the boy, it appears that he already has a child. Her "gift" now has lost its appeal and seems to her to have been more a sentimental notion. Was she just going to hand him the baby and say, "Here, darling, it's all yours!" Jenny does not really want to have a child. She has to remind herself that this does not make her a bad person. For one thing, she has a family history of mental illness, which she does not want to risk passing on to a child. Geof understood her feelings when he married her, but this does not keep Jenny from feeling sorry for herself, guilty toward Geof, and angry with the boy who has changed her mind about having a baby. On reflection, however, she realizes that the boy did not change anything. He only made her confront who she really was and come to terms with her decision not to have a child. She is resolved to help David find out what really happened to his parents. This is the least she can do for him after the "gift" he has given her.[59]

The issue of parenthood is further complicated when Jenny learns that Geof lied to her about the boy's paternity when he claimed that blood tests ultimately proved his role as the father—the test, in fact, proves that Geof is not David's biological father. She feels betrayed by this lie until he explains that he wanted to be the boy's father for the boy's sake. David has already lost one father; Geof could not take another one away. Geof did not believe they would really ever learn who David's real father was. It could have been any one of the guys from high school. He felt ashamed for what they had all done, what they had all been like, and how they all had treated Judy. Geof thought of all the guys as the boy's father. He was going to redeem them by claiming the boy they had helped to create. Geof felt responsible; he claimed the responsibility.[60] Through this investigation and the arrival of the boy claiming to be Geof's child, and therefore Jenny's, too, Jenny is forced to face her own questions about her femininity. Is she a "good" wife if she does not give her husband a child? Is it appropriate to continue to think of a child as the wife's gift to the husband? Jenny begins to explore, in more depth than she had previously, what a child means to a woman and how to define a marriage without a child of one's own. At the end of an earlier novel, *Bum Steer*, the reader learns that Jenny suffered a miscarriage during her investigations in Kansas.[61] The loss of this child is never fully resolved or shared between her and Geof, and indeed, the issue of children is left unspoken until it is forced upon them in *Confession*.

The decision not have a child comes very hard, infused as it is with the very nature of being a wife and woman. The mysteries of the amateur detective make observable the confusions and debates women have with themselves and society as to how they understand themselves as women, wives, and mothers. Blanche White and Jenny Cain do not want to have children of their own, but they take on the responsibilities of another's child. They reshape their families and continue to search for truth through their sleuthing. It becomes clear to them, in several of the books, that their investigations can pose a risk to their children. Blanche and Jenny become driven to continue, not just by the possibility of uncovering a murderer, but by that of finding the person who could harm their child. While there may be extreme situations that explain how murder is possible, these women cannot imagine any reason for hurting a child. David Mayer, the boy Geof and Jenny take into their family, and Jenny and Geoff begin to construct a new family in *Twilight* while Jenny tries to get her new charitable foundation off the ground. She names it for David's mother, Judy, in order to honor her memory and show respect. Jenny and David try to find some common ground between them, sharing several motorcycle rides, for example. These times together work to bridge the gap between them. She enlists David's help in the investigation in *Twilight*, hiring him to protect her. David is injured during the course of the investigation, and Jenny is devastated by the emotional toll of putting a member of a family, at risk.[62] Even becoming injured herself takes on new dimensions since she is now answerable for her actions to a child. Blanche White is injured while investigating in *Blanche among the Talented Tenth*. Once this happens, she immediately makes plans to leave the resort and get her children away from possible harm. Children must always be kept away from harm, and so the sleuth must balance her search for truth against the threat to her family.

P. M. Carlson's Maggie Ryan series includes two young children. Carlson set out to write eight or nine books that followed the life of a woman from one point to another in order to capture the sense of the character changing over time.[63] The reader also gets the sense of a couple experiencing the adjustments of having children and the changing of roles from lovers to parents. The series starts with Maggie in college (*Audition for Murder*).[64] There she meets an actor,

Nick O'Connor, who has come with his wife to be part of the college's production of *Hamlet*. Nick's wife is killed, and Maggie and Nick figure out the identity of the killer. Nick is older than Maggie, and she bestows on him the title of, Uncle Nick. As a friend, she helps him heal after the death of his wife. They continue to stay in contact. He comes to see her as a much more important part of his life, while she continues to remain aloof. In *Murder Is Pathological*, he goes to the university where she is now a graduate student in order to be close to her. She enlists his help in an investigation at the lab where she and her friends work. He comes to the decision that he has to be a part of her life, and if that means just being friends, he will make that work. By the end of the case, however, Maggie is willing to make a commitment to Nick and start a more serious relationship.[65]

In *Rehearsal for Murder*, Maggie and Nick have had a young daughter and must make adjustments in their lives for such a demanding presence. Nick thinks to himself: "No time these days for souls. Or bodies, for that matter."[66] As parents, their time and energies are just sufficient for the new baby and jobs, leaving very little for each other. Nick is worried about his role as parent in a family that now includes a child. As an actor, his income is very unpredictable. The arrival of the child means, to both Maggie and Nick, that they are not quite as liberated and carefree as they thought; now, "[t]he future counts."[67] Nick and Maggie share parenting duties as their schedules allow, but Nick is forced to realize that he only "looks after" the baby, while Maggie is responsible for taking care of the baby, since she is still nursing. He is unsure how to combine parenting and being a husband to Maggie. Maggie is feeling the pressure of being responsible for the bulk of the family's income and her own frustration at being in a body she does not recognize and that follows a new set of priorities (she refers to herself as a "moo-cow" during one argument). Maggie brings Sarah to the theater where Nick is working and straps the baby carrier on him before she heads off to her work. The reader tracks the path of the baby carrier throughout the book as the baby passes between the parents, thus following along with the chores of parenthood along with the details of an investigation.

Maggie becomes involved in a case of kidnapping when a man she recently met asks her to pick up his child from preschool and drop her off at the baby-sitter's. The request is unusual since the two have just met, but Maggie thinks that he asked her since she has her own child with her and therefore seems "safe." Maggie is concerned when she meets the baby-sitter. The apartment does not seem appropriate for the man, Buzz, and the woman does not fit her image of the type of nanny Buzz would hire. Maggie later goes back to the apartment to check up on the child and sitter because she remains uncomfortable about the situation. Maggie looks through the apartment and finds that no one is home this time, and it seems to her as if someone has cleaned up any evidence of the child and nanny having been there. Throughout her investigation, Nick and Maggie continue to stumble through their new roles as parents. The child was wanted and is loved. She has brought new joys to their lives, but each parent is also overwhelmed by the demands on his or her time and self. Where the two were well connected and instinctively knew what the other was feeling, now, they now miss important signals. When Maggie's investigations take her across town to locate the man and his child, she assumes she will just take Sarah, the baby, with her since it is her turn to watch over her, but Nick intercedes and makes sure the three of them go off together to find the necessary information. What involves one, involves them all. Nick discovers that Maggie has been set up as the kidnapper. Now, the safety of their family is at stake, and they must continue to investigate in order to clear Maggie's name. Maggie cannot accept that Buzz is the person behind the kidnapping since it involves his own daughter. No matter how unpredictable or dire Maggie's life gets, she knows that Sarah is the one thing that will not be sacrificed.

Maggie locates the baby-sitter and is able to figure out where the child is being kept. The baby-sitter was not in on the kidnapping, and since she remembers Maggie from before, she tells her where the child is. Maggie takes Sarah with her to find the child, but Nick objects to their splitting up. There is no way around it this time, since Nick has to return to his theater to get his last paycheck. He offers to take Sarah with him, but, Maggie explains: "I'm afraid it's nearly moo-cow time again."[68] After ensuring that the child is returned to her mother, Maggie again comes into contact with Buzz. He asks her another favor, which Maggie recognizes as the ransom drop. She leaves Sarah with Nick before she takes on this new task. She wants to make Buzz pay for what he has done to his family. She also wants to make sure that Sarah is safe and away from the danger she now associates with Buzz. Nick again objects to Maggie involving herself in such a potentially dangerous situation. She replies that if she were not a mother she might have just walked away, but "little girls are important."[69] The murderer in a second investigation in which Maggie and Nick are interested arrives at the theater before Maggie has a chance to leave. Maggie is able to create a connection with this mentally disturbed woman. She wants to take her out of the theater and to the shop where Buzz wants Maggie to make the drop. Nick realizes that Maggie is trying to get the woman away from Sarah, away from the gun the woman brought, and to the police, who must be watching the drop site. She wants to protect herself, Nick, and Sarah, as well as the young woman, who is no longer able to care for herself. The plan goes awry when Nick realizes the woman still has the gun. When Maggie and the woman approach the drop site, Buzz is confused by the two women and follows them back to the theater. Nick still has Sarah strapped into the carrier and goes out a window onto the roof at the first chance he gets in order to ensure Sarah's safety. Buzz walks in on the woman with the gun and thinks it is Maggie with his money. He fires twice. The young woman dying on the ground, however, is not Maggie. Maggie is furious with Buzz and his explanation that "it just happened."

"Yeah, sure it did." Scorn animated her voice. "It's not enough to kidnap your own kid, torture your own wife, steal from your own family! You've got to get yourself a gun too. Go rampaging through the world like your goddamn father-in-law! . . . "

"No! . . . It was Susan—"

"Ah, another woman. Clean break, right? Muffin would never see you again? Well, Buzz old pal, I've got news for you. Even without this murder your illustrious daddy-in-law would have tracked you down like a wounded trophy animal."[70]

The dead girl had a father who ran out on her, too. Maggie is not going to let that happen to Buzz's child. Maggie creates a plausible story for Buzz: he thought the girl had kidnapped his daughter; she was standing there with a gun in her hand so he shot her in self-defense. Buzz has to trust Maggie. She is going to keep his passport, his plane tickets to South America, and his note explaining everything in the bank safe. He also can trust her because she wants his daughter, Muffin, to have a dad, not someone who uses her to skip the country with some strange woman. Maggie plans on keeping quiet about the real truth for Muffin's sake. She and Nick donate the half-million dollars in "ransom" that they take from Buzz in memory of their friend who was killed by the young woman Buzz murdered. Alone with Nick, Maggie criticizes her own role in "inventing" the scenario being played out, in particular, forcing Buzz to stay with his child. The alternative script was a police version that would have ruined Buzz and made his family suffer. It is a messy case that does not leave either of them "satisfied" with the results, but through it, they remember to value what they have in their marriage and family, no matter how difficult life gets. The case helps Maggie and Nick face their frustrations regarding parenthood and the changing nature of their marriage. Their frustrations are those faced by many couples. There are no easy solutions, but the situation with Buzz makes clear where their priorities lie.

What this case illustrates is Maggie Ryan's commitment to children and family. Adults can take care of themselves, but the children must be protected, nurtured, and loved. It is unclear what kind of father Buzz will be to his daughter or if Maggie made the right decision in sending a "murderer" back to his family without having to pay for his crime. For Carlson, it is not essential that the "bad guy" lose. She is more interested in how people react to evil. If the world is unjust, what should be done by a person trying to be good? Morality is always involved and in question.[71] In *Murder in the Dog Days*, Maggie discovers that a woman killed her husband because he had been abusing the children. It was common for him to beat her, but once he started beating the children, she knew he had gone too far. She had stayed in the marriage for the sake of the children, whom he loved. Maggie arranges for the wife to tell her story to a woman police officer whom they can trust. This officer knows that without a legal confession, the police will not have enough evidence to convict. Maggie finds the killer but protects the children: "It's not justice if it hurts a child."[72]

Not all women mystery authors agree with the way Carlson appears to excuse murder for the sake of children. Mystery author Carolyn Wheat, for example, is not sure a child benefits from having a murderer as a father, as in *Rehearsal for Murder*. She argues that the justice system has to have some value. It is the best we have, and murderers should not be allowed to simply walk away.

The detective cannot set herself up as the judge and jury of what is acceptable and unacceptable.[73] Carlson's focus on children is perhaps too extreme, and it has the potential for dangerous repercussions. Since the age of sixteen, children have been the primary focus of the character, Maggie Ryan. The reader learns, in *Bad Blood*, that as an exchange student in France, she became involved with a man she later found out to be married with children of his own.[74] She became pregnant as a result of their relationship, but gave the child up for adoption after realizing that as a teen, she could not offer the child the kind of life she deserved. Sixteen years later, the girl locates Maggie and the two work to create a friendship, despite the pain involved. This experience early in her life added a degree of vulnerability, as well as toughness, to Maggie's character. Her priorities came into focus early in her life. For Carlson, and Maggie Ryan, children must be protected at all costs. It is up to the reader to decide if and when Ryan crosses the line.

Conversations about marriage, for women, are intimately linked with their conversations about children. Jane Lawless is the only woman in this group of amateur sleuths who appears to have made the decision not to have children without experiencing much inner conflict. The issue comes up in only one conversation. In this conversation, which is with a woman who wants children but is involved with a woman who is very set against it, Jane replies that she has never wanted children herself but that she enjoys them very much.[75] For most women, marriage and children are very difficult to tease apart. Women are socially obligated to marry. Having done so, social pressures continue work on them to have children. Wife and mother are made one and the same. The decision to put off either one of these two situations can come at a very high price in terms of social acceptance and self-image.

The murder mystery is about murder, violence, and hopefully, ultimate justice. The woman amateur sleuth is typically a woman with little experience in law enforcement. She lives in a community in which she feels safe and has few, if any, contacts with violent or criminal people. Most have no direct experience with the justice system aside from a lawyer or police officer in the family or a traffic ticket. These women appear ill-suited to their role of criminal investigator. The crimes that invade the peace of their communities are not the anonymous drive-by shootings or liquor store holdups that fill the readers' newspapers and television. They are crimes of passion that stem from relationships gone wrong and expectations unfulfilled. Therefore, any violence experienced by the amateur sleuth as a consequence of her investigating is most often, minimal. It does, however, evokes great feelings of horror by the reader and the other characters around the sleuth, since she stands for "any woman" and is supposed to be safe from such abuse. Hers is a world of nurturing and caring, not of violence. Each attack on her is an attack on the community of which she is a part. The reader is struck by the incongruity of the murder and violence on the tranquil landscape of the home and community. The strength of the woman amateur sleuth is in her lack of training and sense of the criminal mind, as would be found in the women PI or police detective. Her role as "everywoman" illustrates to the reader, not just how any woman can be the "hero," but also the devastating nature of violence. It marks all who come in contact with it, and families and communities are forever changed.[76]

Ellen Hart's Jane Lawless is injured several times during the course of her investigations. In *Hallowed Murder*, her house is broken into and her diary is stolen. This crime is very unsettling to Jane, having been a very personal attack on her home and her most private self. At the end of the book, Jane is handcuffed to a car and made to drive across a frozen lake. According to the killer, if she makes it across without the ice breaking, then God has decided on her innocence. Luckily, Jane is rescued by her brother and a member of the sorority she had been assisting in the investigation.[77] In *Vital Lies*, she is shut in a walk-in freezer after she enters to look for clues. The attack that bothers her the most, however, is when someone steals and then rips up the family photos she kept in her wallet. Again, it is the personal and private attack that is more devastating than the aggressive or physical assault. Photos of Christine, her dead lover, and moments in her life are forever destroyed. In *Stage Fright*, Jane is knocked unconscious when she interrupts an intruder in her garage. In his attempt to flee, the intruder covers her in a tarp and knocks her over. She hits a cast iron stove and is knocked out.[78]

The physical danger to Jane up to this point in the series is minor. Most damage is done to her sense of security and self. The personal attacks are more devastating than the frightened reactions of people trying to deal with the crimes they have committed. *A Killing Cure* puts Jane at the most risk of any of the titles in the series, which Hart has been writing since 1989.[79] It appears that by 1993, she was ready for Jane to face a few more challenges and risks. Combined with the injuries to her body, Jane now also faces injuries to the soul. She commits to a relationship with another woman, only to have to break it off when the woman decides to return to a previous lover. This is a story of personal risks and personal attacks.

In *A Killing Cure*, Jane's father is sent a pipe bomb in the mail by someone who does not want him to continue representing a man on trial for the murder of a respected woman in the community. The bomb turns out to be a hoax but results in her father suffering a heart attack. Jane begins investigating the woman's murder as a way of finding the person responsible for hurting her father. During her subsequent investigation, someone breaks into her house and leaves a music box on her mantel. The person then calls the house to make sure Jane knows that he is watching her and wants her to stop her investigations. Jane is afraid for herself and for her elderly aunt, who has just come to live with her. She also has this woman's safety to think about. The two immediately leave the house for the night, but Jane is frightened by the intrusion, and this fear stays with her as she works to find out who is behind the "joke" of the music box.

Her father's client is responsible for a later attack on Jane. While questioning him about the woman who was murdered and his relationship to her, this man comes to think that Jane is enticing him sexually. He is a very crude man with a very violent history toward women. When they meet again at a nightclub, the man, Emery, tries to assault Jane. He touches her and pins her wrists against the wall as he talks to her. She tells him to get away, but this just excites him more. When Emery forces himself on her with a kiss, she is able to grab his hair and jab him in the eye. She runs away and flags down a taxi cab, but she still feels the man's presence all around her. Later the same evening, Jane's drink at an exclusive women's club is drugged and she is kidnapped and dumped in a shed several miles away. She does not know who is involved in the attack, which leaves her weak and scared of everyone involved in the case. She does not know who to trust. The man who helps her out of the shed, Freddy, is the man who kidnapped her, but in her vulnerable state, Jane is forced to rely on him. She decides that if he had wanted to kill her he would have done it already and she can at least get out safely.

In a final attack, Freddy holds Jane at gunpoint and forces her to go with him in his car to Jane's family cabin, where he plans to kill her. He has already killed his mother-in-law in an attempt, he believes, to save his family. His mother-in-law was going to tell Freddy's wife about his affair. He knew this would mean the end of his marriage and, with his wife pregnant, the end of his chance at a family. In the course of covering up the murder and his affair, he beat up his girlfriend, framed Emery for the murder (a man he believes should be in jail anyway for his violence against women), and set about scaring Jane and her father. He ties Jane to a tree in order to keep her from escaping and drugs her drink so that she will be asleep when he kills her. With no way to fight against his gun, Jane uses her words to fight back. She reasons with Freddy and tries to explain why he should stop the killing and face his wife. She tells him that instead of protecting his wife and child, he is hurting them more. Her death will continue to haunt him. He cannot keep hiding from himself. Then Jane wakes up in her bedroom in the cabin, to find that Freddy has not killed her.

Jane tries to telephone Freddy at home, but his wife tells her he is not there. Jane realizes that he might try and commit suicide, so she calls her father to help save the man. They arrive at the dock where Jane believes Freddy to be and are soon confronted by an explosion on the water. Several minutes later, Freddy swims out of the water. He could not go through with it. He is surprised to find Jane there trying to save him. She tells him the killing had to stop somewhere. He may have tried to kill her, but she still does not want him, or anyone else, to die. He has to face what he has done and hope that his wife will eventually forgive him. The man originally suspected in the murder, and defended by Jane's father, is cleared of the charges. After hearing of Emery's assault on Jane, Jane's father finds several other women who are willing to press assault charges against him. There is some degree of satisfaction for the reader that this criminal will not go unpunished, even though he was not the original murderer.

For the other women sleuths, too, the violence they face is most often minor or infrequent. Amanda Cross makes sure the readers are aware that "Kate has never fired a gun or been beaten up in the course of her work, although, like any city dweller, she might be shot or beaten up in the streets any day now."[80] It is not the mystery that is dangerous to women, it is urban living, according to

Cross. The women amateur sleuths are not usually made a target of violence, but they may have to deal with someone who has killed and is afraid of being found out. In such situations, the women sleuths rely on the resources at hand rather than any training or experience with a gun. Nancy Pickard's Jenny Cain comes up with a couple of innovative ways to defend herself. In *Say No to Murder*, a lobster is used as a weapon. Forced into a lobster pen, Jenny throws whatever she can find at her assailant. She hears him screaming and realizes that it is not the police he is trying to keep away, but the lobster that has grabbed hold of him. In *Generous Death*, Jenny uses a more feminine weapon to restrain a killer. Jenny is chased by the killers, a man and a woman who have been working together, through a local museum while the old building is engulfed in flames. From her hiding place in a bed on display, Jenny unhooks and removes her bra from beneath her blouse and uses it to restrain the killer. She presents an interesting picture to the fireman and police who break into the building, who see a man tied up with a bra and a woman standing beside him with her blouse all buttoned up.

It is most often her gymnastics background that Maggie Ryan employs to defend herself. In *Audition for Murder*, Maggie and the killer chase each other through the scaffolding and lights above a theater. In *Murder is Pathological*, Maggie and Nick are trapped in a room used to euthanize lab animals. Maggie stands on her head and, with her feet, reaches a bowl of sulfuric acid and a chute where tablets of potassium cyanide come down. She keeps the tablets from dropping in the bowl and killing them both with the lethal fumes. In the Maggie Ryan series, Maggie and Nick most often work together to investigate, even in cases that primarily concern Maggie's friends or career. They utilize their backgrounds in theater, dance, and gymnastics, as well as their intelligence, as "weapons."

The "murder" mystery is changing shape under the guidance of many women mystery writers. Amanda Cross, within her Kate Fansler series, redefines what qualifies as murder and violence. Who can be made accountable? When does society care about murder? Several books within the Fansler series do not contain murdered bodies. Kate Fansler does not "live amid multiple murders." Indeed, the sleuth has been criticized by critics for "not tripping over enough bodies." The series, Cross admits, contains fewer bodies than it does novels. It is the intellectual mystery that interests Cross. The reader and Kate embark on the stories together to try to solve life's little mysteries and recognize the rich varieties of human motives.[81] Lives are much more interesting to investigate than deaths. Whether alive or dead, many of Kate's cases involve investigating the lives of unique women. These women are remarkable for their fierce opinions, straightforward demeanor, and richness of life. When they are killed, it is often because they were perceived as a terrible threat to appropriate roles and behavior. While investigating their lives, Kate revels in their insights and their remarkable abilities to form a vibrant life for themselves outside "normal" society. The cost for such incredible lives may, in a few cases, be murder, but for most of these women, it is their lives rather than their deaths that are worthy of remark.

In *Death in a Tenured Position*, Janet Mandelbaum commits suicide. Kate's investigation into her death implicates several members of her department at Harvard University. There is a sense that the society in which Janet lived, including Janet herself, was responsible. She was never able to find a place for her life. The conclusion of the book leaves the reader with disorder rather than order. The restoration of order is a false ideal, according to Cross. The "order" of Harvard University, to which it would like to return, is built upon the systematic exclusion of women. This order killed the woman, just as the established order of masculine society continues to restrict and stifle women in the community.[82]

Solutions to the crimes in the amateur sleuth mysteries come from the details of everyday life and relationships. The detective is primarily a "reader" of texts. The woman amateur detective, as illustrated by the sleuths chosen for this chapter, does not put herself in the position of the traditional masculine detective as she investigates. She is not the authority figure, like a man, who is a part of the established order and determines the solution. The male voice is the privileged voice that tells the other characters and reader of the novel what the text means. There is no acknowledgment that his may be a misreading or that his solution is not the entire solution.[83] The protagonist of the Amanda Cross mysteries, for example, and many of the other women writing detective fiction do not take on the role of the ultimate authority. They do not accept a single vision of reality. Many voices are allowed to speak, and the sleuth is allowed to be fallible. In *The Question of Max*, for example, two solutions are uncovered by Kate Fansler. Both fit the uncovered clues and are plausible. Either can be taken as the "entire" truth and the end of the book. By creating these two solutions, Cross highlights this issue for the reader. Is the last solution presented really the final one, or could there be more? Is the solution accepted by the murderer the same as that understood by his victim? The process of reading these mysteries is a process of reading and rereading the story of the murder. The lives of those involved change as new perspectives are added and evaluated. Each has a truth to tell. The role of the sleuth is to let them all speak and find a space for the truth that is the most plausible, though admittedly, it may not be the absolute truth. Lives are composed of stories. Some we tell ourselves, others we learn from those around us. Feminism suggests that subjectivity is superior to any illusion of objectivity. Involvement is more valued than distance, and compassion should be considered more of a priority than justice.[84] Stories that include the space for disorder and diversity are preferred by these women authors over complete order and certainty. Society's definition of order and justice may very well be unjust.

In exploring the connections between justice, morality, and the legal system, the women's amateur sleuths in this chapter bring the issues of power and control into the equation. They work to create alternative solutions to establishing the expected order through the police. They find ways to inject morality into areas where the official justice system cannot go. In Western society, the people with power and control have greater access to the legal system. They are perceived to be above the law. Power and control can be accrued on the basis of economic wealth, perceived racial superiority, or masculine gender. These amateur sleuth mysteries give the women authors the chance to both illuminate these discrepancies and find solutions other than calling in the police.

Nancy Pickard's *Confession* and Barbara Neely's *Blanche on the Lam* are just two examples of where women mystery authors expose abuses of power and how people deemed powerful by androcentric society can potentially exploit the system for their own benefit. Blanche White discovers the murderous secret of the aristocratic southern family for whom she works as a maid in *Blanche on the Lam*. Blanche discovers that the "lady of the house," Grace, killed several people (her husband's first wife, a gardener on the estate, and a sheriff) as revenge for their getting in the way of what she considered her rightful inheritance of money and attention. She also tries to kill Blanche in order to keep her secrets safe. The family is very rich and powerful, but Blanche can expose their crimes, if not to the police, then at least to the press. Grace was a very disturbed child who grew up to be a very disturbed and dangerous woman because her family refused to believe that anything was wrong with her. In exchange for not calling the authorities, Blanche arranges with the family for Blanche's criminal record to be erased and for her to receive money so that her children can get an education. Even after arranging this settlement, Blanche does not want the lives of those murdered to be forgotten, especially that of the gardener, who had become a special friend. Blanche talks with a reporter she can trust about the family before she slips out of town and finds a new home for her family in Boston. She had always intended to make these secrets public, though she let the family assume she would keep quiet. She cannot let the deaths of these people stay silenced.

In the Blanche White books, there is no "police" solution. Black Americans do not look for justice from the police, according to author Barbara Neely. Thus, she created Blanche to be as moral as possible without calling in the police. She is able to give the guilty their comeuppance without help from the official justice system. Neely uses the Blanche White books to play with the connections between morality and justice. If you do not have the police, can you still have justice? As an author, Neely challenges herself to find solutions without the obvious intervention of the police.[85] In this situation, Blanche never said that she would keep the family secrets. She is not responsible for their assumptions to that effect. She sees her payment as "aggravation money," not "hush money." Blanche used the means that she had available, as well as the two things the family valued mostly highly, money and reputation, to construct some sense of justice for herself and those whose lives had been disregarded.

*Confession* is a brutal departure from the usual "cozy" traditional mysteries in the Jenny Cain series. The reader is exposed to child pornography, child molestation, and the workings of a very brutal and strict, religious-type sect. The murder case brought to Jenny and Geof's attention by the boy claiming to be his son turns out to be a murder/suicide, just as originally ruled by the police. There is no one else directly responsible for the deaths of the boy's mother and the man David believes to be his father. In a strict sense of the word, *Confession* is not a "cozy" mystery. There is no murder to be solved or murderer to be chased through clues and caught. The boy's mother committed suicide. She knew what it would take to get her husband to kill her, and she knew that he would kill himself rather than live with the knowledge of what he had done and what his wife told him about their son's parentage. Jenny and Geof follow the trail of clues, not to the one who pulled the trigger, but to all the people who contributed to Judy, the boy's mother, coming to that decision. Hers was a life of pain and suffering caused by adults with very disturbing ideas of sexuality, childhood, retribution, sin, authority, and forgiveness.

Nancy Pickard paints a very harsh picture of what can happen when power and authority are taken to the extreme. The men in charge of the religious sect who are implicated abuse and torment their members through divine right. They encourage followers to attack those who are unable to defend themselves and disdain forgiveness. Judy's mother and "her customers" manipulate the lives of children for their own gratification, though Jenny defines their actions as child pornography. They construct justifications that do not take into account the lives of the children. Jenny Cain takes the reader through the clues to expose the secrets and horrors of the abuse of power. Jenny and Geof make sure the police take immediate action where possible to save the lives of future children, like Judy once was. It is not always enough, however, to punish those exploiting their power. They do not understand that they have done wrong and continue to believe in their own right to judge and exact retribution. Jenny names her new charitable foundation after Judy. She wants to honor the memory of this woman and have her remembered for more than just her death or suffering. The foundation funds projects often overlooked by traditional sources (which often means "concerning the lives of women"). "Justice" does not just mean making people pay for their crimes; it also means improving the lives or memories of those affected by the crime. For Blanche White, this means clearing her name and making sure that her children will receive the best education possible. Some good will come out of this very bad situation, and it will be done in memory of Blanche's friend, Nat. Similarly, Jenny keeps the memory of Judy alive through the foundation and creates a loving family for her son, David.

Women amateur sleuths come from a wide variety of situations and lifestyles. Prior to the boom in women's mysteries in the 1980s and 1990s, women amateur sleuths were most often nosy British spinsters. Jane Marple set the standard, and few books were published that offered women readers much more. With the renewed popularity of women's mysteries in the 1980s came an incredible opening up of the mystery field for potential women authors. Nancy Pickard explains that most of these women grew up reading Nancy Drew, who has become part of the American psyche. As adults, these women wanted to find a heroine of mystery, adventure, and romance, but nothing was available. It was difficult for these thirty- to forty-year-old women to make the connection with "grandmotherly" Jane Marple. Mystery author Marilyn Wallace adds that as women, they, too, had changed. The women coming into the mystery field had lived through the civil rights movement, the women's movement, and the environmental movement. This was a time when people were taking on issues and making their voices count. The women were part of the new tradition that said, "I can have an impact on the world in which I live."[86]

New voices are expanding the possibilities for women's narratives and pushing the limits of traditional gender definitions. Women are being included in the definition of hero and the chance for adventure. For P. M. Carlson, working mothers are heroes. Her character Maggie Ryan is certainly a hero, who responds to difficulties. In those responses, she provides a model and gives the reader something to think about. For that she is heroic.[87] Neely's Blanche White is a hero, whereas few other black women domestic workers have ever been shown to be. She maintains power over her own life and is satisfied with the rules she has made.

The heroic is not the invincible. Indeed, the hero is the person who struggles with being human. In fiction and society, the universal is most often the masculine. The use of "he" stands in for everyone—male and female. In the mysteries of women, the universal is replaced with the term "human" and is validated with qualities from the feminine—attachment, responsibility, and empathy, for example. The women authors do not merely expand the "heroic" so that it can include anyone and everyone. If everything is heroic, then nothing is heroic. Qualities of the hero—perseverance, tenacity, responsibility to others, compassion, and dedication to those in need—are qualities that women have learned to value. To be heroic is to deal morally and compassionately with life. The sleuth struggles, but she can handle what comes her way.[88]

The women's mystery novels of the 1980s and 1990s continue to include more voices in a wider variety of narratives. The protagonists highlight the connections between feminism and femininity. They explore heroism and familial obligations. Rather than looking for the "right" answers or returning to the status quo, I would argue that it is the adventure that (women) readers are seeking in today's mystery novels. A simple "parlor-room" puzzle does not satisfy today's readers, who are faced with a sophisticated sense of crime courtesy of movies, news, and television. Women are looking for information and adventure. They want to learn about something new and escape into a new slice of life. The amateur sleuth mysteries of women illustrate the adventure of the everyday. Women who are like the readers and live in the same kind of society are shown as smart enough, tough enough, and dedicated enough to solve mysteries and preserve a bit of humanity in their communities. Even the amateur sleuth mysteries set in other times and countries exhibit qualities that contemporary Western women can understand and with which they can empathize.

Feminism and femininity are shown as compatible in women's amateur sleuth mysteries. Women can strive for independence and equality and still "get the man" if that is what they want. They can also lead a fulfilling life if they choose not to marry or have children. There is room for choice. They can construct marriages, with their partners, that are equitable and fulfilling for both parties, and they can also struggle, knowing the relationship can survive if there is trust. Where the women have chosen to marry, the partners are often featured working together to solve the mysteries. The problems involve them both, since they involve one partner. Within the marriage, there is very little sense that the husband thinks of his wife as "nosy," a "snoop," or "busybody." He is attracted to her sense of commitment and ability to get involved. It is the woman's own sense of social expectation that gives her the most concern. Many woman amateur sleuths (especially true for those written by women who entered the field "early" in the current revolution), continue to struggle with the questions: "What kind of woman would do that?" and "What will people think?" As the women who entered the field in the 1980s are joined by younger women in the 1990s, these questions are losing their ability to change women's behavior and expectations. Women authors are hesitating much less. The younger women are not as self-conscious about their feminism and femininity. The boundaries are thus pushed farther out for all women in the field.[89]

The women amateur sleuths in this category are not a homogenous group solely defined as "women." That is not the only quality by which they can be understood or by which they understand themselves. It is not possible to dismiss Blanche White's ethnicity and culture, and she would never think them any less important than her gender. Jane Lawless is a woman who is a lesbian. It is not possible for Jane to separate the facets of her life as she strives to understand her self and her place. Kate Fansler presents the reader with very insightful discussions of aging in America culture. A very strong sense of feminism informs her novels and the construction of their themes and plots. The women mystery authors discussed here each have an incredible sense of character and voice with which they tell their stories. Nancy Pickard, for example, in *I.O.U.,* is able to create a unique and very meaningful voice for her protagonist. In this novel, Jenny Cain experiences the loss of her mother. The writing of this novel is noteworthy for how it conveys a profound sense of despair and loneliness. Jenny is confused, shaken, and incomplete without the presence of her mother, even though the latter had been silent for years due to her mental breakdown.[90] The reader embarks on the rocky journey of recovery and peace that Jenny must take as she investigates her mother's life and what led to her mental breakdown. It is not a murder, but a life, that compels Jenny to search for answers.

Barbara Neely noted, when interviewed, that she came to the mystery novel in part because as an author, she could use the mystery element to engage the reader in subjects they would not necessarily read about otherwise. All great teaching is in fiction, according to Neely. It sends the reader into a pattern that is new. Readers can arrive at new patterns in their own lives as a result.[91] Fiction is subversive in its emotional appeal. It gets to the reader's heart and gut. The abstract is made very human by the mystery author.[92] It is this sense of engagement that attracts readers to these women's mysteries. One of the most important contributions of the women's movement of the 1960s and 1970s, according to mystery author Diane Mott Davidson, was that women learned to trust their own experiences and voices.[93] It was now acceptable for women to have a voice and be honest about how it feels to be female.[94] The contemporary woman amateur sleuth is aware of the conflicts between the individual and society. She is very cognizant of the imperfections in traditional forms of social justice. She also works to embody two qualities often not allowed women in the past: she possesses practical intelligence and the power of action. She demonstrates the possibility of finding solutions—or at least the importance of looking for solutions even if they are not readily at hand—and the need for compassion, courage, and connection.[95] Women's (political) stories are told in their daily lives—in their marriages, their children, their jobs, and their connections.

## NOTES

1. Edie Gibson, "The Sisterhood of Sleuths," *Publishers Weekly* 235.18 (5 May 1989): 38.
2. Cheri L. Ross, "The First Feminist Detective: Anna Katharine Green's Amelia Butterworth," *Journal of Popular Culture* 25.2 (Fall 1991): 77–86.
3. Lois A. Marchino, "The Female Sleuth in Academe," *Journal of Popular Culture* 23.9 (Winter 1989): 89.
4. Carolyn G. Heilbrun quoted in Paula Span, "The Professor and the Mystery Writer," *Los Angeles Times*, 10 November 1989, E10.
5. Carolyn G. Heilbrun writing as Amanda Cross quoted in Gibson, 38.
6. Marchino, 95.
7. Carolyn G. Heilbrun, "The Women of Mystery," *Ms.* 1.5 (March/April 1991): 62.
8. Gibson, 38.
9. Marchino, 96.
10. P. M. Carlson, telephone interview, 5 November 1993.
11. Ellen Hart, telephone interview, 20 December 1993.
12. Hart interview.
13. Maureen T. Reddy, *Sisters in Crime: Feminism and the Crime Novel* (New York: Continuum, 1988), 122.
14. Barbara Neely, telephone interview, 24 January 1994.
15. Neely interview.
16. Amanda Cross, *The Collected Stories* (New York: Ballantine Books, 1997), 3–4.
17. Judith Greber, telephone interview, 28 January 1994.
18. Greber interview.
19. Carolyn G. Hart, "Why Cozies?" in *The Fine Art of Murder: The Mystery Reader's Indispensable Companion*, ed. Ed Gorman, Martin H. Greenberg, Larry Segriff, and Jon L. Breen (New York: Carroll & Graf Publishers, 1993), 71.
20. Carolyn G. Heilbrun, *Reinventing Womanhood* (New York: W.W. Norton & Company, 1979), 171.
21. Heilbrun, *Reinventing*, 172.
22. Heilbrun, *Reinventing* , 175, 177.
23. Heilbrun, *Reinventing*, 174.
24. Heilbrun, *Reinventing*, 182.
25. Betty Friedan quoted in Sheila M. Rothman, *Woman's Proper Place: A History of Changing Ideals and Practices, 1870 to the Present* (New York: Basic Books, 1987), 227.
26. Rothman, 179–80.

27. Rothman, 222.
28. Rothman, 225.
29. Rothman, 187.
30. Rothman, 253.
31. Reddy, 103.
32. Judi M. Roller, *The Politics of the Feminist Novel* (Westport, CT: Greenwood Press, 1986), 23.
33. Nancy Pickard, *Marriage Is Murder* (1987; New York: Pocket Books, 1988), 55–56.
34. Pickard, *Marriage*, 59–60.
35. Pickard, *Marriage*, 219.
36. Nancy Pickard, *Generous Death* (New York: Pocket Books, 1987).
37. Nancy Pickard, *Say No to Murder* (New York: Avon, 1985), 32–33.
38. Carolyn G. Heilbrun writing as Amanda Cross, quoted in Span, E11.
39. Cross, *Collected Stories*, 15.
40. Amanda Cross, *Sweet Death, Kind Death* (New York: Ballantine Books, 1990).
41. Amanda Cross, *Death in a Tenured Position* (New York: Ballantine Books, 1988), 20.
42. Cross, *Tenured Position*, 5.
43. Amanda Cross, *In the Last Analysis* (New York: Avon, 1966).
44. Amanda Cross, *Poetic Justice* ( New York: Avon, 1979), 50.
45. Cross, *Poetic Justice*, 50–52.
46. Cross, *Poetic Justice*, 87.
47. Cross, *Poetic Justice*, 88–89.
48. Hart interview.
49. Barbara Neely, *Blanche on the Lam* (New York: Penguin Books, 1993), 21.
50. Barbara Neely, *Blanche among the Talented Tenth* (New York: Penguin Books, 1995), 11–12.
51. Carolyn G. Heilbrun, "Women, Men, Theories, and Literature," in *The Impact of Feminist Research in the Academy*, ed. Christie Farnham (Bloomington: Indiana University Press, 1987), 221.
52. Cross, *Collected Stories*, 48.
53. Amanda Cross, *The Question of Max* (New York: Ballantine Books, 1984).
54. Amanda Cross, *The James Joyce Murder* (New York: Ballantine Books, 1982), 23.
55. Neely interview.
56. Nancy Pickard, *Confession* (New York: Pocket Books, 1994), 3–4.
57. Pickard, *Confession,* 51–52.
58. Pickard, *Confession*, 58–60.
59. Pickard, *Confession*, 199–200.
60. Pickard, *Confession*, 304–6.
61. Nancy Pickard, *Bum Steer* (New York: Pocket Books, 1991).
62. Nancy Pickard, *Twilight* (New York: Pocket Books, 1995).
63. Carlson may write another Maggie Ryan book, but at this point that is unlikely since Bantam has the rights to the Maggie Ryan series and will get the next volume, while Carlson's current agent is "down on Bantam." Carlson interview.
64. P. M. Carlson, *Audition for Murder* (New York: Avon, 1985).
65. P. M. Carlson, *Murder Is Pathological* (New York: Avon, 1986).
66. P. M. Carlson, *Rehearsal for Murder* (New York: Bantam Books, 1988), 16.

67. Carlson, *Rehearsal*, 35.
68. Carlson, *Rehearsal*, 171.
69. Carlson, *Rehearsal*, 188.
70. Carlson, *Rehearsal,* 203–4.
71. Carlson interview.
72. P. M. Carlson, *Murder in the Dog Days* (New York: Bantam Books, 1991), 224.
73. Carolyn Wheat, telephone interview, 20 December 1993.
74. P. M. Carlson, *Bad Blood* (New York: Doubleday, 1991).
75. Ellen Hart, *Vital Lies* (Seattle, WA: Seal Press, 1991), 105.
76. The horror expressed as a result of the amateur sleuth being injured or attacked belies society's suspicious silence when such abuse occurs in the home. It is somehow more outrageous for the woman to be attacked by a stranger than by her husband.
77. Ellen Hart, *Hallowed Murder* (New York: Ballantine Books, 1993).
78. Ellen Hart, *Stage Fright* (Seattle, WA: Seal Press, 1992).
79. Ellen Hart, *A Killing Cure* (Seattle, WA: Seal Press, 1993).
80. Cross, *Collected Stories*, 4. This claim must be amended since the publication of *The Puzzled Heart* in which Kate is severely beaten by a woman who was involved in the kidnapping of Kate's husband, Reed. Amanda Cross, *The Puzzled Heart* (New York: Ballantine Books, 1998).
81. Cross, *Collected Stories*, 4.
82. Reddy, 14.
83. Reddy, 10.
84. Reddy, 14.
85. Neely interview.
86. Nancy Pickard and Marilyn Wallace, "There's a Revolution in Mystery—And Women Are Leading It!" Author book signing and discussion, Grounds for Murder Mystery Book Store, San Diego, California, 17 March 1990.
87. Carlson interview.
88. Greber interview.
89. Pickard and Wallace.
90. Nancy Pickard, *I.O.U.* (New York: Pocket Books, 1992).
91. Neely interview.
92. Greber interview.
93. Diane Mott Davidson, telephone interview, 11 March 1994.
94. Greber interview.
95. Patricia Craig and Mary Cadogen paraphrased in Marchino, 98.

*Chapter 5*

# Mysterious Women—Feminism, Femininity, Heroism, and the Ordinary

> [Mystery fiction] is virtually the last literary frontier for the American hero—Marilyn Stasio[1]

Delineating the mystery genre into three categories—private eye, police, and amateur—does not exhaust the possibilities within the genre. Indeed, there is no end to the ways it can be subdivided. Bookstores, publishers, authors, and readers recognize categories such as historical (including, but not limited to, medieval, Elizabethan, Victorian, and Renaissance), historical romance, romantic suspense, gothic, psychological thriller, young adult, espionage, Victorian, Sherlockian, cozy (or traditional), and many others. Creating a marketing niche can be as simple as marketing the book under a new classification. In some situations, authors themselves become the marker for the type of book. New authors become "the next Grafton, Paretsky, or Agatha Christie" type. The three categories in this analysis are some of the most basic and well-known ways of dividing the industry, but the others contribute to the complexity of the genre. Historical mysteries, for example, allow readers and authors to go back into history and either reinterpret events or add color to the stories passed down as history. New fictional characters join in sleuthing with names with which readers are more familiar. The readers "learn" about historical periods. They get a feel for the location, dress, habits, and customs, and can fantasize about a favorite time or person. A recent mail order mystery catalog included historical mysteries with sleuths with such names as Charles Dickens, Jane Austen, Fred Astaire, Ginger Rogers, Ben Franklin, and Eleanor Roosevelt. Cases are solved in medieval Wales, feudal Japan, Renaissance Venice, Ancient Rome, and rural, Depression-era Kansas. In another example of mystery classification, romantic mysteries explore the cross-over between romance and mystery novels. The passions of the romance are paired with the rationality of the mystery. Authors and readers thus challenge the critical assumption that women's emotional lives cannot include intelligence or reasoning. Passion and brains are shown as not mutually exclusive.

Most of these categories of mysteries include quite a few women authors. They have successfully pushed their way into almost every type of mystery fiction. There is one category, in particular, in which women have been conspicuously absent. The future of the genre, and where women will be making a significant impact, I would suggest, is in the field of spy/espionage novels. Here, the issues of feminism, femininity, and heroism are again tested against the strength of historical conventions. Men currently, and traditionally, have dominated this market, and many of the traditional lines of demarcation between masculinity and femininity remain. The lines are clearly drawn between appropriate spheres of behavior and worldviews. It is the man, with his quick wit and quicker gun, who is the hero. Women tend to occupy two roles in the spy novel, the evil manipulator who seduces the hero to prevent him from accomplishing his goals, or, if she is not a cunning, manipulative woman, the "prize." A successful case means that the hero "gets the girl." A spy must remain detached from his surroundings and blend in. He cannot stand out or make himself obvious. He is solely focused on his duty and performing the tasks entrusted to him. His dedication to his job is not necessarily due to his belief in the cause or an altruistic belief in his side's inherent goodness, but in the fact that the job allows him to enjoy a life of glamour, adventure, and risk. He is the best in his field and refuses to admit that anyone can beat him.

Women have not typically been attracted to the high degree of violence, international terrorists, gratuitous sex, and casual attitude to life and death characteristic of the spy novel. Women's obligations to family and community make it difficult for female authors or readers to imagine a woman in the position of professional spy. Women readers and authors have had a difficult time translating the narrative fantasies of the spy novel into their own woman-centered fantasies. Spy novel author Ken Follet explains that the fantasy of the man who appears to lead an ordinary life but is secretly doing important things (like toppling governments, killing people, and even saving the world) is a fantasy many men share. Men are trained to seek power over work, money, wife, children, politics, and nations. When women write spy stories, according to Follet, the plot is "often just a channel through which a love story can flow." Women have different fantasies because they are trained to seek, not power, but a powerful man. Follet does suggest that today, women are being trained less effectively for the housewife-mother role. He is in favor of this new development, but continues to explain that it is radical feminists who want to see women develop new motivations. Good women's spy writing will be the result of these radical feminists acquiring male motivations and fantasies.[2]

Recent work by several women mystery authors has shown new ways of interpreting the spy novel and making it interesting for women. For these recent entrants, the spy novel has proved an interesting combination of adventure and thoughtful discussion for women. Women who have made forays into the field include Dorothy Gilman, Marcia Muller, Patricia Cornwell, and Amanda Cross, for example. Each has taken a very different approach to the standards of the spy novel. Gilman's main character, for example, is a woman in her sixties who raised her family and then went looking for something more rewarding than her garden club. This series has been ongoing and quite successful since the mid- to late 1960s. The Central Intelligence Agency (CIA) supposedly hires her as one of their agents because of her age and sex. No one would ever suspect a grandmotherly type of being a spy.[3] Gilman expands on such cultural misconceptions. Mrs. Pollifax succeeds as a spy because she understands how those around her will react to her as an older woman, but she does not solely rely on getting by on looks alone. This is a nice twist on the spy novels' traditional picture of women as dangerously sexy and therefore able to lure men by virtue of their appearance. Mrs. Pollifax is also well educated, understands the dangers of world travel, and is trained in self-defense. The spy novel gives Gilman a chance to turn the model on its head and see what happens in the world of intrigue when an elderly woman is the protagonist.

Patricia Cornwell and Amanda Cross have crossed into this territory in more recent books, albeit in very limited ways. Each has published a book in their respective series that steps into spy territory. Cornwell's *Cause of Death* puts Dr. Kay Scarpetta and her niece Lucy in the line of fire from international terrorists involved in nuclear arms smuggling, hostages, and the potential for citywide devastation.[4] In contrast, Cross, in *An Imperfect Spy*, uses the issue of "women as spies" as the center of her academic mystery.[5] Women are trained by society in the skills of infiltration and subversion, according to this Kate Fansler mystery. Who can better blend in than a woman, who is often overlooked and regarded as a part of the landscape. In this mystery, Kate and her husband, Reed, develop a very interesting relationship with a secretary at Schuyler Law School. This woman, who calls herself Harriet, patterns her life after John le Carre's character, George Smiley. She astonishes both Kate and Reed with her passion for her skills as a "spy." She breaks into their apartment, in one instance, to prove to them that she is capable. As an "oldish" woman, she is invisible and can go anywhere, "like someone in a fairy story."[6] This woman just decided one day to disappear. She did not want to "bow out" slowly and gracefully. She left behind her old life of conventions and appropriate behaviors and became a spy, working outside the norms of society. Society has made spies out of many of its women, especially women in their later years.

Marcia Muller appears to be moving her entire series into territory once reserved for the male spy. Sharon McCone's lover, Hy Rapinsky, worked for and later rejoins a securities firm that seems to Sharon to be more than that. She gathers hints and glimpses of a company involved in espionage and subversion. Through Rapinsky, she become acquainted with this firm and does limited work for them. She confronts Hy's, at the time, former employers in *A Wolf in the Shadows* when she has to rescue Hy from captors in Mexico. She has to find him before his associates in the securities firm can kill him. McCone's new association with high-level espionage puts her in dangerous company (confronting "coyotes" smuggling illegal immigrants from Mexico into the United States, for example) and encourages her to think about her priorities and obligations. This all comes at a time when she is leaving the safety and security of working at the All Souls law office and has to find a place of her own. McCone must decide just what kind of investigator she is. She questions her own ideas about justice and how far she is willing to go to complete a task, as well as the types of cases she in willing to take on. In the novels following *A Wolf in the Shadows*, Muller ventures farther into the territory of the "thriller." Muller, herself, comments that the label "thriller" is primarily a marketing tool. As an author, she does not pay attention to the type of mystery she is writing. It is also a matter of having written the McCone series for twenty years. She needs to continue to push herself and her characters. Moreover, Muller notes that many of the women who entered mystery writing in the late 1970s and early 1980s are in a similar situation.[7] Each is trying to find fresh material and push the characters in order to find more interesting stories and adventures. As they venture into the "espionage" or "thriller" category, the possibilities for women's adventures are expanded. New aspects of the lives of women, and of men, come under scrutiny.

The conventional, mass-produced, formulaic genre of mystery fiction provides a rich venue for women to challenge and critique their place in gendered society. Women were granted the space to create their own stories on two fronts. First, critics have historically overlooked women's writings as unimportant and emotional. True writers were men, who had a "natural" inclination to write the truly insightful and profound. Secondly, genre fiction is dismissed by critics as "uninspired fluff." By writing for the market and the common consumer, authors of genre fiction cannot be confronting real issues, according to the critics. The conventions created for genre fiction are just a way of quickly getting books to market and making money off the masses. Women authors took these opportunities to write about their own lives and to comment on their society, by virtue of their status outside power, control, and authority. The mystery novel is one form of mass-produced fiction in which women have been able to push the accepted and create new possible narratives. They have used the mystery as a form for experimentation, discussion, fantasy, debate, foolishness, and practice.

Regardless of the type of mysteries written by women or the types of women writing them, patterns have emerged that speak to the commonalties of women's experiences. Their perceptions have value in their narratives. They are put up against the dominant frameworks and judged important and worthwhile. I would suggest that one of the most important consequences of Second Golden Age mystery fiction has been the development of community among women, which is inclusive of both writers and readers. The female author is no longer the "madwoman in the attic." Loneliness and isolation have not driven her outside society; her perceptions are not the ravings of an hysteric. She is a "brazen hussy" (a term taken from a Sisters in Crime promotional pamphlet), out leading the charge in honor of her work and that of her peers. She takes delight in taking over a term with which women were historically branded in disgust and condescension. A brazen hussy elicits connotations of being out in public, not hiding her "wares" but rather proclaiming herself to those who pass by, knowing it to cause scandal and titillation. It also connects the women with each other—as long as they wear the label, they might as well wear it together with pride. There are others like them—those who have come before and those who will come after. The female author knows she goes against traditional mores and expectations. She knows what society expects of her, and to a certain extent, it is what she expected of herself. However, she is enjoying the freedom to explore that comes from having the space to create outside traditional scrutiny. The mystery novel, as a form of popular fiction, receives little critical attention. It is dismissed by academics and literature critics who equate value with the canons of "great literature." The mystery is also a format with prescribed rules and conventions, making it relatively easy for a reader to see herself in the place of the writer. It is a form open to new ideas and practitioners. The conventions give the author a guide for construction, but the stories themselves can include almost anything. Within the rules there is great flexibility.

The women of the first Golden Age (and those who came earlier, such as Anna Katharine Green, who have been neglected by history), gave today's women writers a history of their own to find and gain strength from. The men who dominated certain eras in the history of the genre, such as the private eye or police novels, gave women important models of another kind of reality. Women who did not picture themselves in English country manors found a connection with the new urban dramas. Since it was all "just for fun," they could play at imagining themselves in such adventures and writing their own fictional narratives. The history of the genre—its placement outside of the literary canon, the strong tradition of women role models, and its ability to include both masculine and feminine narratives—and the flexibility of its conventions to both contain the stories and free the imaginations of its writers goes far to explaining why this genre has been taken up by women from a variety of circumstances and why it has changed women's literary landscape.

Kathleen Gregory Klein suggests, in *The Woman Detective*, that the mystery genre should undergo a radical and complete change: "women-centered, gender-aware detective fiction can and must reinvent the genre; its beneficiaries will be writers and readers alike."[8] Klein calls for a break with the history of the genre because it has been "no good" for feminism. The future must not resemble or remind readers of the past. On the contrary, however, I would argue that the genre does not, and should not, break with its past. Doing so would continue the very common pattern of silencing women's contributions. Each generation of women writers has had to start anew and search for the history in which they were a part. "At every moment in the history of detective fiction there is a plethora of women writers, many of whom have been allowed to go out of print, but whose numbers hint at a hidden treasure." Women writers have historically been ignored because critics and historians do not take women's writings seriously.[9] "Twentieth-century critics have taught generations of students to equate popularity with debasement, emotionality with ineffectiveness, religiosity with fakery, domesticity with triviality, and all of these, implicitly, with womanly inferiority."[10] Several of the mystery writers interviewed for this book spoke of coming back to mystery novels after years of being told by professors and parents that they should only pay attention to the accepted canon of "great literature." The type of literature they enjoyed and with which they found a connection was viewed as frivolous and uninspired. Only later in their lives, once they had married, taken jobs, raised families, and done what was expected, did they admit to enjoying mystery novels and fantasize about writing their own. Carolyn Heilbrun remarks that most of those writing some of the best-known feminist detective fiction came to it after some years devoted to other careers.[11] For example, when she joined the ranks of women mystery writers, Barbara Neely reports that she did not come to writing as a "twenty-two year-old innocent." She had had a full life of work. She was a competent and capable person who wanted to write and knew what she wanted to write—even if publishers were not interested in publishing it.[12] These women, especially those who began in the 1960s and 1970s, came to mystery authorship without completely understanding themselves as part of a history of women writers. They were separated from the history of the genre by masculine-oriented ideas of literature and canon. It was only in the very late 1980s and early 1990s that women authors began to learn about their past, as well as the present community of women writers in which they found themselves. Not all women authors write to express their feminism or challenge masculine doctrines. Many write out of enjoyment and the possibility of an income. Not all mysteries are rich with the possibilities of feminist critique and interpretation; not all mysteries are even written well. With this in mind, it is still premature to abandon women's contemporary mysteries to the critical scrap heap.

The woman investigator does not succeed because she looks and acts like a man. She neither scorns masculine society—becoming "ultra-feminine"—nor adopts it as her own—becoming an "honorary male." In her introduction to an anthology of stories featuring women sleuths and by women crime writers, Sara Paretsky begins with words written by Virginia Woolf when she first tried to write for publication. Woolf imagined an "Angel in the House" who spoke to her: "My dear, you are a young woman. You are writing about a book that has been written by a man. Be sympathetic; be tender; flatter; deceive, use all the arts and wiles of your sex. Never let anybody guess that you have a mind of your own." Woolf struggled with this voice for many years. She even tried to kill it so she could find her own voice. It is a difficult phantom to destroy because it speaks in many voices and with much authority. Paretsky quotes the first governor of Massachusetts, for example, as one of many examples of authority dismissing the voices of women. In reference to the poet Anne Hopkins, the governor stated that she had "fallen into a sad infirmity, the loss of her understanding and reason." This was due to giving herself to reading and writing rather than to household affairs "and such things as belong to women."[13] The women investigators discussed here exposes the struggles of many women in trying to make a place in a society predicated on a particular set of gender assumptions. They do not preach feminism; they just try to live it. Discussions of feminism in the media in the 1960s, 1970s, and 1980s were often heated, and women felt they had to scream to be heard. Popular debate was divided between groups demanding that women stay home and be good wives and mothers and those who proclaimed that women should compete toe-to-toe with men in the workplace. What appears to have changed in the late 1980s and early 1990s is the volume of the debate. The women authors talk about their characters living feminist lives, not lecturing or looking for converts.

Society has not made such a smooth transition. Despite a possible decrease in the vehemence of debate, society is not androgynous. Masculine behavior and modes of interpretation are assumed by society to be the universal. Qualities such as intelligence and independence are revealed in these women's mystery novels to be gender specific. While they may, at first, appear to be innocuous or neutral terms, the women's novels expose the terms as reserved primarily for the male. The authors ask how society is supposed to understand women like Kinsey Millhone, Arly Hanks, or Blanche White, for example, who are smart and self-reliant. Are these women heroic because of, or in spite of, these qualities? The woman hero in the detective novels of the women considered here does not just figure out "whodunit." She takes the author, characters, and reader on a journey—a quest. It is the journey that is central to these mystery novels, not the dead body. During this journey, gender stereotypes are illuminated, struggles take place over "assumptions" and "essentials," and new types of fantasies and narratives for women are tried out.

The question that began my exploration—and continues to perplex literary critics, popular media, and observers of the genre—is how women (i.e., the "fairer and gentler sex") can be so good at murder, as evidenced by the number of women writing murder mysteries. This question is a simplistic view of one very small aspect of the issue of violence in society. Those who are really "good" at murder—serial killers, for example—are, except for a few isolated examples, men. Women are more often the victims than the perpetrators. The original question is most often asked by popular media as a way of generating thrills and controversy. Women mystery writers include murder in their novels, but the greatest proportion of their work is spent on the lives of their characters. Victims, too, are often introduced to the reader. Each is shown to have family, dreams, expectations, fears, and a life worth leading. The reader experiences this life and feels pain and outrage when it is cut short. Even where the crime of murder is graphic and realistic, as in the Patricia Cornwell books, the details are there to provide the reader with a sense of tragedy and realism. Searching for a link between murder and mystery writing does not contribute to our understanding of why women have been, and continue to be, attracted to the genre and why they have been successful. Most women mystery authors are not "good" at murder; they are "good" at human relations.

The women's mystery novels examine and highlight life. They involve relationships, the details of the everyday, and the construction of community. Murder is a device for focusing attention, but it also signals the breakdown of order in the community. Order must be created out of the chaos. The women are not necessarily looking to restore order in the sense of that which was before. It was because of that "order" that there was a breakdown. The community of the individual mystery novels gives the detective permission to dig into lives and their secrets and to critique what caused the murder in the first place. In the details of the everyday, the detective finds the clues to society's secrets and oppressions. For example, Sue Grafton, in *"E" Is for Evidence*, focuses the reader's attention on a woman's simple act of greeting her husband and fixing a few appetizers while the couple talks with Kinsey Millhone. Millhone notes the woman's attentiveness and submission to her husband. She originally interprets these clues as an indication of her shallowness, but with the addition of later clues, she paints a picture of a woman who is afraid and full of self-doubt. She believes herself unworthy of her husband's love because she is "damaged goods." She hides a secret of childhood abuse at the hands of her brother. The husband kills his wife for what he perceives as these betrayals. He had always felt himself to be the cause of her fears and sexual insecurities. Her family could not confront their own past; their secrets and misguided blame continue to damage the lives of their family members. Clues are in the everyday details, not just forensic evidence. The detective "reads" the lives of those involved as text; looking to put together a narrative that is logical and plausible. She knows that truth is fluid. There is no one method of interpretation. Her job is to find the story that makes the most sense to those involved.

Clues have multiple meanings. The detective must propose and dismiss many stories before she finds the one that is most consistent with the events. The detective signifies to the reader and characters that there is no one "truth." Signs (clues) have various meanings depending on who is telling the story, the location (context) of the story, and/or its purpose. Meaning is determined by who has the power and authority to control it. The detective, killer, police, victims, and suspects each have their own agendas and struggle over the meaning of the clues and how the story of the murder is to be told. In *Towards Zero*, an Agatha Christie character comments that while murder mysteries usually begin with murder, in truth, "murder is the end. The story begins long before that—years before, sometimes—with all the causes and events that bring certain people to a certain place at a certain time on a certain day—in other words, towards zero."[14] In the history to which this Christie character points are the clues the detective must search out and understand. The murder itself is often one of the least significant parts in many women's mysteries. The women's mystery novels discussed here illustrate that the detective story involves reading the details of life as an important narrative.

If, as critic Marilyn Stasio concludes, the mystery novel is the last bastion of heroism in American literature, if women writers are an important portion of the mystery writing population, and if, furthermore, women protagonists are growing in strength and complexity and in dedication to responsibility and connection, then how is heroism being defined in this era? Who is the new literary hero, and how can she transcend the pages of the mystery? Literary heroines have existed throughout the history of the novel, but few women in literature have been called heroic. The heroine is most often praised for her dedication to traditional feminine qualities. She is pure, gentle, generous, quiet, stoic in the face of adversity, and responsive to her roles as mother and wife. She epitomizes the feminine. "Hero" is traditionally reserved for masculine behavior: adventure, facing down enemies, taking risk, aggression, independence, and charging in after adversity. The English language allows men to act heroic and exhibit heroism, but such permutations of the language are not available to the heroine (there is no "heroine-ism"). Men cannot be heroines; it is a gender-specific term that only applies to women. Theoretically, however, women can be heroes; the term is the "universal." For women to do so, however, means struggling against gender stereotypes and risking their femininity. To be "universal" is to be masculine.

Historically, the arrival of a "warrior queen" signals incredible excitement, awe, admiration, and enthusiasm beyond what the heroic male can arouse.[15] She provides a focus for what the country will later call its Golden Age. For women, the warrior queen signals that the tradition of independent womanhood is being kept alive for women during dark times.[16] Historian and critic (as well as mystery author) Antonia Fraser argues that women need female heroes even more than men need male heroes because the women's expectations of independence, fortitude, and valor have generally been much lower.[17]

The excitement surrounding the woman warrior is tempered with fear. Men and women have historically been taught that women are "innate" nurturers. Woman's role is to pacify, not excite. As the weaker sex, she needs male protection. Since women are not "naturally" aggressive, the warrior queen becomes an "honorary male" in her society. She fits neither gender category satisfactorily. Her position is suspect and problematic. She is both feared and envied by the men and women of her community. She is remarkable because of her sex, but her sexuality is often openly questioned. The people of her time, as well as later historians, comment about her sexual voraciousness and/or chastity. The anomaly—her "heroism"—requires explanation. Her childhood is examined for evidence that she shunned domestic duties and play.[18] The warrior queen's legend is constructed by dominant modes of interpretation as an aberration. She is made less a role model than a singular exception. However, feminist analyses, such as Antonia Fraser's *The Warrior Queens*, worked to restore the position of the warrior queen as respected and remarkable historical figure.

"Women in novels written by women have a healthy tendency to be heroes rather than heroines." She has charisma, leadership, individuality, and a sense of professionalism. Heroism is not a question of what is done, but how and why it is done, and for whom. The motives, as well as the nature of the action, affect the quality of the idea.[19] The more difficult it becomes to be heroic under the dictates of reality, the more important heroism is for myth and the imagination to provide.[20] The hero of the novel is a hero "of a life process that is imperishable and forever renewing itself, forever contemporary."[21]

The role of the female hero in traditional crime fiction has not been a comfortable one. She was most often viewed as an encumbrance. She did not run fast enough nor hit hard enough to keep up with the male characters. Most parts for women in crime fiction were passive. They could inspire the heroic, but they could not intervene aggressively or heroically. Part of what appears to be an unwritten rule for traditional women characters is that while they can be abducted and locked up by criminals, they are safe from "vulgar" physical assaults such as kicks, punches, and blows to the head.[22] They are allowed the role of the nurturing heroine, but the role of hero is usually reserved for men and their adventures.

One of the basic themes of the mystery novel is the hero's inadequacy to face his fate or situation. There is always unrealized potential in the hero. Stanley Cavell's "dandy" is most illustrative of this point.[23] The individual does not completely fit into existing sociohistorical categories. The reality of the novel is only one possible reality; other possible realities are contained within it. The hero is a subjective individual who becomes an object of experimentation and representation.[24] The women mystery authors use the plasticity of the novel and the novelistic hero to find room for women to experience adventure and heroism. She does not fit stereotypic definitions of "femininity," but neither is she an "honorary male." She experiments with masculine and feminine attributes—she tries them on. The perceptions of the strong woman have changed during the boom in contemporary women's mysteries. In the first Marcia Muller book, *Edwin of the Iron Shoes*, Sharon McCone was not exposed to much hostility or aggression, and she had little sense of herself as self-reliant. By the later books, particularly in *Wolf in the Shadows*, McCone has matured into a confident, capable, well-trained, and skilled private investigator. Sharon McCone and Marcia Muller have both matured and come to respect complexity. The stories in the women's mystery novels chosen here replay the struggles, anger, and sense of accomplishment felt by women as the category of the "woman hero" evolves.

The warrior women of the detective novel separate action from aggression. For example, the woman detective studies aikido, works out at the gym, jogs, and practices at the firing range in order to better defend herself. The woman detective calls attention to the traditional definition of "feminine" as vulnerable and requiring the protection of a man. The are times when the woman detective feels vulnerable or overwhelmed by the violence and hostility she witnesses. Most of these women detectives do have men in their lives. The men, such as Catherine Saylor's boyfriend, Peter Harman, and V. I. Warshawski's neighbor, Mr. Contreras, do not interpret the women's feelings of vulnerability as a sign of weakness. The women, in turn, do not interpret the men's gender as a guarantee of invulnerability. Violence is debilitating for the men, too. The women authors struggle to reevaluate the gender stereotypes of both men and women.

The analysis of heroism in the mystery novels of women has been discussed with relation to the issue of "feminism." Can we then conclude that the mystery novels of women are "feminist"? What would it take for them to be feminist? Is it necessary that they be feminist? Not all of the women mystery writers, or even those writing mysteries with strong female protagonists, think of themselves as feminists or as writing about feminism. When interviewed, several authors balked at any inference that what they were doing was "political," as the "feminist" label might imply. First and foremost, they write popular fiction for a mass audience. Feminist bookstore patrons may expect to read a story where the focus is on the tenets of feminism, but popular fiction customers do not.

I would contend that while they do not preach feminism, many women's mystery novels introduce a multiple of feminist issues. Rosalind Delmar provides a useful model for the basics of what this feminism means: "At the very least a feminist is someone who holds that women suffer discrimination because of their sex, [and] that they have specific needs which remain negated and unsatisfied."[25] Delmar includes in her definition a call for radical change in the social, economic, and political order. I would moderate this to read a call for change that does not need to be radical to satisfy most women. I would also clarify that women suffer discrimination because of gender assumptions made about their sex. Small changes in attitudes and behaviors taken at the everyday level can have profound consequences in the larger social, economic, and political order. The women authors of the mystery embrace their characters as women and illustrate this by highlighting the details of their lives as independent and intelligent woman.

Feminism recognizes that society discriminates on the basis of perceived gender differences and that change is required if women are to have the opportunity to fulfill their diverse needs and desires. Within this objective there are many "feminisms." Women do not have to share the same sense of identity in order to work toward the same goal. Women of color, lesbians, radical feminists, and working-class women have different expectations and experiences. They are united by the object of their concern—society's perceptions of the "appropriate" woman—whether or not they share a particular social analysis.[26]

The complexities and paradoxes within feminism mimic women's paradoxical position in society. Feminism aims for individual freedom by mobilizing sexual solidarity. It acknowledges diversity among women, but depends on women recognizing their unity. Gender consciousness is at the core of feminism, yet it calls for the elimination of prescribed gender roles. Women are the same species as men, but they are biologically different. They are part of the universal, yet the universal is most commonly described according to masculine prerogatives. It is in these paradoxes that the difficulties within feminism emerge. Women are both the same as, and different from, men; women are both the same as, and different from, other women. Gender is a critical distinction made by society, and yet it is not separable from other factors of identity (i.e., race, religion, culture, class, and age).[27] The debates within feminism and between feminisms, as well as between feminists and society, are complicated by these paradoxes. The object of feminism continues to be the critique, and ultimate elimination, of gender mythologies that continue to constrain and dominate women (and men).[28]

Feminist criticism is a symbolic exchange between the critic and the women whom the author writes about and for. When feminists publicize women's private experiences within public texts, they can be collectively explored. Feminist criticism is performative; it goes beyond restating existent ideas and views. It is committed to the future of women and society. The critic presupposes a degree of freedom in the reader and takes this freedom as a goal. The goal of feminist criticism, and of this analysis of women's detective novels, is a process described by feminist critic Tania Modleski as follows:

> First, it reveals the ideological workings of a system in which women, far from being in a position to give the gifts, are the gifts—indispensable intermediaries between men; second, engaging in relationships of reciprocity with other women, works toward the time when the traditionally mute will be given the same access to "the names"—language and speech—that men have enjoyed.[29]

Authors and readers are acknowledged as part of this collective exploration. By publicizing how women react to a society delineated by gender (through the texts and in the publishing industry in which the texts are located), more women become aware of the debate and can participate. Feminism depends on a multiplicity of voices. Each new woman's detective novel and academic critique expands the number of voices participating in the creation of possible women's narratives.

A variety of literary texts can be studied as attempts to redefine or critique the social order. They offer examples of how the culture thinks about itself, articulating and proposing solutions for the problems that shape the moment. A novel's impact on a culture does not necessarily come from how it escapes from the formulaic, but also from how it uses commonly held assumptions. Conventions are a kind of cultural shorthand. Literary texts can offer a blueprint for survival under a specific set of political, economic, social, and/or religious conditions.[30] Marginal to dominant conversation in literature, women's novels take the position of social outcast and witness. Similar to the detective who is marginal to society and therefore able to comment as an observer, women's novels are well suited to comment on dominant culture.

Reading as entertainment and criticism of gender assumptions do not have to be mutually exclusive activities. Reading for pleasure is not a passive and uncritical experience.[31] Unlike academics or critics, everyday readers approach, read, and use literature. They integrate it into their lives.[32] It is a constructive act. To read a mystery, for example, the reader keeps up with the sleuth. Even if the reader is not trying to beat the detective to the solution, the only way the plot and resolution of the book make sense is if the reader keeps mental notes along the way about possible scenarios or solutions. The perception that mysteries are easy to write contributes to how closely they are read. Many readers see themselves as potential authors. Authors often talk of reading a mystery and declaring, "I can do that." Detective novels are often read with an eye to the mechanics of writing (i.e., structure, format, characterization, and plotting). Readers are also critical of how "good" the mystery is and how well the author succeeded (or did not succeed) in telling her story. The critical attention a reader pays to a mystery contributes to the pleasure of the reading. Readers interact with the mystery novel; they find pleasure, sources for argument, avenues of discussion, and fantasy.

It is not necessary to abandon genre fiction when looking for critical or feminist texts. "Good" things can come from "bad" places. Mainstream, profit-driven, conglomerate-owned publishing houses can produce thoughtful genre fiction. Dominant culture cannot absolutely control social definitions. Popular genres can be appropriated for critical feminist interpretations. In his analysis of network television, Todd Gitlin explains how "good" (critical) television shows can make it through the process that typically produces shows aimed at attracting the largest and most lucrative audience for advertisers. Gitlin explains how the television show "Hill Street Blues," for example, revolutionized ideas of television production, storytelling, and the capacity of the television audience for a thoughtful discussion of crime and violence.[33] Trying to be more "realistic" and stand out from other television police dramas, dialogue was created that often overlapped in the police squad room. The camera moved like a person walking through the room rather than as an omnipotent viewer. Well-crafted television shows such as this one can attract large audiences. Television networks and advertisers are not as concerned about a show's content as much as they are about profitability. Similar arguments can be made for the mass market dynamics found in genre fiction. The gatekeepers (i.e., publishers, agents, and editors) do not care so much about what they produce as much about how much money it can generate. Mystery fiction is a lucrative market. Well-crafted and critical mystery fiction can make as much money in the market as more simple or exploitative stories.

Alternative visions of reality can "leak" out from the dominant ideology. "Leaks" produce alternative definitions of cultural artifacts. Countercultural movements examined by social critics, such as the street culture of England analyzed by Dick Hebdige, are shown to use dominant cultural artifacts and reshape their meanings. In the example of the English street culture, makeup, hair color, seams, zippers, and safety pins become methods of individual expression. Makeup, for example, is typically used by women in subtle shades to highlight and enhance their features in order to make themselves more attractive to men. To the British youth, however, makeup was used by men and women in garish tones and in black and whites in order to startle. Zippers, seams, and safety pins were worn outside and all over clothing, and in the case of safety pins, on the body, to draw attention to what is usually hidden. As the alternative culture attracted more adherents, its sense of style was co-opted by dominant society—showing up in advertising, mainstream fashion, and popular culture.[34] Cultural definitions are, to a certain degree, fluid and changeable. What begins as "alternative" is often worked into mainstream society. The "leaks" provide avenues for resistance and the possibilities of change.

Feminist critic Lillian Robinson argues that women can no longer settle for leaks, however. Dominant culture "ha[s] an army of plumbers on call, not to mention the army itself."[35] Women in the mystery genre do not have to rely solely on creating "leaks" in the system. They have pushed the genre and its industry to recognize the legitimacy of the voice. The female protagonists created with independence, strength, creativity, and connectedness are not just the fantasies of the authors. Many women mystery authors have taken these ideals into their own world. Mystery publishing remains concentrated in the hands of profit-oriented corporate conglomerates, but it is being challenged in its publishing practices by women as fearless and smart as their fictional counterparts.

In 1986, Sisters in Crime was created at the Bouchercon Mystery Fan Convention in Baltimore by author Sara Paretsky and a group of women mystery writers she invited to an impromptu breakfast. The idea was to discuss their mutual concerns about the status of women in the mystery field. The women hoped to develop a camaraderie and talk about what they wanted out of the field. The authors believed they were being reviewed in the important newspapers and journals less frequently and their books taken less seriously than those written by men. They also expressed concern over the issue of sadistic violence against women in some mystery novels. From this first meeting, a steering committee was elected in 1987. The bylaws of the group state that the purpose of Sisters in Crime is "to combat discrimination against women in the mystery field, educate publishers and the general public as to inequalities in the treatment of female authors, and raise the level of awareness of their contribution to the field." Ten years later, the over 2,500 members come from a variety of countries, are both men and women, and cover the mystery field (writers, readers, editors, agents, booksellers, and librarians). The organization is open to anyone with a special interest in mystery writing and furthering the purposes of Sisters in Crime.[36]

Author P. M. Carlson characterized the U.S. mystery field of the early 1980s as an affirmative action program for men. Publishers gave men special encouragement to write mysteries. They accepted twice as many men's books for publication as women's. Reviews gave men special treatment. The *New York Times* reviewed five times as many mysteries by men as by women. The primary mystery author organization, Mystery Writers of America, encouraged its male authors. For decades, its Edgar Award for Best Mystery Novel had never gone to an American woman. It was just assumed by those in the mystery field that men's ideas and men's books were more important, interesting, and "universal" than women's.

The first campaign launched by Sisters in Crime (SinC) was the Media Monitoring Project. The impression of the original group of women was that women's mysteries were not being reviewed in the major newspapers and journals proportional to the number of women writing mysteries. Being reviewed in the press has a direct relation to the kind of career an author can expect. The buying decisions of libraries, bookstores, and readers are largely formed by reviews in trade journals and major newspapers, like the *New York Times*. It was not enough for the women authors to complain that they were not being reviewed in fair numbers. The women of SinC were challenging social assumptions and "commonsense" mystery business practices. Most critics and reviewers believed themselves to be gender blind and fair in their representations of the field. A column by mystery critic Robin Winks of the *Boston Globe* suggests how "fair" people can end up being unfair:

> A year or so ago, one of those rare people who actually appears to read every one of these monthly pieces told me that she had been keeping count, and that women writers and women detectives were seriously lacking representation in my reviews. I told her, truthfully, I believe, that I had no idea whether that was so, as I really wasn't particularly conscious of the gender count. This month I found myself thinking about that statement a bit, for as I sit down to write, I discover that the five books I have liked best are all about women detectives, and that I wasn't conscious of the fact until it was time to address the old Hermes.[37]

The women of SinC educated themselves about the problem. They gathered facts: counting numbers of women's mysteries, reviews, and awards. After collecting the data, SinC made their findings public. Author, P. M. Carlson recognizes that SinC was wise to have good, solid information before informing people about the situation. These women would most probably been dismissed as "hysterical" for claiming unfair treatment.[38] SinC's first letter was sent to the *New York Times* and pointed out that in 1985, only 16% of the mysteries reviewed by the *Times* were written by women. Counts of other major publications showed 15% to be the typical figure. However, women write 40% of the mystery novels published. The Media Monitoring Project continues to be a SinC priority, with new members continuing to volunteer to monitor their local newspapers, journals, and magazines. Annual reports are sent to the respective publications. The 1992 *Book Review Monitoring Project Report* showed progress being made. Of the twenty publications monitored, reviews of women's mysteries were up to 30%—a figure much closer to the percentage of mysteries written by women.

The SinC Monitoring Project is illustrative of how this organization has constructed new forms of protest against discrimination based on gender. Rather than choosing between masculine ideals of business and feminine principles of passivity, SinC works to construct new modes of behavior. Being a commercial writer has traditionally been a competitive and solitary career. The author writes her words alone and then faces a publisher with little information about how the publishing process works or how her treatment compares with that of other authors. Many women authors have historically been reluctant to enter into the industry for fear that their words were not interesting or important enough. The women were often not aggressive in business and let others take control of their work. The authors interviewed here, who began writing in the late 1970s and 1980s, commented on their lack of understanding with regard to publishing and their sense of having to tackle it on their own. SinC has made it a priority to expose the workings of the publishing industry and encourage women to take control of their work—from contract negotiations to marketing. The *Sisters in Crime Newsletter* publishes accounts of the deals made by published authors. Members discuss publishing contracts within the newsletter, informing authors and potential authors about clauses to be wary of and rights to which they are entitled. New authors are able to enter into publishing relationships informed and prepared.[39] "Getting ahead" is being redefined to include helping others in the field.

The goal of each SinC publication is to broaden the availability of mysteries, particularly those by women authors, and encourage new voices to enter the genre. SinC's annual *Books-in-Print* is mailed to mystery bookstores, bookstore chains, and libraries to achieve greater visibility for mysteries written by women (and male SinC members) and to provide the necessary references for ordering. Pamphlets published by the organization are often the result of authors volunteering to pass on experiences and information. *Shameless Promotion for Brazen Hussies* is one such pamphlet, which has been very successful. It is an ongoing project that incorporates the suggestions of published authors on book promotions. Another SinC pamphlet that has been successful in helping new authors get information is *So You're Going to Do an Author Signing*. By taking control of their work, the publishing process, and assisting potential authors, SinC members are not dependent on "leaks" in the system. They are creating space for themselves.

Other SinC services and activities include a national clipping service for authors' book reviews, the Outreach to Women of Color Committee, and consulting with publishers on the publication of the Sisters in Crime Classics Books series, which will reprint books written by women whose work received less attention than merited in a time when women's authorship was more likely to be dismissed. The "World's Greatest Mailing List" was put together by one member for her own use but is now part of the services of SinC and continues to grow as other members contribute to it. It includes listings for mystery bookstores, foreign mystery bookstores, bookstore chains, magazines and journals, mystery bookstores, book distributors, wholesalers, newspaper book editors, book critics, and libraries.[40] Authors use the list to distribute materials for newly published books and are therefore able to reach the largest audience possible. The printing company housing the list can also be hired by the author to develop promotional materials, especially when these are not provided by the author's publishing company.

In addition to pamphlets and lists, SinC has constructed a Speakers' Bureau to assist libraries, organizations, and bookstores looking to reach authors for signings and discussions of their work. SinC attends fan, library, and publisher conventions in order to acquaint buyers and fans of the genre about the wide variety of women's mysteries available. Through SinC, individual authors are able to gain access to trade journals, such as *Publishers Weekly*, in order to advertise their books. SinC also assists in several studies looking at the issue of violence against women—one of the concerns voiced by the original group of women who came together to start Sisters in Crime. The studies look into the portrayal of women in fiction and violence experienced by women in Western society. The group does not believe in censorship, but does want to make readers aware of alternative representations of women. Information about SinC members and their work has been added to a national archive as part of the National Women's History Project. SinC endorses the literacy campaign of the Rutgers Convocation for Literacy, sponsored by St. John Institute of Arts and Letters, Inc. The campaign focuses on what authors can do to promote literacy and includes them lending their publicity to the cause as well as their time to libraries and classrooms.[41] Regional chapters sponsor writer conferences and retreats. They maintain contact with members and meet to discuss books, authors, and the publishing industry. The recent addition of an electronic chapter capitalizes on new technologies and brings more members together via e-mail and on-line discussion groups.

The work of SinC is primarily conducted on a volunteer basis. Past SinC President Margaret Maron comments: "Sisters in Crime runs on the volunteer energy of busy women. So far, we have no paid help. Yet over and over again, I've been struck by how often a vacuum is perceived in Oklahoma or California just days before someone in Georgia or New York volunteers on her own to fill it."[42] The image of the solitary woman writer—a woman with a "room of her own" or the "madwoman in the attic," scribbling away—is being challenged by the image of the woman as member of a community. In just a few years, Sisters in Crime has grown quickly in size and influence by working to combine responsibility with professionalism.

Authors, agents, and editors whom I interviewed credit Sisters in Crime with being an important agent in the changing environment of mystery writing. Many editors, for example, belong to SinC and see it as a necessary component of their job because of the contacts, information, and resources it distributes. Two aspects of the organization were mentioned most often by those I spoke with about the mystery industry: the networking opportunities afforded by SinC and attention the group pays to the importance of press reviews. Many of the women writing in the late 1970s and 1980s did not know any published writers or mysteries by women when they began. The women authors found Mystery Writers of America to resemble an "old boys group." Few awards or convention discussion panels included women or topics of interest to women.[43] SinC creates a community in which women can write.[44] Many in the mystery publishing industry have been impressed by SinC's high level of organization. New and published authors are drawn to the group for its attention to responsibility to its members. Publishers have begun to put more money and effort into acquiring women's mysteries and promoting them, as a result, partly, of SinC's priority on not letting their members' books be ignored.[45]

The degree to which Sisters in Crime has been successful in its challenge to traditional social gender definitions can also be gauged by the degree of criticism and anger the group has elicited from traditional masculine-oriented media, publishing personnel, and authors. SinC threatens dominant cultural definitions of gender and business. The struggle is over meaning and what is "appropriate" for women and the mystery genre—who has the power to control meaning. The dominant interpretive community is fighting to maintain its control over the status quo. The decline in the market for hard-boiled, aggressive, misogynist male detective in an environment more supportive of women and the precepts of Sisters in Crime is one example of the shift in control. The men who write these mysteries tend to characterize SinC as "political" and "antimale." In a recent submission to *Publisher's Weekly*, author Carolyn G. Hart tried to clarify the position of SinC. She stated that Sisters in Crime is not a union or publisher. It does not give awards. Its function is educational rather than political. The group is open to anyone who enjoys mysteries by women. Anytime Sisters in Crime can attract a new reader to books by its members, it attracts attention to all mysteries. The events sponsored by SinC encourage communication and shared knowledge. The regional chapters engage in activities geared to helping their communities. The group does not favor censorship or pornography but recognizes that opinions differ on what should be done about these issues.[46] Just as in the mysteries created by many women authors, attention to the priorities and concerns of women are shown to be of benefit to society as a whole. Society is put in danger when any one group is consistently left out, ignored, and/or discredited.

The repeated theme in this discussion of women and the mystery novel is "community." Sisters in Crime was created by women in the mystery industry who wanted to create a sense of community since it was noticeably lacking in their chosen profession. The characters and stories they develop focus on creating and maintaining community, as well as the dangers of dismissing the need for connection and responsibility. The clues, and ultimately the solution, to the murder are discovered in the dynamics of community. "Restoring order" means strengthening the ties between members of the community or, where necessary, creating a more equitable community where one did not exist. Through the mystery novel, readers and authors, too, are brought together as a community. The isolated act of reading actually joins many readers across physical boundaries and gives them a sense of belonging and connection. Women's mystery novels are written in the vernacular language of the audience, which it does not require professional interpretation by literary critics or university professors to comprehend. By using the common language, these mystery novels are able to represent the community to its readers. Events in the lives of the readers are representable: society represents itself to itself.[47]

The reality of women's mystery novels is of a secular and imagined world that is visibly rooted in the everyday—the everyday lives of women. Many women readers of women's mystery novels imagine themselves as members of this community through the novels' attention to the arbitrariness of the sign. Language is not determined; masculine language can be reworked to reflect the experiences of women. Language reflects relations of power, not a sacred order. The mysteries of the women writers discussed here also focus on the typical experiences of women in Western society. The woman reader is an integral part of the novelistic experience. The reader exists in the same world as her contemporary fictional woman hero. These women detectives live in cities that look like the readers' homes. She faces the same kinds of daily obstacles (traffic, shopping, work) that readers do. These similarities transcend the actual locations and times of the novels. Historical or foreign mystery novels, too, create this kind of connection with the reader. The fictional woman detective can even read the same detective novels as the reader. The fictional detectives often comment on what detective novels they are reading or how one of the "fictional" detectives would handle their situation. The community created through women's fictional detectives is made up of authors, readers, and characters with deep attachments to each other, even when not aware of the others' existence. Men, too, can become members of this group. They can learn the language of the community, and they have done so as members of Sisters in Crime and fans of women-authored mysteries. The success of women's mystery novels comes from women being able to imagine themselves as part of a community of shared interests, language, perceptions, and experiences.

Women have enjoyed and written mystery novels since the nineteenth century, but through the programs of organizations like Sisters in Crime, specialized mystery bookstores, fan conventions, and increased media and publisher attention, they are now able to recognize themselves in the story of the literary hero. Women's mysteries engage the politics of gender. The woman detective critiques the dominant masculine social constructions and illustrates what it looks like when women assume they can live their lives as independent, intelligent, and capable people. She accepts the fact that if she comes into peril, she has to get herself out of it. This is a given, not an issue to work out.[48] The mystery novels of women take the woman mystery reader to a place of adventure, where women are recognized as heroic. In some cases, this adventure is as close as the everyday. Author Julie Smith's fictional female detective, lawyer Rebecca Schwartz, characterizes the situation of today's contemporary woman detective hero as follows:

> Why hadn't I asked about it that morning? It was Rob's interview, not mine—that was why. But now Today's Action Woman was going to get some answers. Maybe I could even say, "Look, Clayton, baby, I want some answers and I want 'em now." I could Bogart the whole phrase, maybe, twisting up the old lip, and I could stand all casual with one hand in my pocket.
>
> But then I saw what was wrong with that picture; I'd turned Today's Action Woman into a man. I looked lousy in a suit and tie. I pulled into the hotel's porte cochere, reminding myself to read more Sharon McCone mysteries so I could get my fantasies right.[49]

## NOTES

1. "What's Happened to Heroes Is a Crime," *New York Times Book Review*, 14 October 1990, 1.

2. Ken Follett, "Why Women Don't Write Spy Novels," in *Murderess Ink: The Better Half of the Mystery*, ed. Dilys Winn (New York: Workman Publishing, 1979), 39.

3. Jean Swanson and Dean James, *By a Woman's Hand* (New York: Berkley Books, 1994), 81.

4. Patricia Cornwell, *Cause of Death* (New York: G. P. Putnam's Sons, 1996).

5. Amanda Cross, *An Imperfect Spy* (New York: Ballantine Books, 1995).

6. Cross, 25.

7. Marcia Muller, author book signing, Poisoned Pen Mystery Book Store, Phoenix, Arizona, 10 July 1997.

8. Kathleen Gregory Klein, *The Woman Detective: Gender and Genre* (Urbana: University of Illinois Press, 1988), 229.

9. Rosalind Coward and Linda Semple, "Tracking Down the Past: Women and Detective Fiction," in *From My Guy to Sci-Fi: Genre and Women's Writing in the Postmodern World*, ed. Helen Carr (London: Pandora, 1989), 40.

10. Jane P. Tompkins, "Sentimental Power: *Uncle Tom's Cabin* and the Politics of Literary History," in *The New Feminist Criticism: Essays on Women, Literature and Theory*, ed. Elaine Showalter (New York: Pantheon Books, 1985), 82.

11. Carolyn G. Heilbrun, "The Women of Mystery," *Ms.* 1.5 (March/April 1991): 63.

12. Barbara Neely, telephone interview, 24 January 1994.

13. Sara Paretsky, introduction to *A Woman's Eye*, ed. Sara Paretsky (New York: Dell Publishing, 1991), vii–viii.

14. Mary S. Wagoner, *Agatha Christie* (Boston: Twayne Publishers, 1986), 73.

15. Antonia Fraser, *The Warrior Queens* (New York: Alfred A. Knopf, 1986), 6.

16. Fraser, 9–10.

17. Fraser, 335.

18. Fraser, 6–12.

19. Jenni Calder, *Heroes: From Byron to Guevara* (London: Hamish Hamilton, 1977), 195–99.

20. Calder, xii.

21. M. M. Bakhtin, *The Dialogic Imagination*, ed. Michael Holquist (Austin: University of Texas Press, 1987), 36.

22. Colin Watson, *Snobbery with Violence* (New York: St. Martin's Press, 1971), 151.

23. Stanley Cavell, *The World Viewed* (Cambridge: Harvard University Press, 1979), 55–60.

24. Bakhtin, 36–37.

25. Rosalind Delmar, "What Is Feminism?" in *What Is Feminism?* ed. Juliet Mitchell and Ann Oakley (Oxford, U.K.: Basil Blackwell, 1986), 8.

26. Delmar, 8–12.

27. Nancy F. Cott, "Feminist Theory and Feminist Movements: The Past before Us," in *What Is Feminism?* ed. Juliet Mitchell and Ann Oakley (Oxford, U.K.: Basil Blackwell, 1986), 49.

28. Judith Stacey, "Are Feminists Afraid to Leave Home? The Challenge of Conservative Pro-Family Feminism," in *What Is Feminism?* ed. Juliet Mitchell and Ann Oakley (Oxford, U.K.: Basil Blackwell, 1986), 242.

29. Tania Modleski, *Feminism without Women: Culture and Criticism in a "Postfeminist" Age* (New York: Routledge, 1991), 43–48.

30. Jane Tompkins, "Introduction: The Cultural Work of American Fiction," in *Sensational Designs: The Cultural Work of American Fiction, 1790–1860*, ed. Jane P. Tompkins (New York: Oxford University Press, 1985), xi–xvii.

31. William W. Stowe, "Critical Investigations: Conventions and Ideology in Detective Fiction," *Texas Studies in Literature and Language* 31.4 (1989): 589.

32. Elizabeth Long, "Women, Reading, and Cultural Authority: Some Implications of the Audience Perspective in Cultural Studies," *American Quarterly* 38.4 (1986): 609.

33. Todd Gitlin, *Inside Prime Time* (New York: Pantheon Books, 1985); see in particular the chapters "Hill Street Blues" (273–324) and "Epilogue" (325–35).

34. Dick Hebdige, *Subculture: The Meaning of Style* (London: Routledge, 1988).

35. Lillian S. Robinson, "Killing Patriarchy: Charlotte Perkins Gilman, the Murder Mystery, and Post-Feminist Propaganda," *Tulsa Studies in Women's Literature* 10.2 (1991): 283.

36. "An Introduction to Sisters in Crime," Sisters in Crime brochure. n.d.

37. Carolen Collins, "Media Committee: Bias in Book Reviews?" *Sisters in Crime Newsletter* 2.2 (1990): 2.

38. P. M. Carlson, telephone interview, 5 November 1993.

39. An area of current interest and concern is electronic rights and how future technologies should be handled by authors, agents, and publishers. Advice has included what sections of the contract should be crossed out and rewritten before signing.

40. Carolyn G. Hart, "A Plea from the Publicity Chairman," *Sisters in Crime Newsletter* 2.2 (1990): 7.

41. "Publicity for Posterity," *Sisters in Crime Newsletter* 3.1 (1991): 1; "Rutgers Convocation for Literacy," *Sisters in Crime Newsletter* 3.1 (1991): 4.

42. Margaret Maron, "State of the Union," *Sisters in Crime Newsletter* 2.2 (1990): 1.

43. Maxine O'Callaghan, telephone interview, 24 January 1994.

44. Marcia Muller, telephone interview, 27 January 1994.

45. Sara Ann Freed, telephone interview, 25 February 1994.

46. Carolyn G. Hart, "Submission to Publisher's Weekly," *Sisters in Crime Newsletter* 6.1 (1992): 5; P. M. Carlson, "Sisters in Crime: Educational, Not Political," Sisters in Crime press release.

47. The ideas of community and language are suggested in the works of Benedict Anderson, *Imagined Communities* (London: Verso, 1983) and M. M. Bakhtin's, *The Dialogic Imagination*.

48. Judith Greber, telephone interview, 28 January 1994.

49. Julie Smith, *The Sourdough Wars* (New York: Ivy Books, 1992), 125.

# Bibliography


"Adult Trade Books Set the Pace in '92." *Standard & Poor's Industry Surveys* 161.6 (1993): M35.

Anderson, Benedict. *Imagined Communities*. London: Verso, 1983.

Anthony, Carolyn. "Crime Marches On." *Publishers Weekly* 237.15 (13 April 1990): 24–29.

Baker, John F. "Reinventing the Book Business." *Publishers Weekly* (14 March 1994): 36–40.

Bakhtin, M. M. *The Dialogic Imagination*. Ed. Michael Holquist. Austin: University of Texas Press, 1987.

Beck, K. K. Telephone interview, 3 November 1993.

Berry, John. "On Commerce and Conscience: A Conversation with Richard Snyder." *Library Journal*, 15 February 1990, 148–152.

Breen, Jon L. Introduction to *The Fine Art of Murder: The Mystery Reader's Indispensable Companion*. Ed. Ed Gorman, Martin H. Greenberg, Larry Segriff, and Jon L. Breen. New York: Carroll & Graf Publishers, 1993, 3–6.

—. "Introduction: Police Procedurals." In *The Fine Art of Murder: The Mystery Reader's Indispensable Companion*. Ed. Ed Gorman, Martin H. Greenberg, Larry Segriff, and Jon L. Breen. New York: Carroll & Graf Publishers, 1993, 211–213.

—. "Introduction: Private Eye Mysteries." In *The Fine Art of Murder: The Mystery Reader's Indispensable Companion*. Ed. Ed Gorman, Martin H. Greenberg, Larry Segriff, and Jon L. Breen. New York: Carroll & Graf Publishers, 1993, 153–155.

Budd, Elaine. *13 Mistresses of Murder*. New York: Ungar Publishing Company, 1986.

Calder, Jenni. *Heroes: From Byron to Guevara*. London: Hamish Hamilton, 1977.

Carlson, P. M. *Audition for Murder*. New York: Avon, 1985.

—. *Bad Blood*. New York: Doubleday, 1991.

—. *Murder in the Dog Days*. New York: Bantam Books, 1991.

—. *Murder Is Academic*. New York: Avon, 1985.

—. *Murder Is Pathological*. New York: Avon, 1986.

—. *Murder Misread*. New York: Bantam Books, 1991.

—. *Murder Unrenovated.* New York: Bantam Books, 1990.
—. *Rehearsal for Murder.* New York: Bantam Books, 1988.
—. "Sisters in Crime: Educational, Not Political." Sisters in Crime press release. n.d.
—. Telephone interview, 5 November 1993.
Carr, Helen. "Introduction: Genre and Women's Writing in the Postmodern World." In *From My Guy to Sci-Fi: Genre and Women's Writing in the Postmodern World.* Ed. Helen Carr. London: Pandora, 1989, 3–14.
Cavell, Stanley. *The World Viewed.* Cambridge: Harvard University Press, 1979.
Cavin, Ruth. Telephone interview, 31 January 1994.
"Chain Sales Rise 18% in Year; Market Share Increases." *Publishers Weekly* (11 April 1994): 10.
Champlin, Charles. "Women Sleuths and the Rise of the Whydunit." *Los Angeles Times Book Review*, 29 October 1989, 15.
Chapman, Sally. *Love Bytes.* New York: St. Martin's Press, 1994.
Charney, Hanna. *The Detective Novel of Manners: Hedonism, Morality, and the Life of Reason.* London: Fairleigh Dickinson University Press/Associated University Press, 1981.
Chase, Elaine Raco. "Waldenbooks to Promote SinC Authors." *Sisters in Crime Newsletter* 5.3 (1993): 6.
Chastain, Thomas. "The Case for the Private Eye." In *The Murder Mystique: Crime Writers on Their Art.* Ed. Lucy Freeman. New York: Frederick Ungar Publishing Co., 1982, 27–32.
Collingwood, Donna, Hal Blythe, and Charlie Sweet. "Susanne Kirk of Charles Scribner's Sons." In *Mystery Writer's Marketplace and Sourcebook.* Ed. Donna Collingwood. Cincinnati, OH: Writer's Digest Books, 1993, 165–167.
Collins, Carolen. "Media Committee: Bias in Book Reviews." *Sisters in Crime Newsletter* 2.2 (1990): 2.
Cornwell, Patricia. *All That Remains.* New York: Avon Books, 1993.
—. *The Body Farm.* New York: Charles Scribner's Sons, 1994.
—. *Body of Evidence.* New York: Avon Books, 1992.
—. *Cause of Death.* New York: G.P. Putnam's Sons, 1996.
—. *Cruel and Unusual.* New York: Charles Scribner's Sons, 1993.
—. *From Potter's Field.* New York: Charles Scribner's Sons, 1995.
—. *Postmortem.* New York: Avon Books, 1991.
Cott, Nancy F. "Feminist Theory and Feminist Movements: The Past before Us." In *What is Feminism?* Ed. Juliet Mitchell and Ann Oakley. Oxford, U.K.: Basil Blackwell, 1986, 49–62.
Coward, Rosalind, and Linda Semple. "Tracking Down the Past: Women and Detective Fiction." In *From My Guy to Sci-Fi: Genre and Women's Writing in the Postmodern World.* Ed. Helen Carr. London: Pandora, 1989, 39–57.
Craig, Patricia, and Mary Cadogan. *The Lady Investigates: Women Detectives and Spies in Fiction.* London: Victor Gollancz, 1981.
Cranny-Francis, Anne. *Feminist Fiction: Feminist Uses of Generic Fiction.* New York: St. Martin's Press, 1990.
Crawford, Mary, and Roger Chaffin. "The Reader's Construction of Meaning: Cognitive Research on Gender and Comprehension." In *Gender and Reading: Essays on Readers, Texts, and Contexts.* Ed. Elizabeth A. Flynn and Patrocinio P. Schweickart. Baltimore, MD: The Johns Hopkins University Press, 1992, 3–30.
Cross, Amanda. *The Collected Stories.* New York: Ballantine Books, 1997.
—. *Death in a Tenured Position.* New York: Ballantine Books, 1988.

—. *An Imperfect Spy*. New York: Ballantine Books, 1995.
—. *In the Last Analysis*. New York: Avon, 1966.
—. *The James Joyce Murder*. New York: Ballantine Books, 1982.
—. *No Word from Winifred*. New York: Ballantine Books, 1990.
—. *The Players Come Again*. New York: Ballantine Books, 1991.
—. *Poetic Justice*. New York: Avon, 1979.
—. *The Puzzled Heart*. New York: Ballantine Books, 1998.
—. *The Question of Max*. New York: Ballantine Books, 1984.
—. *Sweet Death, Kind Death*. New York: Ballantine Books, 1990.
—. *The Theban Mysteries*. New York: Avon Books, 1979.
—. *A Trap for Fools*. New York: Ballantine Books, 1990.
Davidson, Diane Mott. Telephone interview, 11 March 1994.
Dellon, Hope. Telephone interview, 24 February 1994.
Delmar, Rosalind. "What Is Feminism?" In *What is Feminism?* Ed. Juliet Mitchell and Ann Oakley. Oxford, U.K.: Basil Blackwell, 1986, 8–33.
"The Diseconomies of Scale." *Economist*, 7 April 1990, 25–28.
Dunlap, Susan. *As a Favor*. New York: Dell Publishing, 1984.
—. *Death and Taxes*. New York: Dell Publishing, 1992.
—. *Diamond in the Buff*. New York: Dell Publishing, 1991.
—. *A Dinner to Die For*. New York: Dell Publishing, 1990.
—. *Karma*. New York: Dell Publishing, 1991.
—. *Not Exactly a Brahmin*. New York: Dell Publishing, 1991.
—. *Sudden Exposure*. New York: Delacorte Publishing, 1996.
—. Telephone interview, 11 November 1993.
—. *Time Expired*. New York: Delacorte Press, 1993.
—. *Too Close to the Edge*. New York: Dell Publishing, 1989.
Fetterly, Judith. "Reading about Reading: 'A Jury of Her Peers,' 'The Murders in the Rue Morgue,' and 'The Yellow Wallpaper.'" In *Gender and Reading: Essays on Readers, Texts, and Contexts*. Ed. Elizabeth A. Flynn and Patrocinio P. Schweickart. Baltimore, MD: Johns Hopkins University Press, 1992, 147–164.
—. *The Resisting Reader: A Feminist Approach to American Fiction*. Bloomington: Indiana University Press, 1978.
Follett, Ken. "Why Women Don't Write Spy Novels." In *Murderess Ink: The Better Half of the Mystery*. Ed. Dilys Winn. New York: Workman Publishing, 1979, 39.
Fraser, Antonia. *The Warrior Queens*. New York: Alfred A. Knopf, 1986.
Freed, Sara Ann. Telephone interview, 25 February 1994.
Gamman, Lorraine. "Watching the Detectives: The Enigma of the Female Gaze." In *The Female Gaze*. Ed. Lorraine Gamman and Margaret Marshment. London: Women's Press, 1988, 8–26.
Gee, Robin. "Kate Miciak of Bantam Doubleday Dell." In *Mystery Writer's Marketplace and Sourcebook*. Ed. Donna Collingwood. Cincinnati, OH: Writer's Digest Books, 1993, 118–120.
—. "Q&A with Marcia Muller." In *Mystery Writer's Marketplace and Sourcebook*. Ed. Donna Collingwood. Cincinnati, OH: Writer's Digest Books, 1993, 118–120.
Gibson, Edie. "The Sisterhood of Sleuths," *Publishers Weekly* 235.18 (5 May 1989): 37–39.
Gilbert, Thomas. *How to Enjoy Detective Fiction*. London: Rockliff, 1947.
Gilligan, Carol. *In a Different Voice*. Cambridge: Harvard University Press, 1982.
Gitlin, Todd. *Inside Prime Time*. New York: Pantheon Books, 1985.
Grafton, Sue. *"A" Is for Alibi*. New York: Bantam Books, 1987.

—. *"B" Is for Burglar*. New York: Bantam Books, 1986.
—. *"C" Is for Corpse*. New York: Bantam Books, 1988.
—. *"D" Is for Deadbeat*. New York: Bantam Books, 1988.
—. *"E" Is for Evidence*. New York: Bantam Books, 1989.
—. *"F" Is for Fugitive*. New York: Bantam Books, 1990.
—. *"G" Is for Gumshoe*. New York: Fawcett Crest, 1991.
—. *"H" Is for Homicide*. New York: Fawcett Crest, 1992.
—. *"I" Is for Innocent*. New York: Fawcett Crest, 1993.
—. *"J" Is for Judgment*. New York: Henry Holt and Company, 1993.
—. *"K" Is for Killer*. New York: Henry Holt and Company, 1994.
—. *"L" Is for Lawless*. New York: Henry Holt and Company, 1995.
—. *"M" Is for Malice*. New York: Henry Holt and Company, 1996.
Grant, Linda. *Blind Trust*. New York: Ivy Books, 1991.
—. *Lethal Genes*. New York: Scribner, 1996.
—. *Love nor Money*. New York: Charles Scribner's Sons, 1991.
—. *Random Access Murder*. New York: Avon Books, 1988.
—. Telephone interview, 2 February 1994.
—. *A Woman's Place*. New York: Charles Scribner's Sons, 1994.
Grape, Jan. "The Care and Feeding of a Mystery Bookstore." In *The Fine Art of Murder: The Mystery Reader's Indispensable Companion*. Ed. Ed Gorman, Martin H. Greenberg, Larry Segriff, and Jon L. Breen. New York: Carroll & Graf Publishers, 1993, 377–379.
Greber, Judith. Telephone interview, 28 January 1994.
Grella, George. "The Hard-Boiled Detective Novel." In *Detective Fiction: A Collection of Critical Essays*. Ed. Robin W. Winks. Woodstock, VT: Foul Play Press, 1988, 103–120.
Hammett, Dashiell. *The Maltese Falcon*. New York: Vintage Books, 1989.
Harper, Ralph. *The World of the Thriller*. Cleveland, OH: Press of Case Western Reserve University, 1969.
Hart, Carolyn G. "A Plea from the Publicity Chairman." *Sisters in Crime Newsletter* 2.2 (1990): 7.
—. "Submission to Publisher's Weekly." *Sisters in Crime Newsletter* 6.1 (1992): 5.
—. "Why Cozies?" In *The Fine Art of Murder: The Mystery Reader's Indispensable Companion*. Ed. Ed Gorman, Martin H. Greenberg, Larry Segriff, and Jon L. Breen. New York: Carroll & Graf Publishers, 1993, 71–73.
Hart, Ellen. *Hallowed Murder*. New York: Ballantine Books, 1993.
—. *A Killing Cure*. Seattle, WA: Seal Press, 1993.
—. *Stage Fright*. Seattle, WA: Seal Press, 1992.
—. Telephone interview, 20 December 1993.
—. *Vital Lies*. Seattle, WA: Seal Press, 1991.
Hart, James D. *The Popular Book: A History of America's Literary Taste*. New York: Oxford University Press, 1950.
Hawkes, Ellen. "G Is for Grafton." *Los Angeles Times Magazine*, 18 February 1990, 20–25.
Haycraft, Howard. *Murder for Pleasure: The Life and Times of the Detective Story*. New York: D. Appleton-Century Co., 1941.
Hebdige, Dick. *Subculture: The Meaning of Style*. London, U.K.: Routledge, 1988.
Heffron, Jack. "Sara Ann Freed of Mysterious Press." In *Mystery Writer's Marketplace and Sourcebook*. Ed. Donna Collingwood. Cincinnati, OH: Writer's Digest Books, 1993, 145–148.

Heilbrun, Carolyn G. *Hamlet's Mother and Other Women.* New York: Columbia University Press, 1990.

—. *Reinventing Womanhood.* New York: W.W. Norton & Company, 1979.

—. *Toward a Recognition of Androgyny.* New York: W.W. Norton & Company, 1982.

—. "Women, Men, Theories, and Literature." In *The Impact of Feminist Research in the Academy.* Ed. Christie Farnham. Bloomington: Indiana University Press, 1987, 217–225.

—. "The Women of Mystery." *Ms.* 1.5 (March/April 1991): 62–64.

Heilbrun, Carolyn G., and Margaret R. Higonnet. Introduction to *The Representation of Women in Fiction: Selected Papers from the English Institute, 1981.* Ed. Carolyn G. Heilbrun and Margaret R. Higonnet. Baltimore, MD: Johns Hopkins University Press, 1983.

Herbert, Rosemary. "Aiming Higher." *Publishers Weekly* 237.15 (13 April 1990): 30–32.

—. "Mystery Books Today: The Evidence Points to a Rise in Crime." *Publishers Weekly* 234.2 (8 July 1988): 17–21.

Herman, Linda, and Beth Stiel. *Corpus Delicti of Mystery Fiction: A Guide to the Body of the Case.* Metuchen, NY: Scarecrow Press, 1974.

Hess, Joan. *Madness in Maggody.* New York: Onyx, 1992.

—. *The Maggody Militia.* New York: Dutton, 1997.

—. *Maggody in Manhattan.* New York: Onyx, 1993.

—. *Malice in Maggody.* New York: Onyx, 1991.

—. *Martians in Maggody.* New York: Dutton, 1994.

—. *Miracles in Maggody.* New York: Dutton, 1995.

—. *Mischief in Maggody.* New York: Onyx, 1991.

—. *Mortal Remains in Maggody.* New York: Onyx, 1992.

—. *Much Ado in Maggody.* New York: Onyx, 1991.

—. *O Little Town of Maggody.* New York: Dutton, 1993.

—. Telephone interview, 20 December 1993.

Hoffert, Barbara. "Getting Published: A Report from the Front." *Library Journal,* 15 February 1990, 153–156.

—. "St. Martin's: A Genius for Genre." *Library Journal,* 1 September 1993: 140.

"How Publishers Turn a Profit." *Standard & Poor's Industry Surveys* 161.6 (1993): M36–M37.

"An Introduction to Sisters in Crime." Sisters in Crime brochure. n.d.

Jacobus, Mary. "The Difference of View." In *Women Writing and Women Writing about Women.* Ed. Mary Jacobus. New York: Barnes & Noble Books, 1979, 10–21.

Keusch, Lyssa. Telephone interview, 1 March 1994.

Klein, Kathleen Gregory. *The Woman Detective: Gender and Genre.* Urbana: University of Illinois Press, 1988.

Kolodny, Annette. "Dancing through the Minefield: Some Observations on the Theory, Practice, and Politics of a Feminist Literary Criticism." In *The New Feminist Criticism: Essays on Women, Literature and Theory.* Ed. Elaine Showalter. New York: Pantheon Books, 1985, 144–167.

Kraus, Susan J. "Paretsky Spills the Beans." *New Directions for Women* 20.1 (January/February 1991): 16.

Kristeva, Julia. "Word, Dialogue and Novel." In *The Kristeva Reader.* Ed. Toril Moi. New York: Columbia University Press, 1986, 34–61.

"Ladies' Choice." Narrated by Betsy Aaron. Sunday Morning. New York: CBS, 29 March 1992.

"Library Market Is Crucial to Book Industry." *Standard & Poor's Industry Surveys* 160.7 (1662): M35.

Long, Elizabeth. *The American Dream and the Popular Novel.* Boston: Routledge & Kegan Paul, 1985.

—. "Women, Reading, and Cultural Authority: Some Implications of the Audience Perspective in Cultural Studies." *American Quarterly* 38.4 (1986): 591–612.

Lyall, Sarah. "After the Sale of Macmillan, Fears of Concentrated Power." *New York Times*, 15 November 1993, D10.

Mandel, Ernest. *Delightful Murder: A Social History of the Crime Story.* London: Pluto Press, 1984.

Mann, Jessica. *Deadlier than the Male: An Investigation into Feminine Crime Writing.* London: David & Charles, 1981.

Marchino, Lois A. "The Female Sleuth in Academe." *Journal of Popular Culture* 23.9 (Winter 1989): 89–100.

Maron, Margaret. *Baby Doll Games.* New York: Bantam Books, 1992.

—. *Corpus Christmas.* New York: Bantam Books, 1992.

—. *Death in Blue Folders.* New York: Bantam Books, 1992.

—. *Death of a Butterfly.* New York: Bantam Books, 1991.

—. *Fugitive Colors.* New York: Mysterious Press, 1995.

—. *Killer Market.* New York: Mysterious Press, 1997.

—. *One Coffee With.* New York: Mysterious Press, 1995.

—. *Past Imperfect.* New York: Bantam Books, 1992.

—. *The Right Jack.* New York: Bantam Books, 1992.

—. "State of the Union." *Sisters in Crime Newsletter* 2.2 (1990): 1.

Marshment, Margaret. "Substantial Women." In *The Female Gaze.* Ed. Lorraine Gamman and Margaret Marshment. London: Women's Press, 1988, 27–40.

Martin, Richard. *Ink in Her Blood: The Life and Times of Margery Allingham.* Ann Arbor, MI: UMI Research Press, 1988.

Mason, Bobby Ann. *The Girl Sleuth: A Feminist Guide.* New York: Feminist Press, 1975.

Miller, Lauri. "Joe Blades of Ballantine Books." *Mystery Writer's Marketplace and Sourcebook.* Ed. Donna Collingwood. Cincinnati, OH: Writer's Digest Books, 1993, 114–16.

Miller, Nancy. *The Heroine's Text: Readings in the French and English Novel, 1722–1782.* New York: Columbia University Press, 1980.

Millhiser, Marlys. "Mystery Writing as a Second Career." Panel discussion, American Library Association (ALA) Conference, Sisters in Crime ALA Breakfast, Doral Hotel, Miami, Florida, 26 June 1994.

Milliot, Jim. "New Alliances for New Media." *Publishers Weekly* (3 January 1994): 51–52.

Modleski, Tania. *Feminism without Women: Culture and Criticism in a "Postfeminist" Age.* New York: Routledge, 1991.

—. *Loving with a Vengeance: Mass-Produced Fantasies for Women.* New York: Routledge, 1985.

Most, Glenn W., and William W. Stowe, eds. *The Poetics of Murder: Detective Fiction and Literary Theory.* San Diego, CA: Harcourt Brace Jovanovich, Publishers, 1983.

Muller, Marcia. *Ask the Cards a Question.* New York: Mysterious Press, 1990.

—. Author book signing. Poisoned Pen Mystery Book Store, Phoenix, Arizona, 10 July 1997.
—. *The Broken Promise Land.* New York: Mysterious Press, 1996.
—. *The Cheshire Cat's Eye.* New York: Mysterious Press, 1990.
—. *Edwin of the Iron Shoes.* New York: Mysterious Press, 1990.
—. *Eye of the Storm.* New York: Mysterious Press, 1989.
—. *Games to Keep the Dark Away.* New York: Mysterious Press, 1990.
—. "In the Tradition of . . . Herself." In *The Fine Art of Murder: The Mystery Reader's Indispensable Companion.* Ed. Ed Gorman, Martin H. Greenberg, Larry Segriff, and Jon L. Breen. New York: Carroll & Graf Publishers, 1993, 156–157.
—. *Leave a Message for Willie.* New York: Mysterious Press, 1990.
—. *Pennies on a Dead Woman's Eyes.* New York: Charles Scribner's Sons, 1992.
—. *The Shape of Dread.* New York: Mysterious Press, 1989.
—. Telephone interview, 27 January 1994.
—. *There's Nothing to Be Afraid Of.* New York: Mysterious Press, 1990.
—. *There's Something in a Sunday.* New York: Mysterious Press, 1993.
—. *Till the Butchers Cut Him Down.* New York: Mysterious Press, 1994.
—. *Trophies and Dead Things.* New York: Mysterious Press, 1991.
—. *Where Echoes Live.* New York: Mysterious Press, 1992.
—. *A Wild and Lonely Place.* New York: Mysterious Press, 1995.
—. *Wolf in the Shadows.* New York: Mysterious Press, 1993.
"Near-term Sales Outlook Bright." *Standard & Poor's Industry Surveys* 162.19 (1994): M24–M31.
Neely, Barbara. *Blanche Among the Talented Tenth.* New York: Penguin Books, 1995.
—. *Blanche on the Lam.* New York: Penguin Books, 1993.
—. Telephone interview, 24 January 1994.
Nichols, Victoria, and Susan Thompson. *Silk Stalkings: When Women Write of Murder.* Berkeley, CA: Black Lizard Books, 1988.
O'Callaghan, Maxine. Telephone interview, 24 January 1994.
Paretsky, Sara. *Bitter Medicine.* New York: Ballantine Books, 1989.
—. *Blood Shot.* New York: Dell Publishing, 1989.
—. *Burn Marks.* New York: Dell Publishing, 1991.
—. *Deadlock.* New York: Ballantine Books, 1986.
—. *Guardian Angel.* New York: Dell Publishing, 1993.
—. *Indemnity Only.* New York: Dell Publishing, 1991.
—. Introduction to *A Woman's Eye.* Ed. Sara Paretsky. New York: Dell Publishing, 1991, vii–xiv.
—. *Killing Orders.* New York: Ballantine Books, 1992.
—. *Tunnel Vision.* New York: Delacorte Press, 1994.
—. "The Writing That Got Me Started." In *Mystery Writer's Marketplace and Sourcebook.* Ed. Donna Collingwood. Cincinnati, OH: Writer's Digest Books, 1993, 266–267.
Petty, Lorraine. "Plugging into the Independent General Bookstore Network." *Sisters in Crime Newsletter* 5.3 (1993): 6.
Phillips, Kathy. "McCone and the Comic." *Drood Review of Mystery* 10.1 (January 1990): 8.
Pickard, Nancy. *Bum Steer.* New York: Pocket Books, 1991.
—. *But I Wouldn't Want to Die There.* New York: Pocket Books, 1994.
—. *Confession.* New York: Pocket Books, 1994.
—. *Dead Crazy.* New York: Pocket Books, 1991.

—. *Generous Death*. New York: Pocket Books, 1987.
—. *I.O.U.* New York: Pocket Books, 1992.
—. *Marriage Is Murder*. New York: Pocket Books, 1988.
—. "Mystery Writing as a Second Career." Panel discussion, American Library Association (ALA) Conference, Sisters in Crime ALA Breakfast, Doral Hotel, Miami, Florida, 26 June 1994.
—. *No Body*. New York: Pocket Books, 1997.
—. *Say No to Murder*. New York: Avon, 1985.
—. *Twilight*. New York: Pocket Books, 1995.
Pickard, Nancy, and Marilyn Wallace. "There's a Revolution in Mystery—and Women Are Leading It!" Author book signing and discussion, Grounds for Murder Mystery Book Store, San Diego, California, 17 March 1990.
Porter, Dennis. *The Pursuit of Crime: Art and Ideology in Detective Fiction*. New Haven, CT: Yale University Press, 1981.
"Publicity for Posterity." *Sisters in Crime Newsletter* 3.1 (1991): 1.
Queen, Ellery. *Queen's Quorum: A History of the Detective-Crime Short Story as Revealed in the 106 Most Important Books Published in the Field since 1845*. New York: Biblio and Tannen, 1969.
Radway, Janice. *Reading the Romance: Women, Patriarchy, and Popular Literature*. Chapel Hill: University of North Carolina Press, 1987.
"Reading between the Videos." *Economist*, 29 February 1992, 29.
Reddy, Maureen T. *Sisters in Crime: Feminism and the Crime Novel*. New York: Continuum Publishing Company, 1988.
Robinson, Lillian S. "Killing Patriarchy: Charlotte Perkins Gilman, the Murder Mystery, and Post-Feminist Propaganda." *Tulsa Studies in Women's Literature* 10.2 (1991): 273–285.
Roller, Judi M. *The Politics of the Feminist Novel*. Westport, CT: Greenwood Press, 1986.
Ross, Cheri L. "The First Feminist Detective: Anna Katharine Green's Amelia Butterworth." *Journal of Popular Culture* 25.2 (Fall 1991): 77–86.
Rothman, Sheila. *Woman's Proper Place: A History of Changing Ideals and Practices, 1870 to the Present*. New York: Basic Books, 1987.
"Rutgers Convocation for Literacy." *Sisters in Crime Newsletter* 3.1 (1991): 4.
"Sales Aren't Impervious to Economic Slump." *Standard & Poor's Industry Surveys* 159.5 (1991): M31.
Schneider, Debra. Telephone interview, 28 January 1994.
Schweickart, Patrocinio P. "Reading Ourselves: Towards a Feminist Theory of Reading." In *Gender and Reading: Essays on Readers, Texts, and Contexts*. Ed. Elizabeth A. Flynn and Patrocinio P. Schweickart. Baltimore, MD: Johns Hopkins University Press, 1992, 31–62.
Schweickart, Patrocinio P., and Elizabeth A. Flynn. Introduction to *Gender and Reading: Essays on Readers, Texts, and Contexts*. Ed. Elizabeth A. Flynn and Patrocinio P. Schweickart. Baltimore, MD: Johns Hopkins University Press, 1992, ix–xxx.
Scoppettone, Sandra. *Everything You Have Is Mine*. New York: Ballantine Books, 1992.
—. *I'll Be Leaving You Always*. Boston: Little, Brown and Company, 1993.
—. *Let's Face the Music and Die*. Boston: Little, Brown and Company, 1996.
—. *My Sweet Untraceable You*. Boston: Little, Brown and Company, 1994.
—. Telephone interview, 26 January 1994.
Showalter, Elaine. *A Literature of Their Own: British Women Novelists from Brontë to Lessing*. Princeton, NJ: Princeton University Press, 1977.

—. "Toward a Feminist Poetics." In *The New Feminist Criticism: Essays on Women, Literature, and Theory*. Ed. Elaine Showalter. New York: Pantheon Books, 1985, 125–143.

Slung, Michele B. *Crime on Her Mind: Fifteen Stories of Female Sleuths from the Victorian Era to the Forties*. New York: Pantheon Books, 1975.

Smith, Julie. *The Sourdough Wars*. New York: Ivy Books, 1992.

Span, Paula. "The Professor and the Mystery Writer." *Los Angeles Times,* 10 November 1989, E10–E11.

Stabenow, Dana. *Blood Will Tell*. New York: Berkley Books, 1996.

—. *Breakup*. New York: G. P. Putnam's Sons, 1997.

—. *A Cold-Blooded Business*. New York: Berkley Prime Crime, 1994.

—. *A Cold Day for Murder*. New York: Berkley Books, 1992.

—. *Dead in the Water*. New York: Berkley Books, 1993.

—. *A Fatal Thaw*. New York: Berkley Books, 1993.

—. Telephone interview, 25 January 1994.

Stacey, Judith. "Are Feminists Afraid to Leave Home? The Challenge of Conservative Pro-Family Feminism." In *What Is Feminism?* Ed. Juliet Mitchell and Ann Oakley. Oxford, U.K.: Basil Blackwell, 1986, 219–242.

Starrett, Vince, ed. *Fourteen Great Detective Stories*. New York: Modern Library, 1928.

Stasio, Marilyn. "Lady Gumshoes Boiled Less Hard." *New York Times Book Review*, 28 April 1985, 3.

—. "What's Happened to Heroes Is a Crime." *New York Times Book Review*, 14 October 1990, 1.

Stewart, R. F. *. . . And Always a Detective: Chapters of History of Detective Fiction*. Newton Abbot, U.K.: David & Charles, 1980.

Stowe, William W. "Critical Investigations: Conventions and Ideology in Detective Fiction." *Texas Studies in Literature and Language* 31.4 (1989): 570–591.

Swanson, Jean, and Dean James. *By a Woman's Hand*. New York: Berkley Books, 1994.

Symons, Julian. *Bloody Murder, From the Detective Story to the Crime Novel: A History*. London, U.K.: Viking, 1985.

Thomson, H. Douglas. *Masters of Mystery: A Study of the Detective Story*. New York: Dover Publications, 1978.

Tompkins, Jane P. "Introduction: The Cultural Work of American Fiction." In *Sensational Designs: The Cultural Work of American Fiction, 1790-1860*. Ed. Jane P. Tompkins. New York: Oxford University Press, 1985, xi–xix.

—. "The Reader in History: The Changing Shape of Literary Response." *Reader-Response Criticism: From Formalism to Post-Structuralism*. Ed. Jane P. Tompkins. Baltimore, MD: Johns Hopkins University Press, 1988, 201–232.

—. "Sentimental Power: *Uncle Tom's Cabin* and the Politics of Literary History." In *The New Feminist Criticism: Essays on Women, Literature, and Theory*. Ed. Elaine Showalter. New York: Pantheon Books, 1985, 81–104.

Tuttle, George. "The Golden Era of Gold Medal Books." In *The Fine Art of Murder: The Mystery Reader's Indispensable Companion*. Ed. Ed Gorman, Martin H. Greenberg, Larry Segriff, and Jon L. Breen. New York: Carroll & Graf Publishers, 1993, 343–351.

Wagoner, Mary S. *Agatha Christie*. Boston: Twayne Publishers, 1986.

Watson, Colin. *Snobbery with Violence*. New York: St. Martin's Press, 1971.

Watt, Ian. *The Rise of the Novel: Studies in Defoe, Richardson, and Fielding*. Berkeley: University of California Press, 1965.

Waugh, Hillary. "The Human Rather Than Superhuman Sleuth." In *The Murder Mystique: Crime Writers on Their Art*. Ed. Lucy Freeman. New York: Frederick Ungar Publishing Co., 1982, 33–45.

"What's Happened to Heroes Is a Crime," *New York Times Book Review*, 14 October 1990, 1.

Wheat, Carolyn. Telephone interview, 20 December 1993.

Whiteside, Thomas. *The Blockbuster Complex: Conglomerates, Show Business, and Book Publishing*. Middleton, CT: Weslyan University Press, 1981.

Winks, Robin W., ed. *Detective Fiction: A Collection of Critical Essays*. Woodstock, VT: Foul Play Press, 1988.

Winn, Dilys, ed. *Murderess Ink: The Better Half of the Mystery*. New York: Workman Publishing, 1979.

Yost, Nancy. Telephone interview, 2 March 1994.

# Index

## About the Author

KIMBERLY J. DILLEY is a freelance writer. She has a Ph.D. in Communications from the University of California, San Diego.

ISBN 0-313-30330-4
90000>
EAN
9 780313 303302
HARDCOVER BAR CODE